# The Remarkable
# Chester Ronning

The
*Remarkable*
# CHESTER RONNING
*Proud Son of*
*China*

BRIAN L. EVANS

 The University of Alberta Press

 Chester Ronning Centre
for the Study of Religion and Public Life

Published by

The University of Alberta Press
Ring House 2
Edmonton, Alberta, Canada T6G 2E1
www.uap.ualberta.ca

and

Chester Ronning Centre for the Study of Religion and Public Life
University of Alberta, Augustana Campus
4901 46 Avenue
Camrose, Alberta, Canada T4V 2R3
www.augustana.ualberta.ca/research/centres/ronningcentre

Library and Archives Canada Cataloguing in Publication

Evans, Brian L., 1932-, author
    The remarkable Chester Ronning : proud son of China / Brian L. Evans.

Includes bibliographical references and index.
Issued in print and electronic formats.
ISBN 978-0-88864-663-7 (pbk.).–ISBN 978-0-88864-720-7 (epub).–
ISBN 978-0-88864-721-4 (Amazon kindle)

    1. Ronning, Chester, 1894-1984. 2. Diplomats–Canada–Biography. 3. Politicians–
Canada–Biography. 4. Educators–Canada–Biography. 5. Canada–Foreign relations–
China. 6. China–Foreign relations–Canada. 7. Canada–Foreign relations–1945-.
8. China–History–20th century. I. Title.

FC601.R65E93 2013          327.2092          C2013-903525-7
                                             C2013-903526-5

First edition, first printing, 2013.
Printed and bound in Canada by Friesens, Altona, Manitoba.
Copyediting and proofreading by Kirsten Craven.
Indexing by Adrian Mather.

The University of Alberta Press is committed to protecting our natural environment. As part of our
efforts, this book is printed on Enviro Paper: it contains 100% post-consumer recycled fibres and is
acid- and chlorine-free.

The University of Alberta Press gratefully acknowledges the support received for its publishing
program from The Canada Council for the Arts. The University of Alberta Press also gratefully
acknowledges the financial support of the Government of Canada through the Canada Book Fund
(CBF) and the Government of Alberta through the Alberta Multimedia Development Fund (AMDF)
for its publishing activities.

Canada    Canada Council    Conseil des Arts    Alberta
          for the Arts      du Canada           Government

*To China Hands, old and new*

# Contents

# Foreword

## A Remarkable Man in a Remarkable Time

In early spring of 1968, a year remembered for its "revolutionary" activity in Canada, the United States, and Europe, Chester Ronning gave the keynote lecture at the annual theological conference of the Lutheran Theological Seminary in Saskatoon. This is the seminary of the denomination he belonged to throughout his life in Canada that had given birth to Camrose Lutheran College where he was principal for a time and which is now the Augustana Campus of the University of Alberta. The invitation to have him speak was not without controversy. The Cold War had created hostile and fearful attitudes toward China. Despite, or perhaps because of, the longstanding role of Lutheran missionaries to China, the fear of communism and the negative rhetoric about China and its leadership since the revolution shaped the attitude of many in the Lutheran community, including most who came to the theological conference. Everyone knew of Ronning's affection for China and his untiring work to normalize Canada's relationship with China. Many knew he was a socialist and had deep sympathies with the revolution in China.

Within Lutheran circles, lectures given in seminaries or churches are both anchored in biblical texts and sprinkled with them. Biblical texts have a position of central authority, orient the listener, and provide an assurance that the lecturer shares the community's faith and understanding. In his speech, Ronning departed from this pattern. He did not begin with a biblical text and there were none sprinkled throughout his lecture. To the gathered faithful, the oddness of this was only matched by the subject of his talk. He mapped the history of the Christian mission movement in China from its beginnings through his parents' generation, including his early childhood experience in Fancheng. As was always the case, his lecture was sprinkled with stories and anecdotes full of charm that spoke to his love of China and were intended to open up the audience to see China in a new light. He went on to make what for many in the audience that day was a disturbing argument. The Christian mission movement, he said, played an important role in the liberation of China from the oppression of colonialism, internal tyranny, and systemic poverty. It was formative for the revolution in China. A friend of mine attending the seminary that year listened to Chester Ronning and noted the uneasiness that moved through the auditorium. Ronning's thesis was not how most of them understood the mission movement, much less its purpose. But, as was often the case, Ronning's humour and affable spirit were hard to resist. Only at the very end, when he had made his case and wooed the audience to think of China differently, did he, like all great rhetors, return to the familiar and drive home his point. He quoted from one of Jesus Christ's better-known sermons, a text familiar to everyone in the audience that day. It comes at the end of a lengthy discourse in which Jesus is pointing to the many and varied ways we mistake what is central to being righteous and, through focusing on secondary matters, miss doing that work which brings liberty and dignity to all people. With his finest cathedral voice, Ronning concluded with the words from Matthew 6:33: "But, seek ye first the kingdom of God, and his righteousness; and all these things shall be added unto you."

Chester Ronning used his considerable gifts in service to extending justice, liberty, and dignity in all the contexts of his long and extraordinarily fruitful life and did so without rancour, ideological brittleness, or false righteousness. Brian Evans has beautifully captured the spirit of Ronning as he brings us through the various periods in his life. Evans brings his own love of China and affection for Chester Ronning, his skill as a historian, and his sensibilities, which, like Ronning's, were partly honed in the diplomatic service to his country, to this book. As Evans points out: it is time this story was told. I am delighted Evans has placed it before us. He has done so in a way no one else could have and we are richer for it.

David J. Goa, Director
Chester Ronning Centre for the Study of Religion and Public Life
December 2012

# Preface

## *Chester Alvin Ronning*

Chester Alvin Ronning died the last day of December 1984, aged ninety. Those who gathered at his funeral a few days later included family, friends, colleagues, and admirers from Canada, the United States, Norway, and China. During his nine decades Ronning touched many lives and accomplished many things. He received many honours, among them the Alberta Order of Excellence, the highest accolade given by his home province; Companion of the Order of Canada, the highest civilian award given by his country; and numerous honourary degrees. In 1983, to mark his ninetieth year, the government of China held a dinner in his honour at the Great Hall of the People in Peking (Beijing), and later the mayor of the city of Hsiangfan (Xiangfan), Hupei (Hubei), hosted a celebratory banquet and fireworks display to mark Ronning's return home.

Canadian newspaper, television, and radio commentators marked Ronning's passing as that of a great man: a farmer, rancher, teacher, musician, sculptor, soldier, pilot, politician, author, and diplomat, but many failed to note his greatest source of pride: he was born in China. Ronning's Chineseness was so apparent that some of his Chinese friends called him an "egg": white outside, but yellow inside. One was not long in Ronning's company before he referred to his birth at Fancheng, Hupei, where his Norwegian American parents had established a Lutheran church mission. With a smile, he boasted he was the first non-Chinese baby born in Hsiang Yang (Xiangyang) county, and then he would add slyly, a Chinese wet nurse suckled him. From the day of his birth, 13 December 1894, Ronning's life was entwined with the history of China. Fate kept drawing him back to the land of his birth, and when recalling his life, he invariably measured it by key events in the history of modern China.

I first met Ronning in August 1965 in Banff at a conference on international affairs, and again the next year following his special missions to Hanoi. He graciously agreed to be a guest lecturer in my course on the history of modern China at the University of Alberta. For those who did not have the pleasure of spending time in Ronning's company, let me attempt to give some inkling of the manner and character of the man, as I knew him. First, he was a polymath; a natural at everything he attempted from sculpting to diplomacy. He was tall, slender, handsome, loquacious, interested in everyone and everything around him, gregarious, a talented public speaker, engaging, trilingual—at least, fearless, filled with the milk of human kindness, and funny. I say at least trilingual because in addition to standard Mandarin Chinese, he spoke the Hupei dialect, which in its oral form might as well be another language. In addition, while at Camrose Lutheran College, he taught agriculture, music, mathematics, religion, and German. A meeting with Ronning was invariably punctuated with laughter and amazing stories of exotic places and extraordinary people. After Canada, he identified with China and Norway, and latterly with the United States. Thus, he was a proud Canadian with Chinese sensibility, Norwegian calm practicality, and American drive. Throughout his life, he used languages to great effect, communicating easily with people. His intelligence, impish sense of humour, and innate curiosity made him a natural teacher, politician, and diplomat.

I am guilty of waiting far too long to complete this biography. Thirty years ago, Mel Hurtig suggested I meet with Ronning to

interview him with an eye, perhaps, to producing a biography. I travelled to Camrose one afternoon in late November 1979 to discuss
the project with Ronning in his snug little house full of mementos of
China and India. After 6 p.m., we walked to the York Café where we
had superb noodles served to us by a pretty Chinese waitress to whom
we spoke Mandarin. Later, a craggy old farmer came in and spoke at
first to Ronning in Norwegian. He reminded the world-famous diplomat that it was people like him, who walked behind oxen to till the
fields, who raised the funds for Ronning to go to China in the 1920s.

   From May to September 1980, I returned to Camrose many times,
taping interviews with Ronning, who in no way looked or acted his
eighty-five years. I grew familiar with his life story, most of which he
had already published in his own *A Memoir of China in Revolution*,[1]
or was recounted in the National Film Board's *China Mission* (1980),
directed by Tom Radford, or supplemented by Audrey (Ronning)
Topping's *Dawn Wakes in the East*,[2] describing the family trip in 1971 to
Fancheng, their meeting with Chou En-lai (Zhou Enlai), and including
a long essay by Ronning on his return to his hometown. In addition, other writings (including very recent ones) of both Audrey and
Seymour Topping provided more insights into Ronning's life.

   Our conversations tended to dwell on China, but Ronning had
minor memory problems. I found that certain questions or phrases
would launch him into his memories of Chinese history. Ronning,
like many teachers, came to think in set pieces of a certain length.
A number of our interviews contained these set pieces, but often in
retelling a story, Ronning added details I had not heard before. While
I felt competent to ask him questions about China, my knowledge of
Alberta's political history was not detailed enough at the time for me
to ask him the sort of questions about his political career that needed
to be asked. In the end, I felt the material I had gathered in interviews,
along with the written materials he had loaned me, were insufficient
for a biography that would do him justice. I continued to teach, however, and I developed a course on Canada's relations with East Asia,
the preparations for which gave me the broader context of Ronning's
life as a diplomat. In 1984, in Beijing, I interviewed Mr. Huang Hua, a

former Foreign Minister of China and an old friend of Ronning's, and I visited Fancheng, Ronning's birthplace.[3] Along the way, I produced a paper, and a subsequent article, on Ronning and the recognition of China that was published in a collection edited by Paul M. Evans and B. Michael Frolic.[4]

Following Ronning's death, I heard (incorrectly as it turned out) that his daughter Audrey was preparing a biography of her father. I put my project aside and disappeared into university administration. There were other forces at work, however, as Ronning became a subject in which Chinese students were expressing a great interest. While Ronning was still alive, Liao Dong, a graduate student in political science at the University of Regina, produced a master's thesis on Ronning and China.[5] Later, Professor Liu Guangtai of Hopeh (Hebei) Normal University at Shihchiachuang (Shijiazhuang), while on leave at the University of Alberta, took my course on Canada's relations with East Asia. He learned of Ronning for the first time and decided to write his biography. Liu, a meticulous researcher and excellent historian, examined the records of the Department of External Affairs, interviewed Audrey Topping and others who were associated with Ronning, checked the Chinese diplomatic files open in Nanking (Nanjing), researched the papers Ronning had entrusted to me, and published a biography of Ronning in Chinese in 1999.[6] Around the same time, he invited me to China to present lectures on Ronning in English to his classes. Subsequently, I offered lectures on Ronning at other Chinese universities and at the opening of the China Institute at the University of Alberta in October 2006. Two years later, along with Audrey and Seymour Topping, I was invited to speak at the opening of the Ronning Centre at the Augustana Campus of the University of Alberta (formerly Camrose Lutheran College and later Augustana University).

As I prepared my lectures, I realized that a larger body of Ronning-related material had accumulated since my interviews with him in 1980. Tom Radford donated to the University Archives the tapes and transcripts of his interviews with Ronning made for *China Mission*, and Howard Leeson, a political science professor from the University of Regina, deposited with the Provincial Archives of Alberta the

tapes of his interviews with early members of the Co-operative
Commonwealth Federation (CCF) and New Democratic Party (NDP),
including the ones he made with Ronning in 1976. In the meantime, I
read all the copies of the weekly *Camrose Canadian*, from its inception
to Ronning's death, teasing out references to him and items by him—
there were many. Also, in 2003, Andrew Preston of the University of
Victoria published a scholarly examination of Ronning's missions to
Hanoi,[7] and more references to Ronning emerged in biographies and
autobiographies of diplomats and world leaders.

Because my continuing interest in Ronning was known, I was given
items related to him by many people. In addition, documents relating
to Ronning's diplomatic career were published in the collections of
the Department of Foreign Affairs and International Trade (DFAIT), as
well as memoirs of those who worked with him. Faced with a growing
volume of sources, and having advanced into my seventies, I began to
think I might now be equipped to finish a biography. In January 2010,
David Goa, director of the Chester Ronning Centre at the Augustana
Campus of the University of Alberta, invited me to Camrose to give
two lectures on aspects of Ronning's life. The audiences in atten-
dance on those evenings gave me further encouragement and a deeper
insight into Ronning the individual and his influence. Goa directly
encouraged me to press on with this biography, which, courtesy of the
University of Alberta Press, is now before you.

# Acknowledgements

There are many people who have contributed to the completion of this biography and to whom I am indebted. They include my Chinese friends Liu Guangtai, Liao Dong, and Chen Qineng. Alan Meech, Mary Jo Hague, Pat Prestwich, and Lynn Ogden devoted time to tracking down materials, even driving me to and from Camrose. Letters to Ronning's old school friend Peter Stolee were provided to me by his son James. Debra Huller, managing editor of *bout de papier*, generously provided me with items on Ronning and on Tessie Wong. Dr. Victoria Cheung, Tessie Wong's daughter, kindly provided me with family photographs. David Goa, director of the Chester Ronning Centre, has been a constant source of encouragement and support. Through his publications and direct assistance, David Leonard of Alberta Heritage provided insights into Ronning's family life in Valhalla and was kind enough to take me with him on a tour of the Peace River Country. He, along with Audrey (Ronning) Topping, Gilliane Lapointe, James Stolee, and Brian Harris, read drafts of the biography and offered valuable comments and corrections. This is also true of the two anonymous outside readers chosen by the University of Alberta Press. The members of the University of Alberta Press, along with Kirsten Craven, have treated me with their customary patience and professionalism. I am grateful to all those mentioned above for their support and assistance. Needless to say, the responsibility for errors of fact and judgement is mine alone.

Brian L. Evans
Edmonton, 2013

# A Note on Names

Many systems for transcribing the sounds of Chinese into a Latin
script have been employed over the years. The most popular one up to
the mid-1950s was known as Wade-Giles, after its originators, British
academic Herbert Giles and British diplomat Thomas Wade. It relies
on numbers and apostrophes to clue readers in on the proper pronunciation. Unfortunately, few bothered to learn these finer points and
they were ignored. Thus, China's capital city was expressed as *Peking*,
which was to be pronounced *Beijing*, but it was generally pronounced
*Peaking*. After the People's Republic of China was founded in 1949, the
government introduced a new system called *pinyin*, designed better to
reflect Chinese Mandarin pronunciation. Thus, *Peking* became *Beijing*,
and *Chou En-lai* became *Zhou Enlai*.

Because most of the China references in this biography are before
the introduction of pinyin as an international standard in 1982, I have
chosen to use the transcription of the names of the most familiar
people and places as they were written at the time, with the pinyin
rendition bracketed when the name is first used, i.e., Chungking
(Chongqing). That is to say, names are according to the then bastard-
ized Wade-Giles system, except later within quotations where pinyin

is used. It should be noted that Peking, or Beijing, means northern capital, but between 1927 and 1949 it ceased to be the capital and was called Peip'ing (Beiping), meaning northern peace. In 1949, it once again became the capital as Peking (Beijing). Some names remain the same in both Wade-Giles and pinyin, e.g., Shanghai, Fancheng.

Chester Ronning's China, c. 1930s.

# Chinese Childhood

Flying over the "hump" from eastern India to southwest China was perilous, even after mid-August 1945 when the war with Japan was over. During the war, the Japanese air force ranked third, after terrain and weather, on the list of the major hazards facing those who sought to keep open the lifeline to besieged "Free China." On 6 January 1945, forty-five planes were lost because of the weather. By November 1945, the Japanese were long gone, leaving the rugged terrain and the weather to continue to test the skill of pilots. Their flights, made in unpressurized, propeller-driven planes, presented breathtaking views of high mountains and deep valleys dotted with the wreckage of aircraft that had not made it. It was dubbed the aluminum trail.[1]

Among the forty passengers aboard the Douglas C-54 from Calcutta to Kunming, Yunnan province, on the evening of 25 November were Tung Pi-wu (Dong Biwu) and Chang Han-fu, two members of the Chinese Communist Party, returning from United Nations meetings in San Francisco, and Chester Alvin Ronning, a newly recruited member of the Canadian Department of External Affairs (DEA), on his way to fill the position of first secretary at the Canadian Embassy in Chungking (Chongqing). His journey of over fifteen thousand miles from Canada took over two weeks, fourteen flights, and seventy hours in the air, almost all on chilly military aircraft.[2] Now, only one hurdle remained: the flight the next day to Chungking and a landing on the airstrip of Paishihi (Baishiyi) airport, obscured by the clouds that hover perpetually over Szechuan (Sichuan) province.

Ronning was just shy of his fifty-first birthday, a mature age for someone entering the DEA, yet his arrival in Chungking marked the beginning of a remarkable twenty-one-year diplomatic career: his life prior to Chungking was no less remarkable.

●　●　●

Chester Alvin Ronning was born in Fancheng, Hupei (Hubei), China, on 13 December 1894, the second son of Hannah Rorem and the Reverend Halvor N. Ronning, Norwegian American Lutheran missionaries. He was the first foreign child born in the district.[3] Recently arrived in Fancheng, Halvor was yet to complete the mission station.[4] Both Halvor and Hannah were from the cool, thinly populated regions of the temperate zone. They were little prepared for what they faced in hot, humid, and heavily populated central China. The question was, "Why had they come?"

Halvor Nilius Ronning was born on 3 March 1862, on a thriving farm in Telemark, Norway. His father was director of roads.[5] An excellent skier and a local teacher, as a young man, Halvor was attracted to the teachings of the Norwegian Lutheran revivalist Hans Nielsen Hauge (1771-1824), who challenged the established church and emphasized modesty, honesty, hard work, and religion as a personal responsibility. Halvor was keen to be a missionary, but he had little hope of becoming one until the Rev. A. Wenaas, president of the Hauge Synod Seminary in Red Wing, Minnesota, visited his family in 1882. Wenaas convinced Halvor's father that a shortage of ministers for Norwegian Americans presented an opportunity for young Halvor to study theology at his seminary in Minnesota. In 1883, at the age of twenty-one, Halvor, accompanied by his sister Thea, left for the United States to study at the Red Wing seminary, where he tutored

RIVERSIDE AVE. MINNEAPOLIS. —1819—

Hannah Rorem and Halvor Ronning, 1891. [Ronning/Cassady photo collection]

classmates in Norwegian and taught in a parochial school. Upon graduation in 1887, he became a naturalized American citizen and an ordained Lutheran minister. He remained in Minnesota for the next four years as pastor to a three-point parish near Faribault. During those years, Lutheran congregations underwent a revival with an increasing interest being shown in foreign missions.[6]

In 1888, a Norwegian, O.S. Nestegaard, travelled to China, gained admission to the language school of the China Inland Mission, and became an associate of the mission. Enthused with the cause, he wrote letters to friends and the press calling for Norwegians to go to China to spread the gospel. His letters reached a wide audience among Lutherans in the United States. Early in 1890, O.S. Nestegaard Jr. (son) and Mr. S. Netland left Norway on their way to China to join O.S. Nestegaard Sr. They stopped in the United States, where they spent over five months. In Minnesota, they begged Halvor to go with them to China. Their impact upon him was profound:

> Under prayer to God and closer study of the situation at home and in China, it became clear to me that this was just the time and the opportunity to take the lead in this movement and begin an independent Norwegian Lutheran China mission. The pathetic cry, which came to Paul, also came to me: "Come over and help us." It came with such force that I was convinced it was the voice of God and I answered: "Lord here am I, send me."[7]

Unable to convince the Hauge Synod of the urgency of his request to go to China, Halvor and others formed a separate Norwegian Lutheran China Mission Society on 11 June 1890, which sent its first missionaries to China in October of that year. Then, at Faribault, Minnesota, on 18 February 1891, the society assigned Halvor and his sister Thea to the China field.

Meanwhile, in Radcliffe, Iowa, Hannah Rorem also heard the call to go to China. She asked to accompany the two Ronnings at her own expense.[8] Hannah's family was from a farm on the beautiful island of Ombo, Norway, but unable to make a living there, they left for Ottawa, Illinois, in the United States where Hannah was born on 6 November 1871.[9] Finding the farm in Illinois too poor, the Rorems moved to Iowa where Hannah grew up and trained as a teacher. After her father's death in January 1890, she felt

> deeper concern about my soul than I had ever felt before. I now began to feel an inner call to go to the heathen and tell them about Jesus as the Savior of all men. I have felt and feel how weak I am and how unfit for such a great mission, but the Lord has strengthened me so that I have been given the confidence to offer myself, body and soul, for Jesus and His cause, and I now stand ready to go to China as a Bible woman.[10]

She was accepted by the Mission Society and made her way to Faribault.

On 3 November 1891, Hannah, along with Halvor and Thea Ronning, accompanied by O.S. Nestegaard Jr., left San Francisco for Shanghai, arriving there on 1 December. They were but part of the growing number of Protestant Christian missionaries afire with the desire to convert the 400 million heathens of China.[11] They continued some six hundred miles up the Yangtze (Yangzi) river, arriving a week later in the port of Hankow (Hankou), which marks the point where the Han River joins the Yangtze. In Hankow they met the missionaries who had preceded them.[12] The next day they crossed the Yangtze to Wuchang,[13] to set up a mission house in which they were also to learn Chinese. Learning the language was important and continued to be a priority throughout the years of the mission. Writing a decade or more later, one missionary described the transition from not knowing to knowing Chinese:

> The first year of the missionary's stay in China is most trying. How you long to tell its natives what you think about their abominable money system, their dirty streets, their long fingernails, their disgusting way of sucking in their food when they eat. How you would be delighted to tell them about your own beautiful country, its superior money system, immaculate streets, beautiful houses, and the refined manners of the people. Most of all you would like to tell that proud teacher of yours that altho you can not speak Chinese you are able to speak three other languages and know a great many wonderful things of which he has never heard. Fortunately you are able to say little or nothing of all this. But by the time you would be able to tell them, strangely enough, table manners and money systems have diminished in importance till you would be ashamed to speak of them.[14]

In time, the Lutheran missions established their own language schools, but at the outset, Rorem and the Ronnings, along with the other members of the mission, studied Chinese with Chinese tutors to whom they paid five dollars a month. The house in Wuchang had belonged to a Mandarin who had hanged himself. It was said to be full of noisy spirits, frightening to local Chinese, but the foreigners rejected such superstitions. On Christmas Eve 1891, shortly after they began their language lessons, Hannah Rorem and Halvor Ronning married in Hankow. Together they would face the challenges of establishing a new mission station in the interior of China. In 1891, the mission, entirely supported by volunteer donations, had a budget of $10,000, which rose the following year to $15,000. A short time later, the Hauge Synod in Minnesota decided to set up a mission in China as well, and Halvor was made superintendent of both the society's and the synod's operations.

Halvor was not as dedicated a language scholar as the others, preferring to study in the streets. His impressions of China are interesting and very important, as they were the basis for urging others to follow his example. They are also valuable in helping us understand how he saw the problems he and Hannah faced. His letters also give us a snapshot of the sort of China into which Chester Ronning was born. On 26 January 1892, Halvor wrote to his colleagues in Red Wing, Minnesota, from his new home in Wuchang:

Last week I took a walk on the wall surrounding the city. I went down and looked at three Chinese being beheaded near the gate. It was a terrible sight. The heads with the long que [sic] were hung on poles as a warning to other criminals. The headless bodies were dragged outside the wall. There they were left, half naked with their hands tied behind their backs, for several days for people to look at.

On 4 February, he continued his description of life in the city:

Crowds in the narrow streets. Low, tumble-down houses stand side by side as if steadying one another. Here stands a Chinese on the street cooking his food. At his side one is sitting being shaved. Here some are butchering and close by one is repairing shoes. On the other side is a beggar who is busy doing away with insects in his shirt. Even more disgusting scenes present themselves....No Chinese house has a chimney. The smoke finds its way out where best it can. Others are more civilized and have placed the chimney through the wall and out into the street. Well, they don't know any better....Wagons are not used in the streets. Everything, including stones and logs, is carried on the shoulders. Sometimes up to forty, fifty men carry a log.

In such a noisy and congested crowd, one soon gets tired. Add to all this the intolerable smell on account of the terrible filth....On account of the uncleanliness there is much of eye and skin diseases....

[Down by the gate are the previously mentioned, cut-off heads.] Let me tell you that a few days ago I dipped my pen in their blood to send a message to my brethren at Red Wing Seminary. *Remember the China mission. Hurry with the Gospel to the Chinese! Let not their blood come upon you!...*

[From atop of a wall] we can see some small girls creeping along the ground. They can scarcely walk as their feet have been bound and are only two to three inches long. What are they creeping here for? With a small knife they are cutting grass to still their hunger. At such a sight, I become very much depressed and pray daily that God will help me soon to be able to preach the Gospel of Jesus Christ. I thank God and my brethren who found me qualified to be sent to the heathen.[15]

Halvor's description did not apply to the entire urban area. Hankow, the main port of Hupei province, contained an area conceded to foreign powers, marked by European-style buildings on the Bund along the river. One such concession was under British control.[16] In 1893, the Lutheran missions acquired land just outside the British concession and built a home for missionaries on it at a cost of $4,700. The British concession contained the homes and offices of British merchants and officials, along with the headquarters of the London Missionary Society (LMS) represented by Dr. Griffith John, and a post of the China Inland Mission (CIM) under Dr. Hudson Taylor.[17] The Norwegian Lutheran missions relied upon the CIM (with whom the Rev. O.S. Nestegaard Sr. had associated himself) for support and direction. The American Norwegian Lutherans turned to

Missionaries ready for a journey, late nineteenth century. [Evans private collection]

both John and Taylor for advice on where to establish a mission.[18] Quite independently, each suggested the city of Fancheng, located on the Han River, two hundred miles north of Hankow but still within Hupei province.

In the fall of 1892, S. Netland and D. Nelson, two male members of the mission in Hankow, went to Fancheng and purchased a building site. The following spring, they began to build, but after four months they were driven out. Mr. Ding, the Chinese who had acted on their behalf in the land purchase, was beaten badly and thrown in jail for two years for aiding and abetting the foreigners. A year later, in 1894, Halvor Ronning took up the challenge.

Hupei province, in the century following the First Opium War (1839–42), was marked by periods of rebellion and political unrest. In 1860, the Yangtze valley was opened to foreign merchants, missionaries, and opium, each enjoying special privileges and the protection of foreign gunboats, if needed. Hankow lay on the path of the T'ai-p'ing (Taiping)[19] rebels, whose leader proclaimed himself not only to be Christian but the brother of Jesus Christ to boot.[20] By 1864, his revolt was crushed, but aftershocks continued. By the 1890s, when the Ch'ing (Qing) imperial government in Peking proved itself incapable of standing up to foreign incursions and diplomatic pressures, local attacks on foreigners increased. When the Ronnings began their Lutheran mission, the Chinese in the Yangtze valley were already familiar with foreigners and riots against their presence were frequent.

Early in May 1894, the Ronnings, including sister Thea, and their baby son Nelius, born 22 January 1893, left Hankow and made their way by boat up the Han River to occupy the newly designated mission station at Fancheng. In an effort to reduce harassment and threats, they adopted the custom, followed by seasoned missionaries like Griffith John, of dressing as Chinese, with Halvor wearing a false pigtail, or queue,[21] attached to his hat. This did not always provide him protection, however. During his fifteen years in China, he was stoned seven times.[22]

The Ronnings arrived in Fancheng in late May 1894. They brought with them Chinese children, mainly girls, they had found abandoned, or who were left on their doorstep, and to whom Hannah gave schooling. In addition, Hannah was pregnant with Chester. In his attempts to complete the building begun by Nelson and Netland, Halvor had to appeal to the local magistrate for permission, then to the American Consul in Hankow, and finally to the American representative in Peking. The ultimate pressure—an American gunboat—was not possible because gunboats were unable to mount the Han River.

By 13 December 1894, their house was not yet ready, so Hannah gave birth to Chester in a barn.[23] Because she was unable to nurse him, she gave Chester to a Chinese wet nurse to be suckled. With their parents working hard to establish the mission station, Chester and Nelius grew up in the company of the Chinese cook and housekeeper, and played with Chinese children. They learned to speak Chinese with a Hupei accent more readily than any other language. On occasion, Nelius and Chester accompanied their father on boat trips on the Han River to the 1,500-foot Pian (Bian) Mountain near Fancheng, where Halvor selected the stone to be used in building the mission church. They grew familiar with the different types of boats and ships on the river. They learned that no one was rescued if they fell in the river, because it was considered to be the will of the spirits. *Hong chuan*, red boats with a black hutch, were the only ones permitted to rescue the drowning, although Chester recalled once seeing his father use a bamboo pole to save a drowning man.[24]

Establishing the mission was discouraging work, hampered by bureaucratic delays and the growth of petty crime in Fancheng. The climate was oppressive and the family was plagued by illness. To escape the heat of summer, Hannah and the children went to a house on Pian Mountain, while Halvor remained in Fancheng doing mission work. Chester recalled viewing the mountain from their home in Fancheng.

> [W]e could look up and across the Han River from our upstairs verandah to see in the distance a mountain which resembled a majestic, heavily-maned lion resting on the south bank. In the forest of ancient trees on the mountain lion's head, there was an old temple which had been maintained for centuries...In the temple courtyards, magnificent "mu-tan hua," shrub peonies, ancient China's national flower, are carefully nurtured.[25]

He also recalled playing with Nelius and Chinese children on the terraced fields of the mountain, riding donkeys, and catching frogs for the cook to prepare for supper. Later, Hannah gave Chester his own donkey, which he rode daily hoping to emulate his mother, who was particularly skilled at riding Halvor's cantankerous Mongol pony. Chester's first ride on the donkey did not go well. The cook forgot to tighten the cinch of the saddle, so when Chester mounted the donkey, the saddle slid underneath the animal's belly, dragging

Chester around the compound a number of times. Once the saddle was tightened snugly, Chester remounted and rode the donkey around the compound the same number of times as he had been dragged.[26] Graduating to his father's pony, Chester took a ride on its back behind a Chinese boy one day when the family was at their summer mountain compound. The boys were riding the horse without a bridle and the horse headed for an opening in the compound wall. Chester discovered too late why the Chinese boy had ducked his head, striking his own on the capstone. The resulting lump lasted for the duration of the family's sea voyage to Norway on furlough.

In 1895, the Rev. Thorstein Himle arrived from the United States to introduce medical work at the Fancheng mission. Four years later, Dr. J.M.J. Hotvedt relieved him and began to build a hospital. Establishing the mission, its school, church, hospital, and outstations was arduous work and along with the general conditions in Fancheng, it took a toll on the mental and physical stamina of its members. Moreover, late in 1895, Halvor learned of his mother's death in Norway, news that left him depressed and conscious of the distance he had travelled from his roots. While the birth of his first daughter, Almah, on 26 February 1896, provided joy, a little less than two years later, in January 1898, his sister Thea died at Fancheng after a brief illness. She left behind her husband Carl W. Landahl, a Lutheran missionary from Sweden and a graduate of the Red Wing Seminary. They had been married for fifteen months.

Later came the news that the Reform Movement, launched by the young Ch'ing emperor in Peking in 1898, was snuffed out by his aunt, the empress dowager, Tz'u-Hsi (Cixi), indicating that conditions for foreigners in China were likely to deteriorate further.[27] At the close of the decade, increasing antiforeignism and popular unrest throughout China, aggravated by economic hardship, culminated in the Boxer Rebellion, which ultimately gained the support of the empress dowager and the Ch'ing government.

In Hupei province, antiforeign incidents increased, along with assaults on missionaries, some leading to murder. Halvor, anxious to remove his family from danger, was relieved to receive permission to leave on furlough. He hired a junk to take his family down river to Hankow, on their way to Shanghai. Young Chester remembered vividly an incident one night when they had anchored near a small city on the banks of the Han:

> [W]e were suddenly awakened by the terrifying continuously repeated raucous cry of the Boxers, "*Sha yang jen*," kill foreigners.... It was the first and last time we heard that Boxer slogan by a large mob, but for years I carried the memory of that terrifying sound.[28]

With a feeling of great relief, Halvor, Hannah, sons Nelius and Chester, and daughter Almah left Shanghai on 22 April 1899 for furlough in Norway and the United States. They did not return to Fancheng until 3 November 1901. Their voyage from Shanghai took them to Hong Kong, Singapore, Ceylon (Sri Lanka), Bombay (Mumbai), the Red Sea, and Suez, with a stop in Italy, before landing in Liverpool, where they stayed for two weeks while Halvor received treatment for blood poisoning. Then it was off to Skein, Norway, via Germany and Denmark, ending at Bo in Telemark where they remained for three months.

Chester, nursing the bump on his head, was barely five years old, but he remembered that during the two and a half years of the furlough, he, Nelius, and Almah "had to learn Norwegian" and later "were forced to learn a third language—English."[29] Yet, judging by a comment made by Halvor's brother Nilius, who had returned from America in the summer of 1899 for the family reunion, they already had a command of these languages when they arrived in Telemark. Uncle Nilius described the impact upon the local community of the new arrivals from China:

> My brother, with wife and three children, Nilius, Chester and Almah, and with a large number of trunks filled with Chinese curiosities—the children talking Chinese and English and Norwegian—made a sensation, and people from all over the parish came to stare and to listen.[30]

Ronning family in Chinese dress before leaving on furlough, 1899. Chester on extreme left. [Ronning/Cassady photo collection]

The furlough enabled the senior Ronnings to preach, propagate the need for more missionaries for China, and visit their families. By the time it ended in 1901, the Boxer Rebellion had been crushed and the Ch'ing government was pledged to reform. Hannah gave birth to another boy, Talbert, in October 1899, one month after the family arrived in America from Norway. They went to Jewel, Iowa, where Halvor's church had accommodations. From there they paid frequent visits to Hannah's sister on her farm full of animals. One year later, the enlarged family left Jewel for Minneapolis to visit Halvor's brother Nilius. On 17 March 1901, Halvor delivered a lecture on "Missions in China" at the Missions Festival in Minneapolis. Later, they took the Soo Line to Canada to connect with the *Empress of China* in Vancouver. During a station stop in Calgary, they met Norwegian settlers on their way south to the United States to encourage more Norwegians to take up homesteads on Canadian Pacific Railway land at a place they called Bardo, after their home in Norway. It was located southeast of a town called Edmonton, in the territory that was soon part of the province of Alberta. Among them was John Anderson, the brother of Peter, Halvor's Red Wing Seminary classmate, who urged Halvor and Hannah to buy a farm near Bardo for three dollars an acre, with twenty years to pay at low interest. Subsequently, the proposition became a subject of lively debate as the Ronning family sailed toward Yokohama. Chester and Nelius were enthusiastic following their farm experience in Iowa. From Yokohama, Halvor wired John Anderson to purchase 320 acres for them: the Ronnings acquired a Canadian home.

The prospect of a future life in Canada placed a renewed emphasis on the value of learning English, and once back in Fancheng, the Ronning children were expected to keep up all three of their languages.

> During our three formal meals a day, Mother spoke to us in English. We were made to answer in English, and she saw to it that we read books in English. Father spoke to us in Norwegian and we replied in Norwegian, and he gave us our religious education in Norwegian.[31]

Otherwise, they spoke Chinese to each other, and to their parents. At a reunion with their Chinese playmates, Chester was given a rabbit, which he much fancied, and in their father's school he and Nelius were in demand among Chinese students to teach them English. The following year, in September 1902, Hannah gave birth to twins, Hazel and Harold. The growing number of siblings gave Chester and Nelius greater family responsibilities. A Mrs. Groseth taught the Ronning children, along with other missionary children, in a special missionary school set up for them. In addition, Hannah read to them and told stories. Chester was much taken with John Bunyan's *Pilgrim's Progress*. Nelius and Chester took violin lessons from a Swedish missionary,[32] but they put their "fiddles" away and never played them again after Hannah's death.

Fancheng had changed during their absence. The spirit of rebellion, evident before they left on furlough, was more pronounced and more widespread. It had an impact on the mission and on the Chinese community. More well-to-do and politically progressive Chinese were interested in the gospel and the quality of the schooling provided by the mission. In 1904, the mission established the Hung (Hong) wen high school, with Halvor as its principal. However, popular hostility toward the powerful Westerners and to the weak Manchu (Ch'ing) government was palpable. Both were seen as the cause of China's social and economic woes. Sun Yat-sen (Sun Zhongshan) and other intellectuals called for the overthrow of the Ch'ing dynasty and the establishment of a republic, or at the very least, a constitutional monarchy. Sun, who was Western-educated and a medical doctor, was popular among radical students in mission schools, who rallied to his call to revolution.

As he approached his teens, Chester sympathized with these antigovernment and antiforeign feelings. When very small boys, he and Nelius watched in fascinated horror the beheading of opponents of the government, and later, on a trip to Hankow with their father, they saw a Chinese man with a heavy wooden frame around his neck, chained to a concrete block in the British concession. Very upset at the sight, Chester asked for an explanation. His father told him that under treaties with China, foreigners had special privileges allowing them

Halvor, seated in front in Chinese costume, with teachers and pupils of Hung wen school, c. 1905. [Ronning/Cassady photo collection]

to do such things. Chester later concluded that the Chinese were not actually anti-Christian but against the privileges given to foreigners that the missionaries also enjoyed.[33] Chester sensed this antagonistic spirit among the older students in his father's school, who had formed a pro-Sun cell. One of the leaders, Tung Tse-p'ei (Dong Zepei), a friend of Chester's, swore him not to mention their feelings to his father.

Whether Halvor was aware of the coming storm or not, he continued to agitate for more missionaries to be sent out. Indeed, following the crushing of the Boxers, there was a resurgence of Protestant mission activity in China, as Western missionaries set goals of converting the heathen Chinese to Christianity in record time.[34] On top of the burdens of running an expanding mission, Halvor had a growing family to consider. In April 1904, he wrote a charming sketch of his children.

Prisoner in wooden pillory (cangue). [Evans private collection]

[Nelius] is now twelve years old and ought to attend a higher school. His eyes cannot stand much reading out here. Perhaps when he is old enough to attend the university he can [go to America]....He plays the flute already very well. Chester, only ten, is perhaps going to be a writer like his uncle. He writes long stories. Almah, eight years old, is an artist. She paints better than either her father or mother, and that is saying a good deal, isn't it? Talbert is round and fat, but a fine chap. The twins, two and a half years old, run around, and are healthy and happy.[35]

Hannah and Halvor discussed sending their two oldest boys to a mission school in Shan-tung (Shandong), but decided against it. The next year, in February 1905, one more girl, Victoria, was added to the family. That same year, Halvor reported increasing numbers of baptisms of Chinese converts, while the growing Chinese student movement, which included a number of his students, began to have an impact, beginning with organized boycotts of American and Japanese goods. In 1907, the Ch'ing government, attempting to counter this growing hostility, launched a series of reforms in education and government, but physical attacks on missionaries continued.

In July 1906, Halvor, along with other missionaries, undertook a trip by wagon through Honan (Henan) province to Peking. The party was assailed by a mob. Halvor was hit in the head by a stone, drawing blood, but "[h]e thought it unwise to fire his revolver to scare the mob away. [Instead,] [h]e cried to God for help."[36] By August, he began thinking seriously of returning to America. Hannah, plagued by recurring spells of sickness of increasing duration and intensity, needed medical attention. By September, she appeared to recover, but her health further deteriorated and she passed away on 9 February 1907. Shortly thereafter, Halvor once again took the boys by boat to Pian Mountain to find suitable stone for a memorial to Hannah.

Halvor resolved to end his mission.[37] He divided his family in two: Nelius and Chester would be sent to Hannah's family in Iowa, and the five younger children would remain with him for the year it took him to transfer the mission.[38] He accompanied Nelius and Chester as far

Western missionaries journeying from Hupei to Honan, early twentieth century.
[Ronning/Cassady photo collection]

as Shanghai, where the two boys, dressed in strange-feeling Western
clothes, were placed in the charge of Dr. J.M.J. Hotvedt, who was
taking his very ill wife back to California for treatment. The doctor had
two young daughters and Nelius, aged fourteen, and Chester, twelve,
were assigned the task of minding them for the duration of the voyage
while the doctor cared for his wife. Halvor went with Nelius and
Chester on the tender, which took them to their ship moored at the
mouth of the Yangtze. As the two boys waved their new hats in goodbye to their father, Chester lost his in the Yangtze.[39]

Funeral of Hannah Rorem Ronning, Fancheng, February 1907. Halvor and children alongside coffin. [Ronning/Cassady photo collection]

The ship was scheduled to stop in Japan and Hawaii on its way to San Francisco. The boys found the only way to control the very lively Hotvedt girls was to tie a long silk sash around each of them. They took turns anchoring the sashes and watching their charges. Despite this chore, Nelius and Chester enjoyed a voyage filled with adventure. It remained vivid in Chester's memory. When approaching the port of Kobe, their ship went aground, puncturing its hull. All the passengers, except for the Hotvedts and Ronnings, were disembarked and taken to hotels in Kobe. Four days later, the repaired ship,

Halvor bidding goodbye to Nelius and Chester, Shanghai, 1907. [Evans private collection]

with its remaining passengers, reached Kobe. Later, at Yokohama, health inspectors found smallpox among the steerage passengers. All passengers, along with their goods, were evacuated to an island to be steamed. Chester recalled the stay on the island as one full of fun as he and Nelius ran up and down the low hills, free of reprimand, and temporarily relieved of Hotvedt duties. The stop in Hawaii convinced him that these islands were heaven on earth, a view he retained throughout his life. San Francisco was still in ruins from the earthquake of April 1906, so Dr. Hotvedt took everyone across the bay to Oakland where his wife was admitted to hospital. After a few days, during which the boys revelled in marching through the streets behind the Salvation Army Band, they were put on the train to Ames, Iowa. En route, as good American boys, they set foot on the ground of every state they passed through by getting off the train and down from the platforms at every station stop.[40]

After Ames, it was a long buggy ride to their Uncle Albert's farm near Radcliffe. Albert taught them the basics of farming and the boys learned how to shear a sheep, herd hogs, and drive horses. Chester, more timid than Nelius, avoided trying to do things he was not certain he could accomplish in order not to embarrass himself. Despite their age difference, both boys were assigned to grade seven at the Radcliffe school. On their first day, they were mocked with a chant:

*Ching chong Chinaman eat dead rats*
*Chew them up like ginger snaps.*[41]

They were teased to the point where they refused to talk about China. Less resilient than Nelius, Chester cried himself to sleep that night. Eventually, the boys were accepted and learned American history, and how the heroic American colonies rebelled against the oppressive British monarchy.

Yet, the boys did not remain Americans for long. Within the year, they were to meet the rest of the family at Bardo, Alberta. After a month in Minneapolis to visit Uncle Nilius, the boys made their way north by train to Camrose, via Moose Jaw, Calgary, and Wetaskiwin.

Halvor and children reunited at Bardo, Alberta, 1908. Chester is on the far right.
[Ronning/Cassady photo collection]

On arrival in Camrose, they purchased two .22 rifles with money they
saved from the trip. They were ready to shoot gophers. From Camrose,
they travelled to Bardo in a horse-drawn buggy, driven by their Uncle
Tom Rorem, who, with his wife Alice, had moved from Radcliffe the
year before. They stayed with their aunt and uncle for a month until
Halvor and the remaining children arrived from China. The reunion
was joyous, but according to Chester, their youngest sister spoke only
Chinese, the twins and Talbert spoke a little English, while Almah had
maintained her ability to speak Norwegian, Chinese, and English. In
1908, at Bardo, a year after Halvor had said goodbye to his older sons
in Shanghai, the Ronning family was reunited in a new house, built for
them with money Halvor had sent from China.

Soon after their arrival, Chester was given a horse, an Indian pony called Sailor, which brother Nelius did not want, and was asked to ride twenty-five miles south to Dorenlee to collect twenty head of cattle. There, he met Inga Horte, a tall, pretty, Norwegian-speaking girl, who ten years later and four hundred miles further north would become his bride. Born in Nilsville, Illinois, on 2 June 1895, Inga migrated with her parents Ingrid and Anton Horte in 1902 to Dorenlee, Alberta. It was at Dorenlee that Inga heard a language other than Norwegian for the first time. She preferred Norwegian, but she soon learned to speak English without a Norwegian accent.[42]

Chester and Nelius attended school in Bardo and vigorously defended their pro-American and anti-British beliefs, sometimes to the point of blows. But they soon learned the "truth" about how the British motherland had saved Canada from the clutches of rampant American republicanism. They developed a Canadian outlook. "We became very good Canadians and very loyal Canadians. We became very ardent Canadians."[43] Chester, at fifteen, was trilingual, a world traveller, and was learning to see the world from different points of view.

# Bucolic Youth

The Ronning family's interlude in Bardo lasted five years, during which time Halvor became a naturalized Canadian, and remarried. He gained citizenship courtesy of Frank Oliver, a newspaper publisher and politician seeking votes for re-election. On 11 June 1911, Halvor married Gunhild, the eldest daughter of the Horte family of Dorenlee. Although now a farmer, Halvor was appointed as a travelling evangelist and continued as a Lutheran pastor. He also gave lectures about China, emphasizing the great need for overseas missions. In October 1911 came the exciting news of revolution in China, launched by the followers of Sun Yat-sen, whose ideas were inspiring the students at Hung wen school in Fancheng. Indeed, unknown to the general public at the time, Sun had been in Calgary in February 1911, where he gave lectures on his revolutionary ideas and raised money from the Chinese community to finance revolt in China.

Meanwhile, Halvor lost none of his zeal and dedication to the Lutheran faith. More Norwegian families arrived in Bardo from Minnesota and Norway, exhausting the supply of land available. Many settled farther afield, and Halvor feared they would be without proper pastoral attention: "I felt fully convinced that our church ought to do more to guide and gather our people in the founding of new settlements."[1] He yearned for a new Norwegian settlement, properly ministered to by the Norwegian Lutheran Church. The discovery of new agricultural land in the Peace River district, four hundred miles northwest of Edmonton, caught his attention. Chester was left to wonder why.

> It is not easy to understand how my father caught the fever to visit the Peace River. He was an elderly clergyman, who was approaching the age of retirement, with a large family, comfortably settled in a fine house on a developed, excellent farm of rich land in Bardo, only seven miles from the railway station in Tofield and not too far from the city of Edmonton. He nevertheless suddenly decided that he must see the new land which he said could be the realization of a vision which he had cherished for a long time. [As a travelling evangelist in Canada and the United States,] [h]e met hundreds of young people, some of whom came from Norway. They had hoped to acquire land as their grandparents had when they left Norway. Our father gradually developed hopes to be able some day to find some area suitable for a Norse settlement such as the one in which our family was living, Bardo, where land-hungry people could be established to preserve their religious and cultural heritage.[2]

The Grande Prairie area was huge and homesteads were available for the claiming. There was space enough to establish a large community.[3] The only problem was getting there through the low-lying muskeg bogs and densely forested hills where bears roamed. In 1911, the Edson Trail opened from the railhead at Edson to Slave Lake, and on to Grande Prairie. The conditions of the trail were much worse than advertised, and those who survived the journey had reason to feel a sense of major accomplishment. Not until the railway reached High Prairie in 1914 was the trail made obsolete.

During mid-September 1912, Halvor and Gunhild left Bardo in a covered wagon for Edson from which spot they began the treacherous trek to Grande Prairie. Two weeks and three hundred miles later, they gained the southern edge of the Grande Prairie district. The area was already crowded and it was too dry for their purposes, so they continued on north. On Sunday, 6 October, they stayed with a Norwegian family from Bardo who had preceded them. Halvor debated with himself whether they should press on or go back. "I turned to God, and after a struggle with Him, like that of Jacob, I received an answer, 'Thou has prevailed.'"[4] With renewed confidence, Halvor and Gunhild continued to the northwest to a more luxuriant area, which Halvor named Valhalla. There, Halvor and Gunhild filed homestead claims for themselves and one each for Chester and Nelius. Chester's claim was formally described as the "SE quarter of section 12, Township 74, Range 10, West of the 6th Meridian."[5] He was later to give his address as Lake Saskatoon, Grande Prairie, which was the nearest post office.

Returning to Bardo, after a trip that had taken six weeks, Halvor and Gunhild rallied fifteen families, among them members of the Horte family—Gunhild's brothers and sisters—to go back to Valhalla with them in the spring of 1913 over the "Ice Trail."[6] The Ronnings led the caravan of forty teams, of which, according to Halvor,

> We had four teams, three of horses and one of oxen. Two teams drew sleighs heavily laden with provisions. The oxen pulled a bulky load of farm machinery and household effects and the fourth team was hitched to a canvas caboose, in which we had a kitchen range for heat and the preparation of meals and in which we slept at night. We were well stocked with many sacks of crisp toasted "kavring."[7]

They arrived in Grande Prairie on Easter Sunday, 23 March, reaching Valhalla the next day and pitching their tents on the snow-covered ground. Chester and Nelius followed a few weeks later, after they completed the school term at Camrose Lutheran College, where they were taking courses preparatory to entering university. They walked the nearly four hundred miles of the Edson Trail to Grande Prairie. During the summer of 1913, they helped build their father's house at Valhalla. It was a large, two-storey building made of close-fitting, square-trimmed logs, and large enough to house the members of Halvor's family and to provide rooms for newly arrived settlers until they constructed houses of their own. As Chester remembered,

> We found timber about 9 miles west of us but to haul the logs in summer over the sod was so difficult. My father taught us how to use an axe, and I was the one driving the ox team to drag the logs to the trail. Some of the logs had to be as long as the proposed house and the oxen needed frequent rests. Nelius and I then rolled the logs on to the wagon and I drove the oxen. When I see the house now and the size of the logs I think of those nine-mile journeys bringing them. I had a small .22 rifle and I shot prairie chickens of which there were many. We took the breasts of these chickens, salted them down (my step-mother was very good at this) and put them in large crocks for the winter. We also ate rabbits, as long as they were not spruce rabbits, which tasted awful.[8]

Chester, nineteen, a high school graduate, threw himself into farming, clearing, and breaking the land of his homestead, with oxen and horses.[9] He loved the outdoors.

> I needed four oxen to break my land, but I only had two. Olaf Horte had no patience with oxen so I used his. I ploughed about twenty acres (of the thirty needed to prove the claim) and my homestead had no creeks or interruptions. We would go out early in the morning and then nap when the oxen rested, before going again in the afternoon. The oxen were superior to horses because they would plough through roots. My brother Talbert was with me, but he was very young and used to sit atop the oxen with a whip in his hand. One morning I heard something strange—a drumming sound, so I called to Talbert to come with me to see what was the source of the sound. As we climbed up a low hill, the sound grew louder and louder. Suddenly we saw several thousand prairie chickens doing their mating dance. They paid no attention to us as we crawled closer. They scratched the soil's surface over several acres, so much

that I did not have to disc or harrow it. Talbert and I sat there for several minutes and suddenly they took off. The next morning they were back and again we went to see them. It was a sight I never forgot.[10]

Ronning removed the timber and brush from all thirty acres of his land needed to prove his claim under the Dominion Land Act, and more. At the same time, he perfected his horsemanship skills, partly in an effort to catch the attention of Inga Marie Horte, the youngest sister of his stepmother, whom he first met in 1908 when he travelled on horseback to Dorenlee to collect cattle for his father. Later, he and Inga became students at Camrose Lutheran College.

During the winters of 1915 and 1916, both Chester and Nelius studied at the University of Alberta, living in Alberta College South (later St. Stephen's College) on the campus in Edmonton. In the summers, Nelius taught the children of the families at Valhalla, but when he returned to the University of Alberta to study geology full-time, Halvor turned to Chester, who, in April 1916, completed the first two years toward a BSC.[11] In the tradition of "honour thy father," Chester, at twenty-one, began to teach. As he later observed,

Those were the days when everyone and anyone could teach school. They were all born teachers. All the equipment necessary was textbooks and a strap. The school board provided the strap, and the children were required to supply themselves with books.

Chester had taught one class in mathematics when he was at Camrose Lutheran College, but now he was faced with thirty-one young children, all but three of them Norwegian.[12] It was a daunting task to keep the attention of young children, and it convinced him forever that primary school teachers deserve higher salaries than those of university professors.

Despite this experience, Chester decided to become a qualified teacher. He lacked the religious fervour and dedication needed to be a missionary like his father, or like Nelius planned to be. He imagined a future at the lectern, not in the pulpit. To this end, he needed a teaching certificate from a normal school, but frost ruined his crops and he had little money. In November 1916, Chester wrote Rev. J.R. Lavik, principal of the Camrose Lutheran College, with a proposal to enable him to attend Camrose Normal School. Lavik agreed to provide him with room and board in the college residence in exchange for monitoring the students in the residence and for teaching courses in mathematics and agriculture at the college. This arrangement enabled him to enroll at the Camrose Normal School in January 1917 to study for a first-class teaching certificate, but partway through his program, the provincial Department of Education ruled that he lacked a qualification in agriculture. Never at a loss and always inventive, Chester joined the very class he was teaching, wrote the provincial exam, and gained the necessary qualification.

In the spring of 1917, he received a first-class teaching certificate and returned to his homestead at Valhalla. He joined the United Farmers of Alberta (UFA), a group that lobbied the provincial government in farmers' interests. The UFA and the United Farm Women of Alberta (UFWA) were made up of a series of local grassroots organizations that coalesced around issues vital to farmers. Together, they made up a great Prairie-based mass movement for change.[13] It was membership in the UFA that drew Ronning into active politics fifteen years later.

A letter of 22 July 1917 to Peter Stolee, his good friend and fellow student at Camrose Lutheran College, provides a glimpse of Chester's life in Valhalla, and the general outlook of the newly qualified teacher.

> Since coming home Pete I've been having a whale of a time. The first week I spent in chasing around the country electioneering for a prospective member to parliament. The poor soul however was defeated which may or may not have been my fault.[14] After that I spent some time out at the sawmill, which we own together with Olaf Horte. There is a lake there and a boat in which I spent some time hunting with a rifle. The scenery is very wild and weird.
>
> Then Olaf and I spent a few days prospecting for timber in some land to the north of the lake, which has never been surveyed. We

had each a rifle, a blanket, a tin can, a little rice, oatmeal and tea
on our backs trudging thru the country on the "apostles donks."[15]
Many a time Pete I thought of you and wished that you could have
been along, because of all the people I know you are one of the few I
know would have thoroughly enjoyed it. We struck out in any direction whatever climbing trees to take observations, crossing hills
and valleys and climbing over down fall. We did not see a human
being. In fact I dont [sic] think there have ever been any there
besides Indians and maybe trappers in years gone by. The country
abounds with moose & bear wolves coyotes foxes [sic] but most of
all mosquitos[.] I say they preferred us.

At night we built a fire under the spruce trees[,] ate heartily
of our rations, talked until we became hoarse, then lay our heads
on the moss rolled with our blankets and were sound asleep in a
short time in spite of the fact that at times we imagined that lynx
& mountain lions (which are found frequently) were prowling
around. Some of the views we obtained from 100 ft. pines on the
top of large hills were simply magnificent. The mountains lie to the
west & south and the luxuriant growths of trees made the scenery
look almost tropical. We simply had one grand and glorious time
alone with nature, and yet old Solie[16] says it is doubtfull [sic] if one
can see God in nature.

Be that as it may let me tell you Pete I was greatly inspired &
I am certain that if you could have been with me you would have
enjoyed it just as thoroughly.[17]

But the following spring of 1918, Chester left both his farm and
the classroom for a new adventure, this time to fight in the Great
War, a war that his father firmly opposed. In 1915 and 1916, while at
the University of Alberta, Nelius and Chester participated in officer
training and mixed with a number of patriotic students from England
attending the university who thought that enlisting was the proper
thing to do, and whose attitude influenced the Ronning brothers.
Then, in late August 1917, the federal government passed the Military
Services Act, calling for the conscription of able-bodied males over

twenty and suitable for war service. Among those exempt were men whose occupations or studies were deemed to be essential to the war effort. Farmers fell within this latter category. Early in April 1918, without his father's permission, Nelius joined the Royal Flying Corps (the Royal Canadian Air Force did not exist at this time) in Edmonton. The deed done, he went to Valhalla to seek his father's blessing, which he ultimately received. Thus assured, he left early on a Saturday morning by buggy for Grande Prairie, thirty miles away, to catch the Sunday morning train to Edmonton. Saturday evening, copies of the *Edmonton Bulletin* and the *Edmonton Journal*, with front-page stories on the lowering of the qualifications for conscription, arrived in Valhalla. Chester, determined at all costs to avoid being conscripted, persuaded his father to let him go with Nelius. Half-asleep, he rode his horse Sailor through the night, reaching Grande Prairie in time to join Nelius on the train for Edmonton.

Chester wanted to join the Royal Flying Corps, but there was a surplus of pilots and his request was refused. Even Nelius, already accepted, was told he must wait. The Ronning boys filled in a few days helping on a friend's farm in Bardo before another one of Chester's friends advised him to join the Canadian Engineers. Inducted as a sapper, Chester was sent to Calgary to wait for two weeks. Without money, he survived, thanks "to a fellow Chinese who let me sleep in his house and fed me a big breakfast."[18] Finally, he was assigned to escort a dozen Mormon conscripts from southern Alberta to Fort Osborne in Manitoba.

Very soon he regretted his choice of the Engineers. A particularly mean British sergeant-major drilled the new recruits repeatedly and relentlessly under the hot summer sun. Moreover, because Chester was tall, he was assigned guard duty, watching the conscripts at night, lest they attempt to desert. Not soon enough for him, in late August 1918, he left on harvest leave to help out at Valhalla. He was so unhappy with the Engineers that "[e]ven if there had been no crops to harvest, I would have gone."[19] But he had more than harvesting on his mind. Early in September 1918, he married Inga Marie Horte, whom he had been wooing and trying to impress with his horsemanship for some time. They travelled by wagon to Grande Prairie to obtain a licence and later, back at Valhalla, the Rev. Halvor Ronning, Chester's father (and Inga's brother-in-law), performed the nuptial service. That evening, the Valhalla community joined in a celebration and dance. Thereafter, whenever they were together on the day, Chester and Inga marked their wedding anniversary with a photograph.

Reluctantly back in Winnipeg, Chester was overjoyed to receive admission to the Royal Flying Corps as a trainee pilot. Nelius was already in flying school, but Chester took to the skies before him. Neither of them qualified as a pilot before the war ended in November[20] and they returned to Alberta. Released from his military duties, Nelius resumed his studies toward a master's degree in geology at the University of Alberta. He stayed with Chester and Inga, who had settled in Edmonton, north of the river at 9714-106 Street. Chester hoped to get a job teaching. His hope became reality when a former teacher from Bardo recommended him for the position of assistant principal at Queen Alexandra School at 78 Avenue and 106 Street on Edmonton's south side. There, he taught music and had a homeroom class of grade seven girls, some of them in their mid-teens. He taught in his uniform until February 1919, until he was discharged and he had enough money to buy a suit.[21]

In a letter to his friend, Peter Stolee, written 20 December 1918, shortly before he began teaching at Queen Alexandra, Chester outlined his thinking on the joys of marriage and on a balanced education.

Dear Pedro: –

Your letter this afternoon found me in very high spirits. This morning I received my appointment to the asst. principalship of the Queen Alexandra so now my plans for the next six months are fixed. Congratulate me old man. You know the worries of indecision & uncertainty in regard to ones [sic] plans don't you.

I'm very glad to hear that you are going to continue H.S....I can readily appreciate your point of view in choosing CLC. We need students such as you at the school, Pete. Someone as a stabilizer, as

it were....but when engrossed in your books don't forget that important study, sociology, and I think that you will be able to easily bear
the education you have in view. Let your academic standing go
hang if it interferes with your duties as a leader in the social life of
the college.

Take my advise [sic] for what it's worth considering who it
comes from & remember that I have a great storhouse [sic] full of it
and am very generous in doling it out to my friends, who when they
get to know me as you do can generally sift the "well meant" grain
from the mass of chaff.

Aha! Pedro! Your heart longeth for a life such as Conrad is
living. Good for you[.] I'd like to slap you on the back. & "believe me
Zantippe[.]"[22]

It's wonderfull [sic] to have a girl Pedro, who is willing to share
your sorrows and joys and make life really worthwhile living. It
makes one proud to be a man, thankfull [sic] that he is strong and
healthy and brings out qualities that before seemed dormant.

There is a pure girl somewhere Pedro waiting for you to claim
her & when you do, you will be rewarded for having kept yourself
strong, virile & clean. There is no happiness on earth I daresay
greater than that a man gets in his own home.[23]

Your friend,
Chester

In January 1919, Ronning began to teach with great enthusiasm. He
loved teaching, but at the same time he found it to be stressful. Giving
in to his frustrations, for one time, and one time only, he attempted to
administer the strap, as he describes in this handwritten letter to Peter
Stolee on 9 March 1919.

My dear Pedro: —

My work is interesting and demands all my time. I don't even get
a chance to go downtown for writing paper so I use this fools-cap

and it has gotten to be such a habit I neglect to apologize for using it. I find old man that it is necessary to treat these town kids severely if one is not to be run to an early grave or get his hair whitened in a week.

I am beginning to "waver in my faith and believe with Pythagoras that animals have infused themselves into the trunks of men" consequently that pet theory about the strap is rocking on its foundations and one of these days is going to get a tremendous crash. It almost did the other day but when I told the big bullie [sic] of a boy to hold up his hand to receive promised cracks from a rubber hose in my hand, but the victim refused much to my relief, so I packed him home books, bag & baggage not to return until he is prepared to let Justice do its stern duty.

Time for bed Petra so Bonne Nuit!

Your friend,
Chester[24]

In the summer break, to further his qualifications, Chester took mathematics courses—a favourite subject—at the University of Alberta. Dr. E.W. Sheldon, the instructor, rented Ronning his house at 9330-81 Avenue. The house was closer to Queen Alexandra School, so Chester and Inga moved in. There, in September 1919, Inga gave birth to Sylvia, their first child. Chester was present, assisting the doctor. He became an advocate of such a practice and he attended the births of all but one of their six children.

Unfortunately, soon afterward, Chester was appointed as the male assistant at the H. Allen Gray School at 103 Street and 120 Avenue in north Edmonton, some ten miles away. Rather than abandon their new home, Chester bought a bicycle to ride to his new school, occasionally hanging on to the back of streetcars to make better time. For the Ronnings, the joys of their young child, the comforts of a nice home, and the prospect of years of peaceful stability as Chester furthered his teaching career were seductive, but in August 1920, a tragic accident changed the course of their lives.

# Return to Fancheng

The Rev. Halvor Ronning was proud of all his children, but he was extraordinarily proud of his eldest son, Nelius, for whom he mapped out a future as a missionary in China. They each shared a fervent, personal relationship with God. Halvor's greatest wish was for Nelius to further the mission that he and Hannah had begun three decades before. Nelius shared his father's enthusiasm for spreading the gospel, and his father's hope that he would return to Fancheng. At the University of Alberta, Nelius was known for his burning desire to return to China. (Chester, too, hoped to return to China, but he regarded his older brother's wish as a family priority.) While a student in Edmonton, Nelius became involved with the local Chinese community. He assisted a fellow student, Bin Wong, to teach Sunday school to a group of Chinese men at the Metropolitan Methodist Church.[1] His religious devotion was obvious to all. His roommate later wrote:

> Outstanding above every trait was his faithfulness in prayer. All the time I roomed with him at College, he never missed his daily devotion. When he prayed you got the impression that he was talking

face to face with God as a man who knew what he needed and expected to receive it.[2]

Before joining the Royal Flying Corps in 1918, Nelius completed the requirements for a BA in geology and after his discharge he continued his studies, receiving a master's degree in the spring of 1920. During this time, he received offers to go to Burma with an oil company and to go to France with the YMCA to work with the Chinese Labour Corps.[3] But the offer that gave him joy was an invitation to go to China as a missionary for the Young People's League of America. He considered the offer carefully, concluding, "If my decision is not in accordance with God's plan, He will block my pathway and turn me into the path which He has ordained for me to travel."[4] In this mood, in the summer of 1920, he accepted a position as an assistant geologist with the Imperial Oil Company on a summer survey eight hundred miles north, along the shores of Great Slave Lake. On his return, he would prepare to leave for China.

But it was not to be. Nelius and his partner, J.C. MacDougall, while surveying the rock face of the lakeshore from a boat, were caught in a sudden storm and their boat capsized. A search proved futile and the two young men were presumed drowned.[5] The news was devastating to the Ronning family, particularly to Halvor.[6] It also shocked the University of Alberta community:

Most sad is the news which comes to us from Fort Resolution of the probable drowning of Nelius Ronning in northern waters about August 13th....

Around the University there was scarcely anyone more generally known, more highly esteemed, or more worthily beloved than Nelius. From the time when he first came out from the Grande Prairie...he has been a winning and influential personality in University circles. An athlete, a musician, a conscientious student, a sympathetic friend, an off-bearing supporter of every worthy cause, he combined the most admirable qualities in a manner all too rarely seen.

His heart was set on China—the land of his birth, the scene of his parents' early toil and the goal of his sainted mother's wish for him.[7]

The news also saddened friends in China, who wrote:

> When we heard that he soon was coming to Fancheng, it filled our hearts with much joy, but when the news came of his sudden death, it made our hearts heavy. The whole congregation here mourns the loss.[8]

The death of Nelius changed the course of Chester's life. The young teacher, husband, and father, who had only hoped one day to return to China, now felt an urge to replace his brother and revisit the land of his birth as soon as practicable.[9] He did not have the religious zeal of Nelius; his goal was to return as a teacher, rather than as a minister of the gospel. He yearned to witness the modern transformation of China's ancient civilization, and to participate in it. First, however, he would bolster his qualifications as an educator in order to train teachers in China.

\* \* \*

In 1921, while at H. Allen Gray School,[10] Chester searched for suitable opportunities to go back to China and found that the Lutheran Missionary Movement was looking for teachers to go to China, but only those with a degree in education need apply. That fall, he took Inga and Sylvia to Minneapolis, where he attended the University of Minnesota, one of only two universities in North America offering education degrees at the time. He registered in as many courses as he possibly could. In addition, he took lessons on how to play the organ and learned how to wrestle. Within a year, he received his bachelor of education degree and he prepared his family to leave for China. Their destination was Peking, where Chester would undergo Mandarin language training prior to taking up the position of principal of Hung wen middle school (*Hong wen shu yuan*) in Fancheng.

Early in October 1922, Chester, Inga, and Sylvia left Vancouver for Shanghai aboard the *Empress of Australia*, a converted German ship that had come to the Canadian Pacific Steamship Company through war reparations. Three days out, it broke down and had to return to Vancouver. Two weeks later, aboard the *Empress of Canada*, the Ronnings sailed for Shanghai. It was a calm, seductive interlude full of creature comforts, a poor introduction to what awaited them in China.

Ronning was returning to China after a fifteen-year absence. He had left in 1907 as a precocious youth of twelve; he was returning as a young teacher with a wife and child. He looked forward eagerly to setting foot once again in China. He was filled with curiosity about the changes he would see. The same could not be said of Inga. A young farm girl steeped in Norwegian tradition, but with no experience outside North America, she could only imagine the country with which her husband was so enamoured, that had commanded her father-in-law's devoted attention for eighteen years, and that contained the grave of Chester's mother. Inga was ill-prepared for the major culture shock she received from her first encounter with China. In later years, Chester admitted he had underestimated the impact China would have on his wife. Although Western-style settlements in some Chinese cities provided a protective cocoon for the newcomer, the real face of China could not remain hidden for long.

China had undergone great changes since 1907, when Chester last saw it, and there were more to come. The reforms that the Ch'ing government introduced in the first decade of the twentieth century proved to be insufficient to save their regime, and their grip on state power grew ever weaker. On 10 October 1911, the Double Tenth, an explosion in Hankow, touched off a series of revolts throughout China against the Ch'ing government. These events marked the culmination of efforts by Sun Yat-sen (Sun Zhongshan), the Western-educated Hakka from Kwangtung (Guangdong),[11] his followers, reformers, and others to bring about a change in government. Sun, in exile because of his previous attacks on the government, had a price on his head. He travelled the world in disguise and under pseudonyms, raising money from overseas Chinese communities to

Dr. Sun Yat-sen, c. 1910. [Evans private collection]

support his ideas for a republican government in China. An uprising on 27 April 1911 in Canton (Guangzhou), financed by money
raised from the Chinese communities on the Canadian Prairies, was
brutally suppressed, but the Ch'ing regime was on notice. Sun was
in the United States on a train outside Denver, Colorado, when he
learned of the October 10 explosion in Hankow. He returned in haste
to China, travelling via Europe, where he tried, unsuccessfully, to get
support from foreign governments. He reached Shanghai at the end
of December 1911 to be proclaimed provisional president of a new
Republic of China.

The Ch'ing imperial government in Peking called upon its top military leader, Yuan Shih-k'ai (Yuan Shikai), the commander of the north
China (Peiyang) army, to re-establish order. Instead, Yuan negotiated
with Sun. He convinced the imperial family that they had no option
except to abdicate, while at the same time he told Sun that the Ch'ing
abdication depended upon him giving up his position as provisional
president. The Ch'ing gave up power in February 1912, and at the same
time Sun Yat-sen gave up his position as provisional president, leaving Yuan Shih-k'ai (the prototype of future warlords) in charge of the
new government. With his army, he intimidated the national assembly,
which had been elected as provided for in an earlier imperial reform
decree. Yuan pressured that multiparty body into accepting him as
emperor, but he died in June 1916 before he achieved his goal. He left
the central government of republican China in shambles, a prize to be
fought over by his former generals who became warlords, and who, on
their own or in cliques, ruled Peking for the next decade.[12]

China entered the First World War in the spring of 1917. Sun Yat-
sen, who had staged an unsuccessful revolt against Yuan in 1913, was
against China taking sides in the war that he maintained was being
fought among China's enemies. But the Peking government declared
war on Germany, hoping to regain the concessions that Germany had
seized twenty years earlier in Shan-tung province, and which Japan,
as an ally of England, had occupied in 1915. China's declaration of war
was to no avail: Japan managed to hold on to the German concessions
as a provision of the Treaty of Versailles of 1919.

When the news of Japan's victory at the Versailles Peace
Conference reached China, students and other revolutionary-minded
Chinese reacted strongly: China had been duped. They demanded
that their government refuse to sign the treaty. On 4 May 1919, angry
Chinese students marched on government offices and ministers' residences and demonstrated in front of Tien-an men (Tiananmen), the
Gate of Heavenly Peace and entrance to the Forbidden City, where the
last of the Ch'ing emperors, P'u-i (Puyi), continued to live. This period
of protest, now known as the May 4th Movement, launched a wave of
experimentation in the arts and politics. The West's much-vaunted
superiority was discredited by the disaster of the war in Europe,
and the Communist revolution in Russia, with its promises of a new
utopia, caught the attention of some Chinese intellectuals. Secretively,
in July 1921, a small group of Chinese Marxists and revolutionaries met
at a girls' school within the French concession of Shanghai to found
the Communist Party of China.

Meanwhile, Western intellectuals, such as John Dewey from the
United States and Bertrand Russell from England, presented their
ideas at universities throughout China. The first-ever Nobel laureate
from Asia, Rabindranath Tagore from India, shared his philosophy
with eager Chinese students. In January 1923, Albert Einstein visited Shanghai and received a warm reception, particularly from the
Jewish community. Student movements grew more strident in their
nationalism, which was tinged with xenophobia. Missionary schools,
which had introduced a modern Western curriculum into Chinese
education, were subjected to verbal, and sometimes physical, attack.
Foreigners worried about the growing influence of Bolshevik Russia
among students, who challenged the authority of their professors,
of university administrations, the Minister of Education, and the
Speaker of the elected National Assembly. During the years 1920–21,
north China suffered a major famine. Bandit gangs proliferated as vil-
lagers fended for themselves in times of growing economic hardship
and political chaos.

It was into this China of military and political turmoil, economic
hardship, and social experimentation that the Ronnings entered on

3 November 1922.[13] They arrived amid the hubbub and seeming disorder of Shanghai, the most western of China's cities.[14] While all this was familiar, almost routine, to Chester, the noise, smells, crowds, and disarray terrified Inga, who wanted to return to Canada immediately. With Chester's assurance that the atmosphere was normal and there was no physical threat to them, particularly as foreigners, they pressed on, transferring to another ship for the six-hundred-mile journey up the Yangtze to Hankow, and the Lutheran mission hostel on the edge of the British concession. After several days waiting there, they boarded a day coach on a northbound train destined for Peking. The train was only a few hours out of Hankow near Chi-kung shan (Jigongshan), however, when

> [we] were suddenly ordered to lie flat in the aisle which was rapidly filled. The three of us crouched down as far as possible in the narrow space between the seats, and from both sides there was shooting and bullets smashed the windows. Of course this scared my wife to death. We eventually got through and the train returned to Hankow.[15]

The Ronnings had arrived, in fact, during the worst fall for kidnappings of foreigners. Only the month before, two members of the Lutheran American Mission were released from bandit custody to make their way to Hankow.[16] Chester persuaded Inga that it would be safer if they took a downriver steamer to Nanking (Nanjing), where they could board the famous Blue Express bound for Peking. The express, travelling through relatively bandit-free country, "was almost perfect luxury. My wife Inga was impressed and so was I."[17] Although Inga was mollified somewhat, all in all her introduction to China was traumatic.

In those days, the main railway station for Peking was located near Chien (Qian) Men (southeast corner of today's Tiananmen square), and it was the first sight to greet the arriving passengers. The Eight-Nation Expeditionary Force sent to end the Boxer siege of the Legation Quarter burned Chien Men in 1900. A German architect

Food stall by Peking gate, 1919. [Evans private collection]

Peking Opera, 1910. [Evans private collection]

reconstructed it, adding some Western architectural features to its facade. On arrival in Peking, the Ronnings took rickshaws to the North China Union Language School and the nearby Young Lutheran Missionary Hostel, where they were to live for almost a year in relative peace and security.[18] Not long after they arrived, Chester was asked to manage the hostel. He was able to settle his family into a separate two-storey, Western-style building with a courtyard. They employed a Manchu woman to help look after Sylvia, allowing Inga to enroll at the school and to gain a working knowledge of Chinese.

During their time in Peking, Inga and Chester met other foreign visitors, including students, language scholars, architects, and missionary families, among whom was an eight-year-old boy named Ralph Collins, who very much later (in 1971) became Canadian ambassador to China. They travelled about the city, which still had most of its ancient walls intact, and explored the surrounding countryside on donkey back, becoming familiar with temples and other historic sites. At that time the Forbidden City was still occupied by Henry P'u-i, the young, deposed, last Ch'ing emperor, and was not open to foreigners. Chester and Inga attended performances of the Peking Opera starring Mei Lanfan, famous for his superb interpretations of female roles. On one occasion, at Nan Yuan parade ground south of Peking, they met the famous "Christian" General Feng Yu-hsiang (Feng Yuxiang), who baptized his troops en masse using firehoses.[19] They rode donkeys to the Great Wall for picnics and travelled about the city in rickshaws pulled by members of the former Manchu Bannermen elite, who were forced by their loss of status to take menial tasks to keep body and soul together.

Manchu rickshaw drivers met Anvil, a Swedish scholar and student of the great sinologue Bernhard Kalgren, when he arrived at the Peking railway station early in 1923. Ronning had invited him to stay in their house, because the hostel was full. Anvil, however, failed to let Ronning know when he was arriving. The diminutive Swede was confident in his linguistic ability, but it proved no match for a crowd of Manchu drivers. He had twenty-seven pieces of luggage, but each driver agreed to take only one. A riotous din ensued when the convoy arrived at the hostel compound and Anvil attempted to settle his debts. Again, his Chinese failed him. The noise of the argument aroused Ronning, to whom Anvil shouted: "What's the matter with these coolies? They can't understand their own language. I have studied Chinese under the great scholar of their language Kalgren." Ronning took the bewildered newcomer into the house and returned to deal with the drivers, most of whom he knew, and who settled for half the amount they were asking from Anvil. Subsequently, Ronning and Anvil became good friends. On weekends, they boarded donkeys to visit Chinese temples, which Anvil wanted to see as part of his study of religions that had come to China from abroad.[20]

Peking streets were full of colour, with wayside market stalls selling meat, vegetables, fruit, sweets, nuts, and trinkets. Itinerant theatre groups performed, and there were Punch and Judy-type puppet theatres. Kite-flying was a popular pastime among children and adults. The well-to-do lived in homes separated by lanes (*hu-tong*). Each house was organized around a courtyard designed to trap the sun and its warmth. In each courtyard were usually date, nut, and persimmon trees. Ordinary houses were low and grey with tiled roofs and did not have running water. Householders depended upon water carriers for their supply. Night-soil collectors made their regular rounds as well, supplying local gardens with the fertilizer they collected. During the heat of summer, workers using small containers and ladles scattered water on the dusty streets. There were very few automobiles and those who could not afford them relied upon rickshaws or animal-drawn carts. A street car system was planned but not yet constructed. Long-distance caravans made up of heavily laden horses, donkeys, or camels were a common sight as they transported goods to and from Peking and the surrounding area. Adding to the local colour were the police who, having not been paid for months, went door to door, begging for money to make up for their wages.

There was much to learn just being in Peking, but Ronning was there to learn language. He already spoke Chinese with a Hupei accent, whose tones did not match those of the Peking, or Mandarin, dialect, but he soon found that mastering standard Mandarin

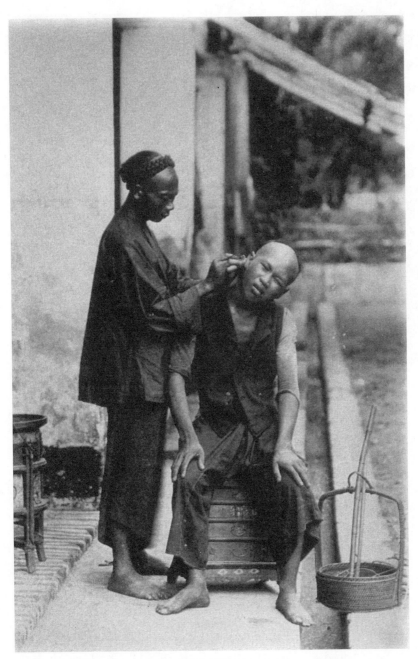

Street barber, 1919. [Evans private collection]

Peking hu-tong. [Evans private collection]

pronunciation was a minor hurdle. He completed four years of language training in one. During their time in Peking, Inga grew familiar and more at home with Chinese culture and society. But the highlight of the year, as Chester recalls in his memoir, was "to come again into contact with Chinese students in universities and middle schools. They were even more active than they were earlier in the century and had a deeper political and social consciousness."[21] They were smarting from China's treatment at Versailles and the failure of the United States to stand up to Japan in their favour.

Indeed, the China of the early 1920s was a far cry from the China Chester knew as a boy. It was no longer an empire but a republic; traditions were being questioned and many were discarded. In a sense, the old Ch'ing empire had become unglued, and it was not certain how China would be put back together, if at all. Society was in flux, but so, too, was the weak republican government, the plaything of warlord cliques that maintained well-equipped fighting forces that they tried hard not to use in battle.[22] During the Ronnings' time in Peking, a major struggle for north China was going on between warlords Wu P'ei-fu (Wu Peifu) and Chang Tso-lin (Zhang Zuolin), with Ts'ao K'un (Cao Kun), a close associate of Wu's, in charge of Peking, and who became president of the republic from October 1923 to November 1924. Meanwhile, the National Assembly, with its cabinet and civil service, attempted to project the semblance of a national government.

In the south, revolution was stirring. Sun Yat-sen, after his unsuccessful revolt against Yuan Shih-k'ai in 1913, fled to Japan where he laid the groundwork for a new revolutionary party later called the Kuomintang (KMT), or Nationalist Party. His goal was to seize power in China and to institute a republic in the style he had originally advocated, in accordance with his Three People's Principles of nationalism, democracy, and livelihood. In Hong Kong, he rallied students to work for the establishment of a republic, but at the same time he urged them to follow the English example of good government.[23] Sun continued to garner support from overseas Chinese, but he was unable to get help from foreign governments. Between 1917 and 1920, he attempted to work in alliance with a warlord in Canton, but it was clear he needed a military force of his own. In 1921, representatives of the Communist International (Comintern) from Moscow began talks with Sun, and, by 1923, his search for foreign support was over. In an agreement with Sun, the Soviet Union promised to provide him political and military support and advisors on condition that the Chinese Communist Party members were admitted as Communists into Sun's Nationalist Party. As a result, Mao Tse-tung (Mao Zedong) became a director of a Peasant Movement Training Institute established in Canton. Chou En-lai became the political commissar of the Whampoa (Huangpu) Military Academy set up by Sun under Chiang Kai-shek (Jiang Jieshi)[24] to train a politically indoctrinated army, faithful to Sun's program. This new army was to be strong enough to challenge the warlords and to lead a Northern Expedition to reunite the country

as a republic. Late in 1924, however, Sun saw an opportunity to negotiate an agreement with the northern warlords. Hoping to avoid costly
fighting, Sun travelled to Peking to seek common ground with them.

The Ronnings left Peking for Hupei province, on their way to
Hankow and Fancheng, in mid-summer 1923, at a time when matters
were about to coalesce around Sun in the south and the warlord Wu
P'ei-fu consolidated his hold in the north and Peking. Hupei province, in central China, straddles the Yangtze River and links south
and north China. The Hankow-Peking railway was a vital economic
and communications link and was guarded well at this time by Wu
P'ei-fu. Wuhan (Wuchang, Hankow, and Hanyang combined), the
largest city in Hupei, was where the republican revolution began
on 10 October 1911. Immediately afterward, the governor of Hupei
province and the army fled, providing the opportunity for the revolutionaries to consolidate their base. The province was the first to
declare its independence in 1911. But in the years after the death of
Yuan Shih-k'ai in 1916, the situation in the province deteriorated
as warlords fought for control, and bandits, such as those who later
attacked the Ronnings' train north of Hankow in November 1922,
roamed virtually unchecked. The gangs were made up of discharged
destitute soldiers and desperate peasants driven to violence by famine
and growing economic hardship.[25]

By the fall of 1923, thanks to warlord Wu P'ei-fu, law and order was
generally restored along the railway as wagons full of armed soldiers
were attached to the trains. The Ronnings were able to travel safely to
Hankow. They stopped for a holiday on the way at Chi-kung shan, a
beautiful mountain spot with a mild climate on the border of Honan
and Hupei provinces. After 1903, Western businessmen and missionaries developed it as a Western-style resort away from the heat
of the plains.[26] It was here that missions held their annual conferences and where they set up schools for their children. The Ronnings
stayed in the house of the Swedish Lutheran missionary Dr. Carl W.
Landahl, whose first wife had been Chester's aunt, Thea, who died in
1898. Later, they continued by train to the Lutheran mission home
in Hankow.

In Hankow, Ronning hired a boat to take his family and their goods up the Han River to Fancheng. The prevailing banditry made finding a willing boatman difficult enough, but Chester increased the difficulty by purchasing a second-hand piano to take with them. He needed a boat with large enough watertight compartments.[27] He engaged a large river junk (*man-kan*) and had the piano loaded on the morning of the day before they were to leave. Because they were to depart very early the next morning, their boat was moored farthest away from the shore and closest to midstream. It was reachable only by crossing the decks of a series of intervening boats scheduled to leave after theirs and tied up between the dock and their *man-kan*. Chester carried Sylvia while he steered a hesitant and nervous Inga over the bobbing and swaying path. But for Inga, the most terrifying part of departure was still to come. Chester had failed to warn her of the ritual that prefaced a long journey by boat: strings of firecrackers were lit, a number of roosters were beheaded, and their blood was smeared on the prow of the boat. With the noise of the firecrackers and the flapping about of the headless roosters, "my wife was scared to death,"[28] he recalled. At last they sailed. Their sleeping accommodation was located on deck. The upstream journey took exactly one month.

On their arrival at Fancheng, the boatman docked well below the mission station and school. Leaving Inga and Sylvia on the boat, Chester walked along the main street leading to the mission. As he progressed, he heard the rude comments about the "foreign devil" uttered by locals, unaware that he understood them. He found the mission house empty, the missionaries were away enjoying the coolness of the mountains. With care, the Ronnings and their goods were moved into the old Ronning family home, but there remained the matter of the piano. It required the efforts of twenty-six workers, and a stout carrying pole, to move it from the boat to the house. On the way, Chester heard some of the ladies of the town speculate that the piano was full of explosives for use by the "foreign devil."

The following summer, Ronning took his family to Chi-kung shan, leaving them there while he returned to Fancheng to teach. This time, he travelled from Hankow by steamer up the Yangtze to Shashi, from

Chester with daughter Sylvia in front of Ronning mission home, Fancheng, 1923.
[Ronning/Cassady photo collection]

where he and a number of missionaries hired a Model T Ford and driver
to head overland to Hsiang yang. There were no roads to speak of, and
they often got stuck. From time to time Chester drove, having had
experience driving a Model T in Alberta when delivering films to rural
areas for Charlie Hosford of the University of Alberta Bookstore.[29]

Chester's appointment was as principal of the Hung wen middle
school, but his purpose in going to Fancheng was to train teachers.
The school, of which Halvor Ronning had been principal from 1903 to
1907, was still in operation with Tung Tse-p'ei (Dong Zepei), Chester's

older classmate and friend, in charge. Tung was a famous local scholar who had attended Halvor's mission school and had passed the Ch'ing (Qing) civil service examinations at a very young age. His success brought prestige to his village, district, and to the Rev. Ronning. According to Chester:

> The Mandarins provided a sedan chair for Tung and he was carried with firecrackers before and aft, and with a yellow parasol carried to shade the sedan chair. The chair was open in front so people could see him. The prestige of my father, as a result of having a boy rise to this position, was great. This was one of the things that enabled my father to build more buildings and to change the roof design of our house, which was located beside a heavenly lamp (*t'ien-teng/tiandeng*). Father's building had to have a different shaped roof in order not to block the spirits from flowing by the heavenly lamp. The roof looked like an M in profile rather than an inverted V. There was a lot of rain in the area and the roof leaked and water ran down into the house. After Tung passed the examinations, father was allowed to change the roof because now the spirits would be kinder.[30]

Later, Tung studied at Cheeloo (Qilu), a Protestant university in Chi-nan (Jinan), Shan-tung. He participated in the student demonstrations arising from the October 10 (Double Tenth) Revolution and the May 4th Movement. Filled with the revolutionary spirit and the ideas of Dr. Sun Yat-sen, he returned to Fancheng to teach at his old school. In 1919, he was described as "one of the ablest teachers...a great student, and a devout Christian."[31] Around that same time, he wrote a piece commenting on the need for Christian education in China and on the sad state of government schools in the area.

> Since these schools are closed at present in this locality, a very large number seek admittance to the church schools. The better class of boys are the ones that come. They come to get a good education, and they know that the church schools do their work. It would

therefore be well if the educational work could be enlarged so as to be able to accommodate a larger number of students. China needs Christian schools. Nothing but Christianity will lift China out of this present chaos. In order to reach the multitude we must have native workers with a Christian education. In order to give the youth a Christian education we must have Christian schools with good and well trained teachers.[32]

When he wrote those words, Tung was Chinese superintendent and a teacher at the school. Later, he was made acting principal. Rather than displace him, Chester insisted to the directors of the mission board that he and Tung be made co-principals. It was a wise decision given the course of future events.

Chester regarded himself as a teacher, not a missionary. Nonetheless, he and his family were living in the Lutheran mission established by his parents,[33] in the same city where his mother's grave was located.[34] Chester also undertook a walking tour of the mission's outstations and explored further in Honan province. He walked for days behind a man and his wheelbarrow, stopping at the inns where he stopped. To the growing numbers of Chinese smarting from years of foreign privilege and high-handed behaviour, the presence of a tall foreigner might have been taken as a provocation.

During this time, there were almost daily reports of missionaries being assaulted, kidnapped, wounded, and even murdered. Sun Yat-sen and his followers did not physically attack foreigners, and they generally had good relations with Christian schools. Nevertheless, they envisioned a future China where foreign interests would be greatly diminished—if not eliminated—and the Chinese people would be in charge of their own country, its economy, and foreign policy. In the heat of the expanding revolution, they could not readily distinguish between foreigners who were wedded to their special privileges and those who were sympathetic to the revolution. Thanks to Tung Tse-p'ei, others knew of Chester's pro-revolution views. He was the only foreigner on the staff of the school.

Within Hung wen school, the students and all but one member of the staff were followers of Sun Yat-sen. At least two students had gone to work with Chou En-lai at the Whampoa Academy in Canton, while others undertook to work with peasants in the surrounding country-side to teach them about the revolution. All of them participated in boycotts of foreign goods. This was brought home to Chester in dramatic fashion one day in the midst of a class.

A student opened the door, walked quietly in, and whispered something to the boy next to the door. He in turn passed something on to the chap sitting next to him. Some message was passed from ear to ear until the whole class knew something, which I did not. A few minutes later the whole class rose and walked silently out into the hall. I followed them, wondering if this was some expression of anti-foreign feeling being directed against me, since I was the only foreigner. But the halls were filled with all of the several hundred students, and they walked silently out of the school. I joined the other teachers. If they knew what was going on they said nothing. We followed the students down the street to the city gate facing the Han River. From the gate we saw hundreds of students coming out of the gates of Hsiangyang across the river. They boarded junks going upstream and forcibly seized all foreign kerosene and tobacco, stacked it in piles, drove holes in the kerosene tins and set fire to the tobacco and kerosene. It was all part of the boycott campaign throughout China against Japan and Great Britain.[35]

On 12 March 1925, Sun Yat-sen died of cancer in Peking, where he had gone a few months earlier to attempt to seek a peaceful settlement with the northern warlords. He was soon disabused of his hopes and realized that his long-planned Northern Expedition from his base in Canton was necessary. His body was placed inside a crystal coffin sent by the Soviet Union and then placed in a temple outside Peking. It was later put in a specially built mausoleum on Purple Mountain at Nanking.[36] Sun's death was felt deeply by his followers and particularly among young idealistic students like the ones attending the Hung wen school.

Further incidents heightened antiforeign feeling, particularly against the British. On 30 May 1925, Western and Sikh police, outside a jail in the International Settlement of Shanghai, fired on a crowd, which was protesting the arrest earlier that day of student activists. Nine people were killed, fourteen hospitalized, and fifty or more wounded. The incident touched off strikes, protests, and boycotts of foreign goods. Strikes spread to Canton and Hong Kong following a second incident on 23 June 1925, when foreign troops fired on protesters on Shameen Island, Canton, killing over fifty and wounding over a hundred more. The ensuing strikes lasted in Canton and Hong Kong until October 1926.

A third incident that raised antiforeign—particularly anti-British— feeling to a high level involved the forward thrust of the Northern Expedition, which Sun's successor, Chiang Kai-shek, had launched from Canton on 1 July 1926. In alliance with the Chinese Communist members of the Kuomintang (KMT), Chiang's Soviet-trained and equipped troops proceeded toward Shanghai, while the Communists, accompanying KMT leftists, mobilized peasants on their way to Wuhan. It was agreed by all, including Chiang, that Wuhan would be the new capital of the united country. At Wan Hsien (Wanxian) on the Yangtze above Wuhan, beginning on 27 August 1926, the pro-Chiang governor of Szechuan, warlord Yang Sen, seized two British vessels that had refused to transport his troops. British gunboats fought back, and then, with reinforcements, on 5 September, fired on Wan Hsien city, killing hundreds of Chinese civilians. The 30 May, 23 June, and Wan Hsien incidents all involved the British, against whom feelings rose to a fever pitch. The other foreign powers refused to back the British, who now began to adjust their policy to one more conciliatory toward the revolutionaries.

But banditry was still a factor in Hupei province, and bandits did not hesitate to attack foreign missionaries. The bandit leaders "the Old Foreigner" and "White Wolf" were the same ones whose followers had attacked the Ronnings' train in 1922. Late one night in Fancheng, the gatekeeper roused Ronning to tell him that bandits had taken the city of Tsao Yang (Zaoyang) to the northeast, wounding two missionaries in their attack. The next morning, after learning of a failed attempt to send medical aid to the wounded, Ronning crossed the river to ask for the assistance of the warlord temporarily in charge of Hsiang yang. He gave Ronning a Model T Ford one-ton truck converted to carry soldiers, with a driver (one of his lieutenants) and a number of soldiers armed with rifles and fixed bayonets. They travelled all afternoon over treacherous roads until nightfall when, on the horizon, they saw the flames of burning villages. Driving on through the villages, they eventually reached Tsao Yang, only to find that the missionaries had been rescued and sent to the Hsiang yang hospital. Not wishing to encounter the bandits, Chester and his party immediately set out on the return journey. Back at Hsiang yang hospital, they found that one of the missionaries had died, but his wife remained alive.[37]

Bandit attacks on foreigners were exacerbated by the growing success of the revolutionary movement, spearheaded by the Northern Expedition, which called for an end to special privileges for foreigners and the return of foreign concessions to Chinese control. At Shanghai, in March 1927, leftists, Communists, and workers led by Chou En-lai rose up and established the Shanghai Commune as they prepared to greet the forces of Chiang Kai-shek. Earlier, on 15 March, the British, faced with the approaching Northern Expedition, decided it would be prudent to return their concession in Hankow to the Chinese, as the situation along the Yangtze from Hankow to Shanghai was descending into chaos.

The British Consul in Hankow ordered British subjects, including the Ronnings, to leave China.[38] Inga, however, had come down with scarlet fever and was not well enough to travel immediately. Since her arrival in Fancheng, she had borne two more children: Alton, in the Hsiang yang hospital on 13 May 1925, and Meme (Mei Mei) on 16 September 1926 at Chi-kung shan. Raising children during uncertain conditions was trying. In later life she recounted "how she fought with the spiders and scorpions and how she once met up with a centipede so big she was afraid to step on it. Instead, she attacked it with a butcher knife, but when she cut it up all the parts started to crawl away."[39] When she was well enough to travel, Chester searched for a boatman willing to take foreigners through hostile territory. A member of the Red Spear Society volunteered to take the risk and to contract with three other boatmen to take the Ronnings, and a group of American missionaries, to Hankow.[40] The Red Spear Society, previously affiliated with the Boxers, had been revived to protect river traffic from bandits who preyed on boats becalmed in the serpentine curves of the Han.

The distance by river, from Fancheng to Hankow, was nearly six hundred miles. Depending upon the size of the boat, it could take one month to travel upstream, and with unfavourable winds (or no winds), it could take only slightly less time to travel downstream. The four boats were equipped with spears and broad swords kept handy to ward off bandits, but they were put out of sight at Ronning's request in order not to frighten the women and children. After two days, the boats were moored at a city called Chong Hsiang (Zhongxiang), awaiting favourable winds. Ronning, who understood the local dialect, overheard a warning given to the boatmen that the wind would not favour them as long as they had foreigners on board their boats. Ronning and the others prepared for the worst, but a wind sprung up, defusing the tension.

At Hsa Yang (Shayang), about halfway to Hankow, at an S bend in the river, they encountered upstream boats that had been attacked by bandits—blood and dead bodies still decorated their decks. The Ronnings' boatmen refused to go further. After two days of fruitless argument, Ronning and one of the missionaries went ashore to telegraph the mission in Hankow about the delay. Stopping in a teahouse on the way back, they were confronted by hostile students. The students in the Wuhan area had become more and more radical in their actions in support of the revolution. Challenging Ronning and his companion, both clad in long scholar gowns, the students cried:

"Look at those foreign devils. Destroy the foreign devils. Down with imperialism." Ronning jumped on a table shouting in his Hupei accent: "You are absolutely right! Down with foreign imperialists. Let us destroy them! That is exactly why I want to go down the river and across the Pacific to attack them from the other side. Together we can crush the imperialists!"[41]

Stunned, the students burst out laughing at the spectacle of a tall stranger addressing them in a Hupei accent. They accompanied the two "foreign devils" back to their boats and persuaded the boatmen to continue to Hankow.

The remainder of the passage downstream was frightening, with antiforeign epithets shouted at them from the shore, along with threats of violence. By the time they arrived in Hankow, the city—including the foreign concessions—was occupied by left-wing KMT troops and Communists who were part of the Northern Expedition. They were working to form a new government at Wuhan. Foreigners seeking refuge were spending nights on foreign gunboats in the river. Safe inside the Hankow Lutheran mission hostel, Ronning sought to find out what was happening. He caught wind of the growing tensions between Chiang and the Communists. He encountered a teacher from Fancheng who had accompanied the Northern Expedition. His view was that Chiang Kai-shek had sold out the revolution and had become China's Napoleon.[42]

In March 1927, foreign powers (Britain, the United States, Japan, Italy, the Netherlands, and France) concerned about the strength of the Communists and the heightened xenophobia of the Northern Expedition were anxious to protect their economic interests. They rushed warships up the Yangtze to station them off Nanking.[43] The crisis in China captured headlines worldwide as foreigners streamed out of Shanghai on ships destined for Europe, Japan, Canada, and the US. Although foreigners were being advised to leave China, missionary societies generally left the decision to leave up to the missionaries themselves, who were better able to judge their local circumstances. Nevertheless, from early February 1927, scores of missionaries made their way to Shanghai where they were met by representatives of their churches, assigned accommodations, and assisted in booking passages on outward-bound ships. The exodus continued into May.

Ronning family before leaving China, 1927 (Sylvia, Inga holding Meme, and Chester holding Alton). [Evans private collection]

On 30 March, at Hankow, the Ronnings boarded the *Tungwo*, a Jardine Matheson steamer bound for Nanking and Shanghai. Nanking was a battleground as Kuomintang and Communist forces fought for control of the city. Chiang, now suspicious of the motives of the government in Wuhan, was determined to make Nanking the capital of the new Republic of China. Within the walled city, foreigners were attacked physically and their property destroyed. The British and Japanese consuls were killed. Nearly two dozen foreign warships were gathered in the river. British and American ships shelled the city. In the south end of the city, the Ronnings watched escapees being let down in baskets outside the city walls as they fled to awaiting ships.[44] Two gunboats, one British and one American, fired shells into Nanking to provide cover for the refugees, some of whom boarded the *Tungwo* as it continued to Shanghai, arriving on 5 April.[45] The foreign concessions in Shanghai were under siege behind barricades of sandbags and coiled barbed wire, manned by foreign police and soldiers. Following two days spent in accommodations behind the barricades, the five Ronnings took the only passage available to them—steerage on the next *President* liner bound for San Francisco. En route to Japan, Alton came down with pneumonia and the whole family was moved to first class for the remainder of the voyage.

From 12 April 1927, Chiang Kai-shek began to turn on the Communists in Shanghai, massacring them and their supporters. In addition, he began a purge of the ranks of the KMT as he set about establishing his government in Nanking. He was now threatening[46] the leftist government in Hankow (Wuhan), which sought the advice of Stalin, whose wisdom proved to be misguided and unrealistic. The Communists, prime targets of Chiang's ongoing purge, took refuge in the mountains of western Kiangsi (Jiangxi) at Chinkangshan (Jinggangshan). On 1 August, Chou En-lai and He Long led an uprising against the Kuomintang in Nanchang. Although they were put down, 1 August 1927 marked the founding of the Chinese Red Army, later called the People's Liberation Army. The Ronnings left Shanghai before Chiang began his bloodletting. Only later did Chester hear the story of Chou En-lai's escape from Shanghai and the events that followed, including the execution of some Hung wen students and Tung Tse-p'ei.[47]

In Hankow, a letter had awaited Chester, offering him the position of principal of Camrose Lutheran College. He accepted. To Inga, the prospect of returning to quiet and peaceful Camrose came as a great relief. Her introduction to Chester's China in such "interesting times,"[48] while raising three young children far from home and family, had been frightening and traumatic. "China filled [her] with fear and dread."[49] She entertained no thoughts of returning. Even Chester, drained by the stress of their final six months in China, needed a long rest before taking up his new task. Yet, he looked back on the years 1922–27 as a time when he deepened his knowledge and understanding of China, its culture and modern revolution. At Hankow and Nanking, he witnessed the gathering fury of the revolutionary forces, and he saw the origins of a civil conflict, the denouement of which he would witness twenty-two years later.

# Principal and Politician

By the late twentieth century, the province of Alberta had become a conservative one-party state. Unfortunately, this implies that politics in Alberta were dull, predictable, and have always been so, which is far from the truth. As Roger Epp has written:

> Needless to say, Alberta is now a very different place in its highly urbanized society, its political (or anti-political) culture, its oil-based economy and prosperous national profile....Alberta's lively history of rural activism is now buried at least two generations deep in local memory, or is present only in the thin residue of the UFA farm-supply co-ops and, until recently, the Alberta Wheat Pool.[1]

That is now, but the then of the 1930s was a particularly lively and interesting period in Alberta's political history, when world and local economic crises impacted human affairs in dramatic ways. By 1930, Alberta had had its initial phase of government by the Liberal Party,[2] replaced in 1921 by the political activists of a farm movement. Indeed, in the last years of their power, the Liberals realized that farmers were dissatisfied and they bent over backward to please the UFA, the United Farmers of Alberta. Although members of the UFA were of the opinion that the Liberal government did not reflect sympathy for their problems, the UFA had earlier chosen to remain a movement aloof from direct involvement in party politics. To keep it that way, Liberal premiers Arthur Sifton and Charles Stewart did pretty well whatever the UFA, under its leader Henry Wise Wood, demanded. The Liberals' dependence upon the UFA had become a standing joke.

In 1921, the UFA decided to contest the provincial election as a farmers' party. They nominated candidates in forty-five out of the sixty-one ridings. Thirty-nine were elected, sufficient enough for the UFA to form a majority government. They were said to have no platform and their leader, Wise Wood, declined to take the job of premier. Indeed, they even asked the outgoing premier, Charles Stewart, to continue running the government. Forming a government had not been the UFA's objective, its main goal was to protect and promote the vital interests of its members. At first they received little respect from city folk, who joked that the steps of the legislature should be strewn with straw to make the new government members feel at home.[3]

The first UFA premier, Herbert Greenfield, was a farmer, leading a varied group of agrarian conservatives, American-style populists, and utopian socialists. He served until 1925 and was succeeded by John Edward Brownlee, an Edmonton lawyer who had been active behind the scenes from the beginning. Some have argued that despite the personal scandal surrounding his conduct with his secretary that eventually brought him down in July 1934, Brownlee gave Alberta the best leadership it enjoyed in the twentieth century. "Alberta was once central to the agrarian movement on the Canadian prairies, and home of some of its most radical elements."[4]

The UFA came to power shortly before Ronning left to teach in China and it was still in power when he returned to Alberta. It was during the last years of the UFA government and under Premier Brownlee that Chester Ronning entered politics.

Late in the summer of 1927, Ronning took up the position of principal at Camrose Lutheran College (now the Augustana Campus of the

CAMROSE, ALTA

The new principal of Camrose Lutheran College, 1928. [Ronning/Cassady photo collection]

University of Alberta), which had been offered to him while he was in China. He did not begin immediately upon his return, because he was exhausted and needed time to recuperate. He was ready, however, by the fall term. His salary was "tremendously low" and, for the first year, he, Inga, and their three children lived across from the Canadian Club (later the library) in a dilapidated house with an outdoor privy.[5] On the other side of the house was open country. The approach to the college was by a boardwalk with no trees to line it. As Ronning approached the college on the first day of the fall term, his first day as principal, all was quiet, with not a human being in sight. A cow was grazing in front of the main building, so Ronning picked up a few stones to chase it away. "I did not want people to think it was a cow college."

He entered the main building to find it empty. He went to what he had been told would be his office and waited. Not one of the teaching staff arrived on time. After half an hour, he heard a boy sneezing his way up the walk. He was from near Lethbridge, but because of his hay fever, his father felt he "could spare him" and so sent him to the college. Ronning registered him. Eventually, members of the teaching staff drifted in. Ronning "worked for the next years to make sure that the faculty arrived on time the first day of school." The college was very sympathetic to students who registered late because of fall harvest work, but no excuse was accepted for those from the town. Ronning held that a serious student who stayed home to do farm work could catch up. He got little argument on the point from the college Board, most of whom were farmers.[6]

Halvor Ronning was among the local Norwegian farmers who had pressed for a Lutheran school, but the main initiative came from the United Norwegian Lutheran Church in the United States, from whence many of the settlers in the Camrose region came. Of the twenty-five representatives who met in 1910 to launch the college, about one-third were Haugeans.[7] The college opened in the fall of 1911, incorporated under the government of Alberta to provide a liberal education in the arts and sciences, but the Board's own agenda was to provide students with a basic Christian education within Norwegian tradition, culture, and language. J.P. Tandberg from the United States served as president for the first two years. He was followed by Pastor J.R. Lavik, with whom Ronning made his arrangements in 1917 to enable him to study for a teaching certificate at the Camrose Normal School. Lavik also placed emphasis on the Norwegian aspect of the college's program and also on the need to provide religious instruction in Lutheranism in support of the church's work within the broader Norwegian settler community. In order to graduate, Lutheran students were required to take instruction in their faith, while non-Lutherans were enjoined to attend services in their own religion.

Although his father was a convinced Haugean, Chester's approach to running the college was less religious and more open to letting cultural understanding grow from the bottom up, through individual initiatives. Far from pietistic, a term with which Haugeans were at times tarred, Ronning emphasized the Haugean traditions of hard work and practicality, and looked to the folk high schools founded in nineteenth-century Denmark as a model.[8]

In his fifteen years as principal, Ronning sought to improve the teaching and curriculum of the college. He gained a reputation as a progressive in the field of education. From his experience in China, he knew the danger of sticking to outmoded conservative traditions. Familiar with the nature of the Alberta educational system from his days as deputy principal at Queen Alexandra and H. Allen Grey schools, he was more secular in approach than his predecessors. Ronning was against rote learning and against teachers teaching to the final exams, rather than imparting a love of learning and inquiry. He had a knack for making new students feel at home, giving them confidence in their ability to succeed. And, as principal, he was willing to fight, literally, for it. One of the many stories about Ronning's style as principal is set during the Depression and concerns a financial crisis. Ronning toured the district in 1936, seeking donations for the college's Silver Jubilee fund. He was selling the idea of education and its importance, particularly during tough economic times. He called on a family of five brothers in the town of Viking. Four of them donated, but the fifth absolutely refused. Ronning challenged him to wrestle. If Ronning won, the man would donate, and if he lost, Ronning would cross him off the list. Ronning was tall and thin, and he barely defeated the strong, husky farmer. Five dollars were donated, but for his efforts Ronning suffered three broken ribs and a torn shirt, which was new that morning.[9]

In 1928, Ronning was able to build a small house on the edge of the college campus. It really was not large enough for his growing family, beyond Sylvia, Alton, and Meme. As his daughter Audrey recalled:

> It was the right size for the five of them, but when I was born in St. Mary's, then my sister Kjeryn and brother Harmon, the house became rather crowded. Dad built two bedrooms in the attic and one in the basement beside the coal bin. He also built a playhouse of split logs and a red roof with flying eaves like a Chinese pavilion, where we could sleep in the summer and play house.[10]

With the exception of Harmon, the youngest, all of Ronning's children eventually attended classes at the college.

As principal of Camrose Lutheran College, Ronning was a prominent member of local society. He did his work well and was very popular both within the college and in the surrounding communities, which were made up of Scandinavian settlers, who were, for the most part, Lutheran. One resident confided:

> At that time the College, a residential high school, offered courses, Grades 9 to 12 inclusive, plus a post-secondary business course. Many of the students were from rural areas and had never before lived away from home. Ronning welcomed them with empathy. In the opening day general assembly of students and teachers, he would welcome these teenagers, some as young as fourteen, in an enthusiastic, warm and fatherly way, stating that he and the faculty members understood that it would take a few days to become adjusted to the new environment but that he had every confidence that they could do it well and quickly. The fact that he believed in students and their potential to succeed inspired them to do so. Who would disappoint the man who thought they could?

Students respected him and he never had a discipline problem in his classes.[11]

One of Ronning's great pleasures was to conduct the college choir. Under his direction, it finished in the top ranks at provincial music festivals year after year. Indeed, music played an important role in Ronning's life and he was overjoyed on his return from China when, on a visit to his younger brother Talbert in Minneapolis, he heard a radio for the first time in his life.

> I heard Bing Crosby singing songs and I was intrigued and amused by it. I neglected my duties to my father and my family and they could not understand why I was so involved. I sat all night listening to Bing Crosby. I resolved that I must have one of these things when I came to Camrose. Not long after I got a radio of the sort that you do not need earphones.[12]

The radio served him well, not only for music but also for politics.

While a young homesteader in Valhalla, Chester had joined the UFA and travelled around in their interest during the election of June 1917, learning a lesson on how difficult it was to buck the old-line parties. Nonetheless, he was firm in the belief that "farmers were more interested in the development of this country and the enlightenment of the people."[13] He had been delighted when the UFA was swept to power in 1921, shortly before he left for Minnesota, and later China.

The farmers in Camrose knew of Ronning's past connections to the UFA and a farm member of the college Board of Governors asked him to become a UFA candidate. The UFA wanted people who were intelligent, articulate, and knowledgeable about the farmers' situation. They saw in Chester Ronning an ideal candidate. He hesitated, however, because "I did not think I was capable of analyzing the situation so soon back from China."[14] But he agreed because he found the farmers, led by people like Henry Wise Wood, were more acquainted with developments than were townsfolk. In 1930, he put his name forward as a candidate for the federal seat of Camrose. It was reported, "Mr.

Ronning, in a hamorous [sic] way gave a sketch of his life, and asked for the co-operation of the people of this district in securing his nomination as Progressive candidate for the house of commons."[15] He lost the nomination to the sitting UFA member, W.T. Lucas.

Ronning's next opportunity came in 1932. He was drawn into provincial UFA politics by the growth in Alberta of a social democratic movement that melded certain parts of the UFA program with a provincial movement for social and economic reform, founded and led by William Irvine, and a national movement led by James Shaver Woodsworth, a utopian socialist.[16] These groups, along with labour organizations, met in Calgary in the summer of 1932 to form the Co-operative Commonwealth Federation (CCF), which much later (1961) morphed into the current New Democratic Party (NDP). In Calgary, they drafted a provisional platform. The CCF, according to Woodsworth, should not enter politics directly but remain a group of organizations, with no individual party memberships. Its draft program called for large-scale nationalization of industry and essential services, and for government-run programs such as health care and insurance for the sick, elderly farmers, and the unemployed. Its aim was to reform or do away with the capitalist system, which had lost a great deal of its appeal with the Great Depression and the onslaught of the dirty thirties.

That same summer, Vernor Smith, Member of the Legislative Assembly (MLA) for Camrose, died, and a by-election was called for 25 October 1932. The UFA nominating meeting was set for late September. This time Ronning won.[17] In his speech, he recounted how he had been associated with the UFA since his early days in the Peace River country. The UFA had established a government of the province and the farmers' movement had established the wheat pool: two great ventures. "The aims of the UFA had finally been defined, in his opinion, in the recent manifestoes as enunciated in the Co-operative Commonwealth Federation." He "felt that the banks must be nationalized along with other public enterprises."[18]

Ronning was a natural campaigner. He was tall, strong of voice, quick of wit, and knowledgeable. During the campaign, he drove

# VOTE I
### For
# Chester Ronning
## U. F. A. Candidate

He Stands For

## CLEAN, HONEST, EFFICIENT Government
### and the
## WELFARE of the COMMON PEOPLE

### Mark Your Ballot:
# RONNING, CHESTER ALVIN 1

Published by Camrose Provincial U.F.A.                    Camrose Job Press

Poster from Camrose by-election, 1932. [Evans private collection]

around the country seeking support, but he "did not campaign in the town because townspeople were dead against UFA."[19] In those days, radio was in its infancy and there was no television; face-to-face meetings were of prime importance. A candidate had to go from settlement to settlement, speaking before small gatherings. Heckling was common and slanders from one's opponent nearly the norm.

Politics in Alberta was not so violent as in China, but there were still powerful forces at work. Alberta, the province, was formed in 1905. Previously, it had been part of a region whose affairs were directed from the central government in Ottawa. After 1905, it had is own elected government located in its capital, Edmonton. Alberta was mainly a farming province, settled by immigrants from all over the world: Russians, Ukrainians, Poles, Austrians, Czechs, Italians, Danes, Norwegians, Swedes, Finns, Americans, Chinese, Japanese,

French, English, Scots, Irish, Welsh, Germans, and many more. In the 1920s, the population was around three-quarters of a million and very loosely knit. In politics, there were socialists, communists, liberals, conservatives, and even fascists vying for followers. Special interest groups were also organized to compete with the traditional Liberal and Conservative parties whose base was in the more heavily populated provinces of central Canada and who followed similar policies in the new province. Economic depression, drought, dust storms, and locusts, however, made conditions on the Prairies different from those in central and maritime Canada.

Ronning later described his first steps in the 1932 by-election campaign:

> In 1932, the United Farmers of Alberta (UFA) asked me to be their candidate to contest a by-election for the Legislative Assembly of Alberta. That summer, the UFA had joined the Co-operative Commonwealth Federation (CCF), headed by James Woodsworth. I happened to be the first person in Canada to run on the provisional CCF platform.
>
> Not long after my campaign started, a supporter told me that a very damaging whispering campaign was spreading rapidly through the constituency about me. In his opinion, if I did not stop it, I would stand no chance of winning against my opponents. I asked my new friend what part of my dark past had been discovered. He said: "They say you were born in China. They also say," he went on, "that your mother was unable to supply you with milk, and that cow's milk was not available in China. Is that really so?"
>
> From the way he asked the question I got the impression that he would not vote for me if my reply was in the affirmative. So I had to explain that I had no intention of refusing to give credit to a kind Chinese woman who had saved my life so that I could contest this election as a farmer's candidate.
>
> My friend finished by saying: "The worst of it is that they say that since you were brought up on Chinese milk, you are partly Chinese."

I interjected that according to that logic, I might have absorbed some of the traditional wisdom of the great Chinese philosophers, which should make me the best possible member of the Alberta Legislature to represent the farmers of the Camrose Constituency.

I tried to end our conversation by asking my friend to start a whispering campaign about my opponents.

"What do you know about them?" he asked.

"I have it on fairly good authority," I said, "that they were brought up on cow's milk."

I told this story at every public meeting I addressed after that, and the audiences seemed to appreciate the logic.

I won the campaign, but I was thrown out on my ear in the next round. The electorate must have decided that I had not acquired the sagacity of the Chinese sages after all.[20]

Much has to be said to explain Ronning's last two sentences, with which he breezily dismisses his political career. Winning the by-election required more than just having a good story to tell.

Until his death on 19 July 1932, Vernor W. Smith was Alberta's Minister of Railways and Telephones and very important in Brownlee's cabinet. He won the Camrose seat in 1921 when the UFA swept to power, winning it again in 1926. In 1930, he won handily over his only opponent, a Liberal and a farmer from New Norway, S.M. Westvick. Westvick was once again the Liberal candidate for the by-election. He was expected to win, but his chances were put in doubt by the entry of a Conservative candidate, a Camrose businessman, F.P. Layton. The election was hotly contested, with all the provincial party leaders coming out to support their candidates. Ronning's placards encouraged voters to place their trust in him for a number of reasons, the fourth of which was because

Chester Ronning is a young man who, through years of active membership in the UFA is well qualified to represent an agricultural constituency. He is thoroughly imbued with the principles of the social, economic and financial reforms advocated by organized farmers throughout the whole of Canada...he has the courage and ability to fight for those reforms and principles for which our organization stands.[21]

The UFA had a comfortable majority in the legislature and the loss of the seat would not have damaged it much. J.E. Brownlee, the UFA premier, had not supported Ronning's nomination. He preferred a conservative farmer, so, in this case, Ronning was a sacrificial lamb. His candidacy provided an opportunity to test the new affiliation between the UFA and the CCF; he was a UFA candidate running on a CCF platform. The election took place when times were rough and uncertain. The Great Depression had hit Alberta particularly hard. Farmers were hurting from low grain prices, high freight rates, and high mortgages. There was high unemployment, with the jobless drifting into the cities and protesting their situation. The UFA government was accused of delaying relief measures while at the same time taking the province further and further into debt. The government in Ottawa was Conservative. Its thinking was generally out of harmony with that of the UFA provincially and with UFA federal Members of Parliament (MPs). Provincially, the UFA's hold on power was weakening and the press called for a combined Liberal/ Conservative alternative.

Near the end of the campaign, at a meeting in New Norway, when loudspeakers had to be placed outside for the overflow crowd, both the Conservative and Liberal leaders attacked Premier Brownlee. The Conservatives blamed him for the deficit because he did not follow their advice provincially and ignored the leadership offered by Ottawa. The Liberals accused him of spending too much money on the University of Alberta and assigning its president to too many commissions so he was unable to do his job effectively. A major local issue was the fate of the Camrose Normal School (now restored as a continuing care facility), which Vernor Smith had promised would remain open, but which the Liberal leader had said should be closed. Brownlee was being very coy about the matter. Ronning endorsed a resolution calling for the school, where he had studied for his teaching certificate in

1917, to remain open. Personally, he regarded it as an essential part of Alberta's educational system.

On Election Day, 81.1 per cent of the Camrose electorate turned out; lines formed outside rural polling stations early in the morning. The roads were dry and good, the weather fine. The voting was by preferential ballot; voters were to indicate their first and second choices. Ronning received 45 per cent of the first-round votes, the remainder being split between his Liberal and Conservative opponents. Ronning had a 560-vote lead over Westvick, but all depended upon the second choices on the third-place Conservative ballots. The election had taken place on Tuesday, but the second choices had to be counted all together in Camrose once the rural boxes had arrived. It was Friday before the final vote was known. The question was just how many of Layton's second-place votes would go to Westvick and whether they would be sufficient to overtake Ronning. The Liberal fear was that many of the Layton votes would be "plumped," that is to say, without a second choice indicated. A good number were, and Westvick finished four hundred votes behind Ronning. Brownlee expressed his satisfaction with the result, but the *Calgary Herald* blamed the Conservatives for splitting the vote and allowing the UFA candidate to triumph. The Edmonton press generally agreed that Ronning had won thanks to a split opposition vote. Premier Brownlee, however, attributed the victory largely to Ronning's fine personal reputation. Ronning offered three observations as reported by the *Camrose Canadian* on 2 November 1932:

First, "that governments usually go down to defeat in times of depression and the present by-election would indicate that the people of the Camrose constituency still have confidence in the UFA government;" secondly, "one of the reasons for victory is that people see hope for the future in the constructive policies of the UFA movement"; thirdly "that the 'class government' argument has lost its affect." The farmers nominated a school teacher and he was a supporter of the Co-operative Commonwealth Federation through which the UFA has extended the hand of co-operation to workers in towns and cities, joining them in working for better conditions in Canada.

In early November, Chester Alvin Ronning was officially proclaimed the Member of the Legislative Assembly for the constituency of Camrose, Alberta. He now had to get down to work.

The Legislative Assembly session opened on 9 February 1933, with the press expecting little from it, and, after it was over, confirming that nothing much had happened. Observed the *Edmonton Bulletin* of 10 February 1933:

> The provincial legislature re-assembles amid the most serious, the most critical, conditions that have ever afflicted the people of Alberta.
>
> It does not promise to be a very cheerful session. But the last way to enter upon a session of that kind is in a spirit of funk.
>
> The public will echo the hope expressed in the concluding sentence of the Speech (from the Throne). "[T]hat no ill-considered action of today shall jeopardize the welfare of the future."

Fifty-three days later, 3 April, the *Bulletin* summed it up:

> It cannot be said that the session of the legislature has been outstanding. Nothing remarkable was done in the way of new legislation. No new lines of important public policy were struck out.

This was a particularly jaundiced view of a session in which the new member from Camrose made his mark. In keeping with custom, Ronning was frog-marched between two government ministers up to the Speaker's chair to be introduced to the house. The first Norseman to be elected an MLA, Ronning saw himself as an unofficial general representative for the forty thousand Albertans of Norwegian descent. The next day, at the request of Premier Brownlee, Ronning was given the unusual opportunity to make his maiden speech by seconding the Speech from the Throne. Brownlee advised Ronning to consult the

Speaker regarding style and content. Ronning did so for style but kept the content to himself. His speech made clear that he was a determined follower of the CCF and one who believed in socialist principles. The *Edmonton Journal* said he had "made a splendid impression on the house."[22] He began with a tribute to his predecessor who had died in office, before decrying the economic conditions of the times.[23]

> "Instead of reaping the logical benefits of our labors we are plunged into the depths of economic distress and are surrounded by poverty destitution and want." He went on, "Have we placed human welfare and moral character at the top of our scale of values? Or have we perhaps sacrificed the interests of humanity upon an altar of greed?"

In his speech, Ronning then pointed to the difficulties of farmers, later reciting the stories of members of his constituency, desperate farmers caught by insurmountable mortgage payments. Without pause, he passed on to the subject of education, a subject dear to his heart as a teacher.

> The lack of opportunities for our young people, who are trained to share the active life of the people is perhaps one of the worst features of the present situation. Society owes them such opportunities.

Ronning was also concerned about the state of medicine in the province.

> It is a serious matter in ordinary times to have sickness in the family. In times like these, it is a catastrophe.

He praised doctors for their splendid work.

> [M]any of them are doing regardless of remuneration. But most of the people in rural districts are getting along without much needed

medical services. They are anxiously awaiting the day of State Medicine and look forward to the report of the Committee which has been investigating the possibilities.

Then he sang the praises of the UFA government.

> I come fresh from the people of my constituency with a renewed approval of the honest and efficient government, which has characterized the present administration, with an expression of confidence in its able leader and with a definite mandate to press for courageous, progressive and constructive legislation.
>
> One cannot misinterpret the results of the Camrose by-election. The issues were clear-cut. The record of the government was capably defended and strenuously attacked. The advanced policies of the UFA as embodied in recent Manifestos were enthusiastically championed and bitterly denounced.

He acknowledged there was dissatisfaction:

> [B]ut it was a dissatisfaction with the capitalistic system and a feeling that it had outworn its usefulness to man and is in its death throes. There was a desire for change but it's a desire for a change to a system that will ensure greater economic opportunity for the masses.

He continued:

> It was this feeling that led to the formation of the Co-operative Commonwealth Federation. The creation of this Federation has given the people a new hope, a new enthusiasm. Never before have the people been so interested in the vital issues affecting not merely their economic welfare but having a far-reaching effect on their moral, spiritual and cultural welfare.
>
> The people have been rapidly sinking into a hopeless state of mind. An attitude has been prevalent that has been fertile soil for

those who seek relief through violence and force. The UFA program has been branded as Communistic. The fact is that these policies are the most effective weapons against Communistic methods. The Communists themselves recognize this and correctly regard the forces of reaction as their best allies.

Turning to himself, he announced:

Again our policies have been attacked as atheistic and godless. My personal answer has been that it is on account of being brought up in a Christian home and because my life has been deeply influenced by Christianity that I am so enthusiastic about the co-operative commonwealth ideal. A study of the principles involved will reveal that the ethical bases are thoroughly Christian.

He concluded his speech with:

When one considers the intricacies of the situation and the stupendous proportions of the problem, he is perhaps tempted to let things work themselves out. We are told that Nature's law of supply and demand has always operated and will operate again if we but give it a chance. It would be a great deal easier to discard reason and patiently wait for the return of prosperity. When one sees the evil consequences and catches a vision of an era founded upon righteousness and reason, he sheds all hesitation and shoulders his allotted share of responsibility with eagerness.[24]

Ronning was clearly anticapitalist and afire with the ideals of social democracy. His speech over, the opposition Liberal and Conservative leaders took him to task. But that was not all. Premier Brownlee called him aside to caution him about the stridency of his remarks. He had his eye on Ronning as a possible Minister of Education. Ronning, however, did not take the bait and stuck to his principles. Thereafter, he was considered to be one of the small group of radical, socialist-leaning members of the UFA caucus.

Ronning agreed to supply the *Camrose Canadian* with a weekly summary of happenings in the legislature. His first report sums up the reception to his speech:

> The debate on the speech from the throne was particularly interesting to me. The old party leaders used certain stray statements made by me as texts on the basis of which they proceeded to attack the progressive policies of our movement. I enjoyed the paternal spankings as much as they apparently delighted in administering them.

But then Ronning had the last laugh. He goes on:

> The leader of the Liberals, Mr. Howson, took away all the smart of his sarcastic reference to our "home-robbing" policy when he stole our thunder and with considerable emotion advocated a Federal bank.
>
> Another pleasant surprise came when an old Conservative member from Calgary painted a vivid picture of the disastrous results in Alberta of uncontrolled competition and the functioning of "soulless corporations." He did it more effectively than any radical thinker could possibly have done.[25]

By the date Ronning had taken his place in the Assembly, Brownlee had already won ownership of provincial natural resources from Ottawa and the government had already passed an act to assist farmers faced with high debt, but that act was up for amendment when Ronning arrived. The amendment was to give the act more teeth. A spokesman for the mortgage holders, whose wives and children, according to him, faced poverty, addressed the assembly. "It was un-British to punish them in the way the amendment proposed," he said.[26] Ronning, who that morning had received a number of letters from farmers who faced losing their farms after thirty years of effort, entered the debate, pointing out that it was even more "un-British" to deprive farmers of the equity in their farms after they had worked for decades to stay afloat. The amendment was passed.

Back in Camrose on the evening of Saturday, 11 March, Ronning attended a banquet in his honour hosted by the Camrose Lutheran Church. One hundred and thirty-five people were present. Ronning was asked to say a few words. During his remarks, he touched on the principles of the UFA. He said that he did not deserve the honour being shown him by those present.

> It was quite fitting in his opinion that a banquet on such an occasion should be held in the church, for the church as a whole, should be interested in the affairs of government and should take an active part in solving the problems of the day.[27]

Returning to his place in the legislature, he rejoiced when the estimates for the Camrose Normal School were passed on 28 March,[28] but it is clear that as the house approached prorogation, Ronning, who sincerely believed that all members had the interests of Albertans at heart, was growing tired of the pettiness that was coming primarily from the Liberals. He gained some satisfaction when a Liberal member, who made an issue of the extravagant travel expenses of the UFA cabinet, was squelched when the records showed that the travel expenses in the last year of the Liberal government had exceeded the current UFA expenses by $9,699.00. It was with some relief when the session closed that Ronning returned to teaching at the college and conducting the choir.

In June 1933, Ronning was named a delegate to the Regina meeting of the CCF to draft its manifesto. The group photo of the convention attendees shows a young, thirty-six-year-old Chester Ronning, fifth row back, well left of centre—a political position he was to hold for the rest of his life. He returned to Alberta fired up by the Regina Manifesto and eager to defend the CCF in the house against any further attacks that called it communistic. But the 1934 session of the legislature turned out to be a bit of a damp squib as it saw the stage set for the final year of the UFA government.

During the session, Ronning ceased to provide the *Camrose Canadian* with regular weekly summaries. He did, however, invite his class to the legislature to witness it at work. In early March 1934, he gave a major speech in the assembly that was critical of the educational system.[29] It was a thoroughgoing attack on the content of the curriculum and on the manner in which students were being taught. Old subjects should be cast out and history and current events emphasized. The current system was rigid and depended upon examinations too much. Teachers were judged on the outcome of the examinations. The examination system had served the past; it was time for new approaches. In the same speech, he once again took on critics who called the CCF communistic. As he sat down, those around him loudly applauded, but a reporter covering the speech thought it left the cabinet looking rather cold. A month later, Ronning gave his full support to a report by Dr. Atkinson on the need for preventive health care to be taught in Alberta schools.[30]

Shortly after, members of the cabinet debated whether or not Dr. Alexander, head of the University of Alberta Classics Department, could be a CCFer and remain a professor.[31] Premier Brownlee stated the government's position that any civil servant could join a political party and work for it as long as he did not take part in election campaigns. To this, the Conservative Party leader added that should his party come to power, any professor who had taken part in an election campaign would be dismissed. None of this affected Ronning because he worked for a privately funded institution.

But there were more important concerns for the UFA government, the main one being the growth and strength of the Social Credit movement under William Aberhart, a Calgary schoolteacher, evangelist, and charismatic speaker. Social Credit study groups were springing up all over the province, although Aberhart denied it was a political movement. In March 1934, the Agricultural Committee invited Aberhart to the legislature to explain his ideas. His visit preceded that of Major Clifford Hugh Douglas, the inspirer of Social Credit, who was making his way from New Zealand and who was later hired by the UFA as an economic advisor. Ronning was already well briefed on Major Douglas's theories and on Aberhart's approach to them. For years, Ronning listened to Aberhart's Sunday radio broadcasts from Calgary. He listened as Aberhart, the founder of his own evangelical sect, begged members of the public to buy bricks to build the Prophetic Bible Institute. He expounded his theory that God had built the pyramids of Egypt and that their dimensions held the secrets to the future of humankind. Then, according to Ronning, one summer when Aberhart was in Edmonton marking provincial examinations, he read a popular novel describing Social Credit.[32] He was hooked, not in a political sense but in a metaphysical one. He stopped talking about pyramids and devoted himself to his version of Social Credit. A dynamic speaker, Aberhart attracted followers by promising to get rid of the (unnamed) "fifty big shots" whom he said controlled the banks, to reform the monetary system, and to remove the burden of debt.[33] It was an appealing message of hope to Albertans mired in desperate times. Parts of Aberhart's message echoed the CCF manifesto.

Ronning studied Major Douglas's theories through books supplied to him by friends in Saskatchewan. He knew that Social Credit had a major flaw: provinces cannot control money and credit, which, under the British North America Act, were Dominion responsibilities. Aberhart illustrated his presentation to the Agriculture Committee with a chart showing how blood circulates through the body, keeping the body functioning using existing supplies with no new blood added. The same he argued was true of money in the economy; it was just as essential to keep money circulating. Circulating money like blood became a popular theme with Aberhart, and the blood diagram festooned Social Credit literature. He showed deference to Major Douglas, who was due to arrive in early April.

The Agricultural Committee adjourned and the members retired to the lobby of the Corona Hotel conveniently located on Jasper Avenue at 107 Street, a short walk from the legislature. It was a fine hotel, the site now occupied by an LRT station and a Tim Hortons. Aberhart was also in the lobby, seated on his own. Ronning went over to speak to him, to point out the *fallacious* (a favourite term with Ronning) reasoning behind the Social Credit monetary system—Social Credit theories could not succeed in a province because the Dominion government has control over money. According to Ronning: "He looked at me, put a flabby hand of his on top of mine and said: You understand Social Credit. Join us! We are going to sweep the province at the next election. I will make you Minister of Education."[34]

A month later, the session over, Ronning returned to Camrose. The *Camrose Canadian* of 18 April 1934 took note:

> Mr. Chester Ronning, UFA member, Camrose, has resumed his duties as principal of the Camrose Lutheran College. Mr. Ronning was not prepared to make a statement as to his own personal estimate of the value of the session just closed.

Instead, he saved his report for the joint meeting of the UFA and UFWA meeting in early May, when he gave a speech lasting more than an hour.

> He stressed the inability of the provincial government to carry out many progressive measures in education, health and other departments due to lack of funds, declaring that the situation could not be remedied to any extent so long as private hands were permitted to control the credit of the country. [He] admitted having painted a somewhat gloomy picture of existing conditions but qualified his statements by expressing the thought that "humanity is on the march" and eventually through leadership and education the necessary changes will be brought about.[35]

Ronning was correct. There was a march toward progress in Alberta, but William "Bible Bill" Aberhart was leading it. On 23 July 1934, in Camrose, Aberhart drew an audience estimated at fifteen hundred.[36] He expounded his Social Credit theories but denied that he had a plan for the province. When he finished, his young assistant, Ernest C. Manning, assured the crowd that "the introduction of the Social Credit system in Alberta would not conflict with either the Bank Act or the British North America Act."[37] A Social Credit study group was established in Camrose following the meeting. Aberhart's progress was hardly blunted when, in September, the Douglas Credit League of Canada, the self-defined "true keepers" of the Major Douglas flame, disowned him and his brand of Social Credit.[38]

Ronning, meanwhile, continued his own crusade, hammering home the message of the CCF, delivering a wide-ranging speech to a joint meeting of the UFA and UFWA in Camrose, emphasizing that the government was unable to do many things "due to lack of funds, declaring that the situation could not be remedied to any extent so long as private hands were permitted to control the credit of the country."[39] In October, he addressed the Camrose Inspectorate teachers' convention on a theme close to his heart, asserting

> that the schools of today are not meeting the demands of modern society. There are, he contended, settlements in Alberta where the teaching of English is deteriorating from year to year under the influence of non-English teachers reared in the community. Secondary education of the future will focus attention on contemporaneous life. The Camrose Normal School...should be an experimental school for rural education. The teacher must be freed from uninformed local control, and the whims of uninformed opinion.[40]

The 1935 session of the legislature, Ronning's last, was not a happy one. At the outset, two UFA members crossed over to the Liberals, and personal scandals overtook two prominent members of the government: Oran McPherson and Premier Brownlee.[41] In retrospect, Ronning blamed the press and the Liberals for making dirty politics out of private matters, but no matter, the UFA was daubed with the charge of immorality. The previous July, Brownlee was forced to step down as premier. Richard Gavin Reid,[42] a less skillful politician, replaced him. Toward the end of the session, things got so bad that Oran McPherson, UFA member for Little Bow and former Minister of Public Works, and Charles E. Campbell, owner and publisher of the *Edmonton Bulletin*, fought at the top of the marble staircase just outside the assembly. The house was debating a bill to restrict newspaper reporting, introduced in the wake of the coverage given to the private affairs of the UFA cabinet. Ronning, the closest witness to the fight, told the *Camrose Canadian* reporter: "Mr. Campbell is said to have hurled an unlovely epithet at Mr. McPherson, which caused the latter to exclaim, 'No Campbell can call a McPherson that name!' whereupon he struck the *Bulletin* manager....Mr. Campbell was unconscious for a period of three or four minutes."[43] Campbell's head split open when it struck a marble plinth. Such goings on were fodder for Aberhart and his radio broadcasts, which featured skits called "A Man from Mars" and starred, among others, Ernest C. Manning.

Ronning tried to salvage something from the session, giving his full support to a bill to incorporate teachers as a profession. The bill went through, but a provision for compulsory membership, considered essential and desirable by the teachers themselves, was stripped away. During the session and after, members of the UFA, notably Brownlee, gave speeches excoriating Aberhart's brand of Social Credit. Aberhart had originally said that the existing government could implement his ideas, but such a proposal had been rejected by a UFA convention in Calgary earlier in the year. The Social Credit study groups now became political campaign offices spread throughout the province. When the premier dropped the writ for an election on 22 August 1935, the battle was joined.

Ronning had already been warming up with speeches attacking Social Credit, indicating the impossibility of it being implemented in Alberta under current circumstances. In early June, he was unanimously affirmed as the UFA candidate for the Camrose constituency. He said that if it had not been for the extraordinary situation, he would not have let his name stand. His major opponent was W.N. Chant, the Social Credit candidate. Early posters for Ronning urged people to vote for him because: "The Government has brought the Province through the greatest depression in the world's history, and is appealing to the people for a renewal of their confidence." Meanwhile, Chant's posters proclaimed, "Social Credit Sets You Free!"[44]

Although Premier Reid had attended Ronning's nomination meeting, Ronning invited former Premier Brownlee, still tainted by

personal scandal, to campaign with him. In addition, Ronning had
the active support of three stalwarts of the CCF: William Irvine, Elmer
Roper, and Mary Crawford. As voting time drew near, Ronning's placards proclaimed, in part,

> Vote for Chester Ronning, and use: THE INFLUENCE OF PROVINCE
> TO URGE DOMINION to:
>   1. Control INFLATION so that DEBT's [sic] can be PAID,
>   2. Pay INSURANCE for Unavoidable Crop Failure,
>   3. FREE CANADA from the domination of PRIVATE FINANCE,
>   4. Recapture right to ISSUE OUR OWN CREDIT and secure REAL
>      SOCIAL CREDIT—"We Will Do It!"

To which Chant replied:

> Elect a Social Credit Government on August 22nd
> Cease Borrowing from Outside Sources.
> Obtain A JUST PRICE for Goods and Services.
> End Poverty in the Midst of Plenty.
> Maintain A Democratic Government.
> Insure Economic Security and Freedom.[45]

In his nearly three years in the legislative assembly, Ronning had
worked hard, reporting regularly to his constituents through meetings,
letters, and the newspapers while maintaining his work as principal
and teacher at Camrose Lutheran College. But the personal scandals
involving prominent members of the UFA government, notably the
premier, gravely damaged the reputation of the government. No one
could say that the government was dishonest, because it was not, but
it was seen as immoral. The August 1935 election campaign unleashed
the full fury of the Social Credit movement. Voters in the province,
particularly the farmers, were willing to place their trust in Aberhart
and his promise of a $25 a month dividend to all adult Albertans.
According to newspaper reports at the time, all he needed, he said, was
one hundred good men to put the province right.

None of the UFA survived; the whole UFA slate was thrown out, swamped by the Social Credit tide that gained 54.2 per cent of the 86.6 per cent voter turnout. It was not from lack of Chinese philosophical sagacity that Ronning lost, but it was due in large measure to the CCF's failure to get its act together as a provincial party, relying instead upon the increasingly discredited UFA. Well into the future, the CCF would be associated with the collapse of the UFA. The populism and radicalism that the CCF might have harvested was reaped by Social Credit, which was attacking many of the same targets while promising miraculous hope and extraordinary benefits to a populace worn down by the dirty thirties. Ronning finished a distant third, some three thousand votes behind Chant. Down, but never out, he continued with his CCF work, while Chant became Minister of Agriculture in Premier Aberhart's new cabinet.

The CCF convention in Edmonton in July 1936 elected William Irvine president and Ronning vice-president of the Provincial Association of CCF Clubs. Elmer Roper and Mary Crawford filled out the executive. Early the next year, the UFA held its convention amid speculation that it would leave politics all together. Certainly, the *Vegreville Observer* encouraged it to do so, and added:

> As to the CCF, one can only say that farmers, rightly or wrongly, are not Socialist and as a class cannot be persuaded to join the CCF, which is definitely Socialistic in its teachings. Mr. Wm. Irvine, ex-MP for Wetaskiwin, is perhaps the best exponent in Alberta of the CCF doctrines; but not even Bill Irvine can make a dint in the fiercely individualistic attitude of most Alberta farmers. Oratory at the UFA convention may carry the day for the CCF, but if it does then both the UFA and the CCF are wiped off the slate for a long time in the future.[46]

The CCF did not take the advice but began working on a new program for Alberta. Ronning kept busy making speeches related to the new CCF program and on the growing crisis between Japan and China. At the same time, he led the Silver Jubilee fundraising campaign for the Camrose Lutheran College. In January 1938, he presided in

Camrose over a debate among the UFA, Labour Party, and CCF clubs on the new CCF program. The aim of the program was to "[r]eplace the present capitalistic system by a social order in which domination and exploitation will be eliminated and in which equal opportunity for all will be possible."[47] The CCF clubs followed up with a regular series of meetings and debates, and the CCF began to promote itself as a distinctive party with a decision to accept individual memberships and to participate as a party in forthcoming elections. Finally, in January 1939, the UFA formally withdrew from politics, leaving the CCF a clearer field to set up constituency organizations throughout the province.

In early April, on Good Friday, at a CCF-sponsored meeting to discuss the farm crisis, Ronning avowed:

> If the efforts of the CCF are consecrated, if we are serious about doing something, not for political advantage, but to solve the problems facing the world today, I know no day too sacred. The spirit of Christianity and of Christian organizations is being threatened by a system depriving the common people of a just reward for their efforts...the principles of today's system rest on an unChristian foundation and one that is inadequate...from the CCF point of view wars are inevitable under the present setup, with brotherhood absolutely impossible with nations organized along present industrial lines.[48]

On 23 June 1939, Ronning was once again nominated to be a candidate in the next provincial election, this time as a CCFer running on the CCF platform. In a long acceptance speech, he tied his belief in the CCF into his life story, ending by staunchly refuting any "suggestion that the CCF was Un-British...the CCF platform states there is no intention of interfering with any religious group or with the rights of minorities."[49]

Although Social Credit won the Camrose seat handily in the 1935 election, Chant fell out with the premier two years into their mandate and was sitting as an independent. Moreover, an Independent Unity Association had sprung up in Camrose.[50] The next provincial election looked to be interesting. Then, at a CCF meeting in Edmonton on 2 August 1939, Elmer Roper, who represented the labour unions, was named president of the Alberta party and Ronning its provincial leader. Ronning's years of dedication to the party's ideals and program had been recognized. E.F. Garland, a well-known CCFer, was reported to have said of the forty-four-year-old Ronning, "[I]f he did not kill himself in the cause he could become a second Woodsworth."[51]

And it appeared Ronning was determined to be just that as he began with a frenetic burst of activity and energy. He went to Ottawa to meet with Woodsworth and other leaders of the federal party. On his return, he began a hectic series of meetings to prepare the party not only for a provincial election but for a federal one as well. He set up study groups, organized petitions, wrote long letters to the paper, issued policy statements, condemned Prime Minister Mackenzie King, and prepared to run candidates in every provincial riding. He attacked the program of the Independent Unity Party in Camrose and issued the CCF program for the province. Moreover, he took to the airwaves, taking a leaf out of Aberhart's book, with broadcasts every Tuesday over CJCA and every Saturday over CFRN.[52] He undertook a 2,400-mile tour by car of the northern constituencies and later he flew down to Calgary and Lethbridge to tour the south.[53]

Ronning grew more and more confident of the CCF's chances in the provincial election. The CCF ran thirty-six candidates, hoping for the level of success that the party had achieved in BC and Saskatchewan. It was stressful and exhausting work because it meant long meetings, innumerable speeches, a great deal of travel, late nights, and time away from his home and family, on top of his job as principal. With the provincial and federal elections held close together,[54] the CCF in Camrose ran ads featuring both Ronning and Sigurd Lefsrud, the federal candidate. Ronning was up against J.D. Neville, the Independent candidate, and D.B. Mullen, the new candidate for Social Credit. In the dying days before the late March vote, Ronning was faced with comments circulated by both the Social Credit and Independent campaigns that a vote for CCF would mean a government the same as that in Germany.[55] In the end, both Ronning and Lefsrud lost, but Ronning came within seventy-four votes of Mullen, the winner. Ronning thought the results were good considering how recently the CCF had entered as a party, and the Camrose constituency was not finished with him yet.

Postelection, Ronning slowed his pace, consolidating the constituency organizations that had been put in place before the election. He was able to take a break in June to attend the convention of the Lutheran Church of America in Minneapolis and to watch his father receive an honourary degree from St. Olaf College. On his return, he continued to advance the cause of the CCF and, in October, he expounded further his views on education in an address to the high school teachers' convention in Edmonton.[56] In November, fate stepped in with the sudden death of Mullen, the Social Credit MLA. Pressure was put on Ronning to run again in the by-election. He was nominated unanimously on 23 November at a CCF convention, and he geared up for yet another battle. Premier Aberhart suggested that since the death of a Social Credit member had made the seat vacant, there need be no battle at all: it should be filled by acclamation. This brought a laugh from the editors of the *Vegreville Observer*, who commented: "There will be a election in Camrose all right, unless Mr. Ronning, the CCF candidate should unhappily overeat and pass out during the Christmas festivities."[57]

Social Credit chose C.I. Sayers, a farmer from Meeting Creek, and set the election date for 6 February 1941. This time, Ronning's posters proclaimed: "Follow the Lead of Britain CCF *Policy Identical with British Labour Party*," with some finishing with "GOD SAVE THE KING!"[58] But it did not work. In the two-way fight, Ronning finished 546 votes behind Sayers. Beaten but unbowed, Ronning proclaimed, "As Soon as There is Another Election We Shall Contest it...For (the) CCF Movement is A Crusade."[59] But members of the press advised Ronning and his colleagues to give up on the province and to concentrate on the Dominion. Instead, Ronning took on Neville, the former Independent candidate, in a war of words that went on for weeks in the letter columns of the *Camrose Canadian*, accusing the Independent candidate of not being independent at all but of having made pro-government statements before the election that affected the outcome.

Nothing was gained. As if for diversion, Ronning took the college choir to Edmonton, where they received exceptionally high marks and high praise, and he worked on a master's degree at the University of Alberta. He maintained his schedule of speeches and radio talks, but with the worsening situation in Asia and in Europe, one detects there was a certain restlessness within him. Late in January 1942, he was unanimously chosen as president of the provincial CCF and he presided over a reorganization of the provincial party. In a broadcast in April, he indicated that it was necessary to vote yes in the coming Dominion plebiscite on conscription, something that Camrose and all Alberta did. In June 1942, when Royal Canadian Air Force (RCAF) recruiters passed through Camrose, Ronning offered his name and shortly thereafter happily handed over his political duties to Elmer Roper, who had just won a by-election in Edmonton. He could not have continued his duties in any case because he had been called to rejoin the RCAF to work in Ottawa, decoding Japanese radio messages.

In August 1942, with his newly awarded master's degree, he took a leave of absence from the college, "with a heavy heart," for the duration of the war and headed for Ottawa.[60] Yet, he would come back to Camrose for one more stab at politics, allowing his name to stand as the CCF candidate in the June 1945 federal election. Taking a brief leave from his duties in Ottawa, he campaigned by radio and made a limited number of stump speeches, before flying off to obligations in England. Again he lost. By V-J day in August 1945, he had a choice to make: he could return to Camrose and the college, where he was aware of growing unhappiness among the more conservative board members about him, or he could accept an offer from the Department of External Affairs for a one-year posting to the Canadian Embassy in Chungking, China. He chose the latter, but his belief in democratic socialism remained strong.

## Diplomat in China

By the outbreak of World War II, Ronning's career in politics was nearly over. He was forty-five years old. Through his years as principal at Camrose Lutheran College, and from his experience as political candidate, elected representative, and party leader, he had a wide circle of friends and associates. Added to these groups were his friends and relations who came to him through his membership in the Lutheran Church and by the fact that he was of Norwegian descent. As a result, he was well known in western Canada and in the states of Minnesota and Iowa in the USA. Although Ronning's father had accepted Canadian citizenship, other members of the Ronning and Rorem families remained in the United States. Moreover, there were the families in Norway. Ronning was a tall tree with prodigious roots. Those roots extended across the Pacific to China, to students and friends from his childhood and his days as school principal at Fancheng, where his mother was buried. All of these roots and connections were to be of importance in the second phase of Ronning's career, but there was nothing in them to indicate that he was destined to become a diplomat, let alone an important and famous one. In fact, with war in Europe developing, Ronning, too old to join the

active forces and with his political career in the doldrums, continued
as principal of the college while completing a master's degree at the
University of Alberta.

Among Ronning's connections, one crucial to his later career
was missing: he had little presence in Ottawa, the capital of Canada
and the home of its diplomacy. The Canadian foreign office, known
as the Department of External Affairs (DEA), was founded in 1909
but by 1940, its staff was still sparse, although made up of very intelligent people, among them Rhodes Scholars. Outside of an embassy
in Japan, most of Canada's diplomatic activity was European- and
American-directed. The department had little expertise relating to
Asia. If it needed advice on China, it could turn to Canadian Protestant
missionaries who were, in general, from southern Ontario and former
classmates of members of the department, or make use of British
and American expertise. Canada had sent many missionaries to
China, perhaps more per capita than any other Western country. The
Protestant missionary effort was headquartered in southern Ontario,
and the Catholic one in Quebec. Methodist and Presbyterian missionaries, whose churches joined together as the United Church of
Canada in 1925, worked in Kwangtung (Guangdong) province around
Canton (Guangzhou), in Szechuan (Sichuan) province at Cheng-tu
(Chengdu), and also in Taiwan and in north-central China. Anglican
missionaries were also active north of the Yangtze. These missionar-
ies were an important factor in formulating and carrying out Canada's
China policy.[1]

In 1942, when China and Canada were allies in the war against
Japan, Canada undertook to exchange its first diplomatic representatives with China. The DEA, in its search for a suitable person to
represent Canada in Chungking (Chongqing), asked the missionary
community in Toronto for advice. There were offers from a number
of missionaries to fill the post. In the end, Prime Minister Mackenzie
King, through the department, chose a retired general and former
politician from British Columbia named Victor Wentworth Odlum.[2]
He was then serving as Canadian high commissioner in Australia.
Ronning, out in western Canada, was virtually unknown in Ottawa as

a China Hand, although he was known to Social Democrats through the Co-operative Commonwealth Federation (CCF) in Alberta. He was not from a Canadian missionary family and was not well known in the Ontario missionary community. His father had become Canadian after he had served as a Lutheran missionary in a Norwegian American mission in China. Ronning's connections, when he taught in China in the 1920s, were with the American Lutheran missionary community. In 1942, however, when the Canadian government began looking for people with facility in Asian languages they found Ronning. He was offered three years residence in Ottawa, where he worked until V-J day in August 1945.

During the war, Ottawa society was small and close-knit. Ronning, never one to hide his light under a bushel, soon became known to other members of the military and to the civil service. He made friendships with others who had China experience. He lived for over two years on his own, staying at first at the local YMCA, sharing meals in Chinese restaurants with other China Hands. He was still, however, the principal (on leave) of Camrose Lutheran College. While he established new connections in Ottawa, he remained close to Camrose, returning there on leaves until his family joined him in Ottawa in September 1944. Ronning's wartime work was very important. He was in charge of a Discrimination Unit using foreign radio signals and intercepted codes to track the positions of enemy submarines and shipping. Unable to crack the Japanese code, the unit, nonetheless, was able to predict Japanese naval attacks by monitoring the volume of radio traffic to and from ports under Japanese military control. Ultimately, the unit was able to provide sufficient warning time for Allied aircraft and ships to prepare to defend themselves against an attack. In the Atlantic, by triangulating radio signals from U-boats, they were able to pinpoint their positions to enable Allied planes to attack them.

As previously noted, in June 1945, just one month after the ending of the war in Europe, Canada held a federal election, with Ronning once more a CCF candidate for Camrose. He did well but he lost the election. His active public career in politics was now over, and, although he was still on leave as principal of the college, he was open to new challenges. Shortly before V-J Day, the DEA asked him to interview and to test the Chinese language skills of potential candidates for appointment to the Canadian Embassy in China. With Japan's collapse, Canada was anxious to increase its diplomatic capacity in China as Ambassador General Victor Wentworth Odlum, in discussions with Chiang Kai-shek, had worked out a program for greater Canadian involvement in the postwar reconstruction of China. Ronning interviewed three candidates and found them below standard. He was then asked to write the department's entrance examination, after which he was offered the position of first secretary in Chungking. It was an extraordinary invitation. He was nearly fifty-one, an age when most diplomats were in mid-to-late career, and his academic background was unusual compared to that of the Rhodes Scholars whom the DEA attracted. The department's policy was to hire generalists, but Ronning was engaged because of his special knowledge of China and of the Chinese language.[3] He was given the rank of first secretary to take into account his previous career, age, and, no doubt, master's degree. Another factor was the prejudices of General Odlum, the ambassador who had a very keen sense of rank and was at odds with the other officers at the embassy, ignoring those with Asia expertise.

At the time, little did anyone, including Ronning, dream he was destined to have a diplomatic career of major importance to the development of Canada's relations with Asia. On receipt of the offer, he consulted his family. His teenage daughters, Audrey and Meme, were enthusiastically excited, while his wife Inga was much less so, but she agreed since, after all, it was only for one year. Ronning did not look beyond one year, after which the department and he could part company through mutual agreement, unless other arrangements presented themselves. He wired Camrose Lutheran College to say he would not be back for another year.

On 12 October 1945, Ronning and his family returned to their house in Camrose and he prepared to travel to the land of his birth. Later in the month, he was discharged from the Royal Canadian Air

Force with the rank of Squadron Leader and high recommendations that stood him in good stead with the DEA. On his way back to Ottawa to begin his travels to Chungking, Chester met his brother, Talbert, who came up from Minneapolis to see him in Winnipeg. Talbert was just back from China. Following in his father's footsteps, he became an ordained minister and took up a mission in China in the 1930s. He spent the five war years only sixty miles from Japanese lines, in the Lutheran United Mission in Teng S'ian (Deng Xian), Honan, just north of Fancheng. As was their lifelong habit, he and Chester spoke to each other in Chinese. According to Chester, Talbert's "accent was that of an old farmer from Hupei. I could not have recognized him as my brother if I did not know who he was. He had escaped from China as the Japanese advanced."[4]

Apart from his language skills and previous experience of China, the department was hopeful that Ronning's farm background and social democratic views might assist them in rounding out their picture of China beyond the Kuomintang-centred vision offered by the patrician Ambassador Odlum.[5] General Odlum was two-and-one-half years into his posting and not particularly happy. He had served in Europe during World War I, and briefly again at the outset of World War II, before being named high commissioner to Australia. China, particularly Chungking, was a major cultural shock to him. He could not get over the filth, lack of sanitation, and the dishonesty he observed all around him. He found the Chinese government to be corrupt and its army weak. He was astounded to find that the soldiers did not fight the Japanese, but instead traded with them. Nonetheless, Odlum saw his job as one of making China take notice of Canada. During the war, Canada had started to become a major industrial nation, and the general was afraid that the Chinese would overlook it to concentrate on Britain and the United States when it came to future trade and development. He felt Canada was greatly outnumbered by the British and Americans, who had embassy staffs of three hundred each.

As Ronning was to write of Odlum in March 1946, "He has succeeded in a special way in establishing most cordial relations on a personal basis with a great many Chinese individuals, especially in government and Chinese Army circles."[6] Odlum, who once told Mao Tse-tung that it was easy to be honest in the Communist areas of Yunnan province because there was nothing to steal, had done a good job in getting to know Chiang Kai-shek, but much of his reporting to Ottawa was based on information supplied by Tao Xisheng, Chiang's secretary, who was reputed to have ghostwritten Chiang's opus, *China's Destiny*.[7] In Ottawa, the Under-Secretary of State for External Affairs, on first meeting, found that Odlum's "assurance and confidence in his own judgment is rather frightening."[8] The department counted on Ronning to provide an additional dimension.

Much water had flowed down the Yangtze since April 1927 when Ronning last saw China. On his departure, he witnessed the occupation of Nanking by Chiang Kai-shek, who broke up the United Front with the Communists and turned violently upon them. The Communists, who had set up headquarters in Hankow, had received very bad advice from Stalin, who completely misjudged both the nature of the Chinese Communist movement and Chinese society. They were driven underground and into the mountains where they regrouped.

Temporarily rid of the Communist annoyance, Chiang set about consolidating his power in the lower Yangtze region, establishing the apparatus of government, initiating parts of Sun Yat-sen's Three People's Principles, and proclaiming the new Republic of China as the government of all of China. It was not true, of course, because he still had to deal with warlords, and, eventually, the Communists again. Nonetheless, he enjoyed the goodwill of many world governments and was supported by Western missionaries, particularly because on 1 December 1927 he married Soong May-ling (Soong Mei-ling), an American-educated daughter of Charles Soong, who, among other things, was a publisher of Bibles in Shanghai. May-ling let it be known that Chiang was taking instruction toward converting to Methodism. Later, Madame Chiang, as she was known, became the "face" of the new China in North America and its most prominent spokesperson. In 1934, she and Chiang launched a movement for social reform called the New Life Movement, basically to teach the Chinese proper manners and behaviour. It became noted for violently enforcing its rules and for frowning upon Western habits and dress, when adopted by young Chinese.

The break with the Communist Party of China (CPC) in April 1927 put an end to the support Chiang was getting from the Soviet Union, whose military and political advisors returned to Moscow. Casting about for replacements, Chiang found military help and top-notch military advisors from Germany. The German generals, who later went on to serve Hitler, devised a strategy to enable Chiang to eliminate the Communists. In the early 1930s, on their advice, he launched a series of Annihilation (Bandit Suppression) campaigns that featured blockhouses to cut off CPC lines of retreat and heavy aerial bombing. Meanwhile, the Japanese invaded Manchuria (northeast China) in September 1931 and two years later established the puppet state of Manchukuo under Henry P'u-i, the last emperor of the Ch'ing dynasty. China's appeals to the League of Nations proved useless. The Manchurian warlord Chang Hsueh-liang (Zhang Xueliang), on Chiang's advice, withdrew, moving his troops to northwest China near China's ancient capital of Sian (Xi'an).

The annihilation campaigns proved failures and the Chinese Communists escaped to begin their epic Long March, a trek of a year's duration (1934–35) to the northwest to Yen-an (Yan'an) north of Sian. En route, at Tsunyi (Zunyi), out of contact with Moscow, they elected Mao Tse-tung as their leader and accepted his Sinified version of Marxism, Mao Tse-tung Thought, as their ideology. The remnants of the party, on arrival in Yen-an, lived in caves, licked their wounds, and set about building a party and army structure based on Mao's view that the leading revolutionary class in China was the peasantry. They developed techniques of guerilla warfare, which were used effectively behind Japanese lines, and they began a propaganda campaign condemning Chiang's failure to counter the Japanese invasion.

Chiang remained steadfast in his determination to eliminate the Communists because he regarded them as "a disease of the heart," while the Japanese were "a disease of the skin."[9] He ordered the

warlord Chang Hsueh-liang to crush the Communists in Yen-an.
This was in December 1936 and Chang refused. Chiang flew to Sian
to enforce his order only to be kidnapped by the rebellious Chang. He
was released only after the intervention of the Chinese Communists
through their negotiator Chou En-lai. Chiang flew back to Nanking
on Christmas Day with Chang Hsueh-liang as his perpetual prisoner.
A deal had been struck for a United Front between the KMT and the
CPC, with Moscow's blessing and provision of military support against
the Japanese (that ended with the Soviet-Japanese neutrality pact of
April 1941).[10] On 7 July 1937, following an event known as the Marco
Polo Bridge (Lugouqiao) Incident, the Japanese army invaded north
China, extending their control along the east coast down to Shanghai
and up the Yangtze valley. Chiang and his government were forced to
abandon Nanking and to move up the Yangtze to Chungking, taking
with them factories, educational institutions, and the apparatus of
government, along with their military. In turn, the Japanese set up a
puppet state covering their occupied portion of eastern China. The
brutality of the Japanese assault, characterized by the Rape of Nanking
in December 1937, turned world sympathy to the beleaguered Chinese
regime. Newsreels in cinemas regularly showed conditions in China,
and campaigns to raise funds for the Chinese victims of war sprang up
across Canada.

All of these events Chester Ronning followed at a distance, but
he offered a number of public lectures in Camrose describing the
situation in East Asia and expressing his views on the problem. In
December 1943, in a lecture to students at the Camrose Lutheran
College, he praised Sun Yat-sen's liberal ideas: "As long as the Chinese
maintain and cherish these ideals, and are willing to sacrifice for
freedom as they are doing today, freedom cannot be withheld from
them."[11] In addition, numerous missionaries on leave, or returning
from China, spoke about conditions in China. In July, the month
prior to Ronning's departure for Ottawa, one of the most prominent
Canadian Protestant missionaries, Rev. James Endicott, of the West
China Union University, on a tour of Canada, delivered speeches pre-
dicting the end of the British and other empires in East Asia. And, like

other China watchers of the time, Ronning became aware of what had transpired in the Chinese Communist movement after 1927 through the publication, in 1937, of Edgar Snow's *Red Star Over China*. Snow not only discussed the history of the Communist cause but also gave descriptions and biographies of its leaders, along with transcripts of interviews with them.

With the attack on Pearl Harbor on 7 December 1941, Chiang gained the United States and Canada as allies against Japan, along with Britain, whose Asian empire was being invaded by Japanese troops. Indeed, Canada declared war on Japan before the United States did.[12] This spurred Canada to recognize China, and the two countries exchanged ambassadors. In June 1942, Madame Chiang Kai-shek was given an unprecedented opportunity to address the Canadian Senate and House of Commons in a joint sitting. She dazzled her audience with her beauty and her command of the English language, using words such as "ochlocracy" and "immane," sending MPs and senators rushing to their dictionaries.[13]

More important, however, was America's entry into the war against Japan. What had previously been volunteer unofficial assistance to China in the form of the American Volunteer Group under General Claire Lee Chennault became official. In 1943, US President Franklin Roosevelt dispatched General Joseph Stilwell to Chungking to be Chiang's chief of staff and to train the Chinese army and bring it up to a standard to fight the Japanese. Stilwell was also to be commander-in-chief of the China Burma India theatre (CBI). Vinegar Joe, as he was known, spoke Chinese and had served in China earlier in the century. In attempting to do his assignment, he found himself at odds with Chiang Kai-shek and Chennault. It seemed America and China were at cross-purposes. The United States was strengthening Chiang in order to defeat Japan, but Chiang wanted to preserve his forces to fight the Communists in the civil war he knew would come following Japan's inevitable defeat at the hands of the Americans. Matters came to a head between Chiang and Stilwell, with Stilwell succeeding in getting Roosevelt to order Chiang to put all of his troops under his command. Enraged, Chiang demanded, and got, Stilwell recalled on

19 October 1944 and replaced shortly after by the less abrasive General Albert Wedemeyer.

America and Chiang also did not see eye-to-eye on the question of civil jurisdiction and governmental reform. President Roosevelt had a vision of China as a democratic bulwark in Asia following the war— open, of course, to American business. As such, he promoted Chiang in world meetings of the Allied leaders. The problem was to reconcile the KMT and the CPC differences through negotiations. Technically, the Americans should have had a major say in bringing the two sides together, and American negotiators thought they did. Unfortunately, they viewed the problem through the prism of American political practice and had little appreciation of the depth of bitterness and distrust between the Communists and the Nationalists. Much blood had already been shed and each side faced the reality that, after the war, when the Japanese and the Americans were gone, another major and bloody fight would ensue.

The Americans, who were dispatched to Yen-an as official observers, were struck by the simplicity, dedication, and élan of Mao's Communists. The Communists appeared to be doing their utmost to engage the Japanese through creative guerilla fighting. Some of the American visitors to the caves of Yen-an mistook the Communists for simple agrarian reformers. In contrast, the wartime corruption, inflation, and general surliness of the KMT and its followers in Chungking led some American observers to question the American policy of near-unconditional support for Chiang. But, in short, the US needed Chiang more than Chiang needed the US, to the point that a cynical Harry S. Truman, having assumed the American presidency in April 1945, was prompted to refer to Chiang as "Generalissimo Cash My Check,"[14] as he was known to many in the West. To humour the Americans, both the KMT and the CPC carried on negotiations, giving way, seemingly, on minor points, but each knew the other well enough to know that what they gave would be unacceptable to the other, and vice versa.

When the war ended suddenly in mid-August 1945, both sides had yet to prepare their physical positions and they used the truce

Yen-an headquarters of the Chinese Communist Party, 1934–48. [Evans private collection]

negotiations brokered by the great General George C. Marshall as a cover under which to do so. Chiang's supporters felt that if America was serious about helping Chiang, it would provide large numbers of American ground troops to help him consolidate his hold on China. The best they got was American air support to fly Chinese troops to the northeast to attempt to fill the vacuum left once the Soviet troops withdrew. The Soviet Union, having broken its earlier pact with Japan, entered the Pacific war at the last moment early in August 1945. When its forces withdrew, they took most of the industrial equipment from North Korea and Manchuria, leaving caches of arms for the taking.

It was at this point, more or less, that Ronning entered the picture, in time to witness the final drift to civil war, as the KMT moved its capital back to Nanking, took its seat in the newly formed United

Nations, and developed a core of sympathetic followers in the United States, made up of business and religious interests, known forever as the China Lobby.[15] On 26 November 1945, First Secretary Ronning arrived in Chungking from Canada, following an arduous fifteen-day journey, sixty-eight hours of it in the air, at times in unheated military airplanes. "I had more than a little difficulty," he wrote, "explaining to a fellow traveler how with a Norwegian father and an American mother I could be born in China and still claim to be a Canadian." "It beats the Dutch," was his final comment.[16]

There was no one to meet him at the Paishihi (Baishiyi) airport, located thirty-five miles outside the city. He rode in a truck driven at speed over winding and treacherous muddy roads to the American Army Headquarters, where a jeep from the Canadian Embassy met him. Ambassador Odlum greeted him on the steps of the embassy, located in a compound on the street named the Fairy Grotto. The compound was cramped, filled with families, dogs, and chickens. Ronning found the human content of the embassy to consist of "the ambassador, Gen. V. Odlum, four Chinese girl stenographers, two Chinese male clerks, about 14 servants including 2 chauffers [sic], wash woman and garden boy and small me."[17]

Chungking was not one of China's salubrious cities. While fog shrouded it in winter, it trapped tremendous heat during the summer, and the city was known as one of China's furnaces. Theodore "Teddy" White, correspondent for *Time* magazine stationed in Chungking during the war, wrote this thumbnail sketch of the joys of the city:

> The city taken over by the Central Government as its house of exile was known even in China as a uniquely unpleasant place. Perhaps the newcomers found the weather even more irritating than the people. There were only two seasons in Chungking, both bad. From early fall to late spring the fogs and rains made a dripping canopy over the city; damp and cold reigned in every home. The slime in the street was inches thick, and people carried the slippery mud with them as they went from bedroom to council chamber and back. There was no escaping the chilly moisture

except by visiting the handful of people who lived in modern homes in which coal was burned. The crowded, huddled refugee population, cramped together in their jerry-built shacks, could only warm their fingers over expensive charcoal pots or go to bed early. Everyone shivered until summer came; then the heat settled down and the sun glared. Dust coated the city almost as thickly as mud during the wintertime. Moisture remained in the air, perspiration dripped, and prickly heat ravaged the skin. Every errand became an expedition, each expedition an ordeal. Swarms of bugs emerged; small green ones swam on drinking water, and spiders four inches across crawled on the walls. The famous Chungking mosquitoes came, and Americans claimed the mosquitoes worked in threes; two lifted the mosquito net, while the third zoomed in for the kill. Meat spoiled; there was never enough water for washing; dysentery spread and could not be evaded.[18]

It was here Generalissimo Chiang Kai-shek and his government rode out the war, protected from the full destructiveness of Japanese bombs by the rugged terrain, the low clouds, and fog. Once the war was over, the government prepared to move back to its original capital at Nanking, which they had had to abandon in 1937.

Ambassador Odlum, himself a general, greatly admired Chiang Kai-shek and was working on proposals for Canada-China co-operation following the war, but he was at odds with his own staff. He did not consult his officers, Counsellor Dr. George Patterson[19] and Third Secretary Ralph Collins, both knowledgeable about China and Asia. They left, vowing never to return while Odlum was ambassador. Brigadier Orville Kay, the military attaché, resigned his position and returned to Canada. Because of the difference in their ranks, Odlum forbade Kay to send reports to Ottawa and would only communicate with him in writing. Kay's replacement, Brigadier William Bostock, who arrived one month after Ronning, accepted the general's power of command and did not make a great issue of it. Ronning, closer in age to Odlum, and who, like Odlum, had served in the armed forces in both World Wars, recognized Odlum as "every inch the soldier."[20]

Odlum regarded Ronning as the one member of his staff suitable for him to talk to and consult.

Ronning arrived just in time to monitor the negotiations between Chiang and Mao, between Yen-an and Chungking. Through Wang Ping-nan (Wang Bingnan) of the Yen-an information office, the Canadian Embassy was kept up-to-date on the progress of the negotiations. During this time, Ronning met people on both sides of the civil conflict and he made friendships that would endure throughout his life. Ambassador Odlum took Ronning with him on his meetings with high-ranking officials, with Ronning increasingly acting as his interpreter. On his arrival in Chungking, Ronning had been open to all views, but soon, through first-hand encounters, he began to show sympathy for the Communist position.

The ambassador's residence was organized like an Edwardian household, staffed upstairs and down by well-meaning Chinese servants with whom Ronning established an easy relationship. The embassy had a projector and three short films—one on salmon, one on bronco busting, and one featuring the Toronto Symphony Orchestra (TSO)—but no one knew how to operate the machine until Ronning arrived. Because of fluctuations in electrical power, he rigged up a large transformer sufficient to play the sound. While the films on the salmon run and on bronco busting were almost as good without sound (particularly to a Chinese audience), the one of the TSO was not, and it was Odlum's favourite. When the ambassador viewed it, however, he always reminded Ronning of the cost of the extra electricity to the Canadian taxpayer.[21]

Electricity, or rather the lack of it, was a major problem. Most of the embassy staff went to bed early because there was no light and no heat. Bedrooms were cold in the winter, yet Odlum allowed everyone just one blanket. The room where Tessie Wong (Wong Yaoying), the embassy's receptionist/secretary, and her sister Katherine typed Odlum's reports and letters was heated by a small charcoal stove, but Odlum rationed the briquettes, preferring to issue the Wong sisters with knitting gloves.[22] Ronning typed letters home by candlelight, "hunting and pecking" in the gathering gloom. When he went to bed,

Chungking embassy staff, 1945. Ambassador Odlum centre top, Ronning in front. [Sau W. Cheung private collection]

lying on a cotton pad atop a wooden slat frame, he had only a thin cotton cover for warmth. The sheets were clammy and damp. The Wong sisters found him an extra "illegal" blanket, but he was perpetually cold and suffered from asthma. The rainy, foggy weeks of winter chilled a person to the bone. To keep warm, Ronning sometimes had as many as four hot baths a week.

> So you see I keep clean even if I am continuously cold. We all go to bed early. We need to after the early rising and the strain of attempting to keep the blood from stopping altogether in your veins. It is too cold all day to relax so you are really tired by 8:30 or 9:00. Anyhow, there is no furniture comfortable enough in which to relax. Everything in the line of comforts is pretty primitive in this over crowded [sic] war time [sic] capital of China.[23]

He looked forward to visits to Chinese government offices and other embassies where there was some warmth.

Ronning's quarters upstairs, like the whole compound, were rat-infested. He tried to outwit them but failed. They even ate his bar of soap, which he had dangled from the ceiling on a string over his bed in an effort to preserve it. During the day, the noise of traffic and the cries of hawkers filtered up from the street. At night, the compound echoed with a cacophony of bawling babies and barking dogs. Then, all too early, the roosters crowed their urgent wake-up calls. Within a week of his arrival, Ronning outlined his morning routine to his family:

> Our chief boy, Liang by name, is very solicitous of our every want. He wakes me by turning the light on at 6:30. While I rub my eyes and say a few words to him in Chinese, he brushes my clothes, folds my socks, underwear and shirt and arranges them all in handy places within easy reach of the chair before which he puts my slippers and my already highly polished shoes. A second boy has been attending to the brushing of my shoes. The hot water arrives and I dress and shave. A musical gong sounds in the hall and I join the

ambassador for breakfast. The food is much better than I thought. We have tangerines, oranges and pomelos followed by eggs and toast with a little Canadian butter (only once a day). We finish with a big steaming cup of weak coffee. Weak because it costs about $10,000 a pound.[24]

Early in December 1945, Ronning took a drive in the embassy jeep to deliver some presents from Mah Him of Kingman, a town near Camrose, to his family in Chungking. He also visited the Lutheran mission where he met young men from Talbert's mission at Deng Xian and three of his own former students from Fancheng. His previous world was linking with his new one. In addition, he wrote his family,

This week I have had the pleasure of meeting Dr. Jim Endicott, a prof. from the West China University, who is a very promonent [*sic*] friend of the Communists. I learned many things from him and will pass them on to you when my own mind is more clear on the issue.[25]

And then, to Ronning's surprise and delight, someone discovered it was his birthday on the thirteenth of December and some of the members of the embassy gave him a party that included cake and flowers. He reciprocated by taking the Wong sisters on picnics using the embassy jeep in which the ambassador had forbidden them to ride. Ronning had them crouch down low whenever they drove past the ambassador. In time, he came to regard Tessie Wong as a daughter and her well-being was to become a matter of great concern to him in the future.

In January 1946, Ronning was put in charge of moving the embassy to Nanking. He faced two major tasks: flying to Nanking to find suitable locations and housing for the embassy and its staff, and then returning to Chungking to pack up the embassy's goods and chattels and take them downriver by boat to Nanking. His flight to Nanking was continually postponed and he did not reach the city until early February; the embassy move was not completed until the end of

Ronning wheeling Tessie and Katherine Wong, Nanking, 1946. [Sau W. Cheung private collection]

May. Meanwhile, he accompanied Ambassador Odlum to a number of events and meetings. Although chosen for his linguistic ability, Ronning felt rusty, hesitating to speak in public. Just before Christmas 1945, he went with Odlum to the Central China University where the ambassador delivered a speech. In fact, the university was located in Wuchang and was only in Chungking for the duration of the war. Most of the students were from Ronning's home province of Hupei. After the ambassador finished and his speech was translated, they called on Ronning, and

> they suddenly announced that I would speak in Chinese. I had absolutely no warning but I had to get up and say something. I started out rather hesitatingly but gained momentum rapidly. I told them a few stories that were associated with Hupei, which they received with considerable enthusiasm, particularly the students from the Hsiang yang district who had the same accent. When I said that I had once shouted that I also was in favor of smashing imperialism in response to a mob of angry students who yelled, "Down with imperialism," the whole student body broke out into prolonged thunderous applause. The ambassador wondered what in the world I had said. I did not inform him. When I got excited... [I] spoke must [*sic*] faster than I thought I was capable of after so many years absence from China.[26]

On 30 December, he was called on to translate when a famous Communist general, Yeh Chien-ying (Ye Jianying),[27] "a strong well built man with bright and sparkling eyes," called at the embassy. "I did the translating and really got warm for once. In fact I was nearly soaked with perspiration before I was through."[28] Ronning provided the same service on 2 January 1946, when Chou En-lai and his wife Teng Ying-chao (Deng Yingchao) came to the embassy for dinner accompanied by their eight-person negotiating team. It was Ronning's first time to meet Chou,[29] although he was fully aware of Chou's history and how he came to be second to Mao Tse-tung in the Communist Party. He had half an hour's conversation with Chou, whom he found to be "quiet and forceful." He was "very favorably impressed" with the Communist leaders he met. "They seem to be on fire for the welfare of China." He continued, "My opinion is that it will be a good thing for China to have the Communists brought into the government."[30]

On 9 April 1946, Ronning had his second encounter with Chou En-lai and Teng Ying-chao. His earlier positive impression was greatly reinforced.

Last night the Ambassador and I had a big Chinese feast as the guests of General Chou En-lai, number two Communist, and a number of other prominent Communists among them was Mrs. Chou. She is a very pleasant, serious and clever woman. We had an elaborate "*hai-shen*" feast with "*Tien-chi*"—Field Chicken—frog legs to a barbarian. The flavors were superb.

General Chou impresses me very much. He is a big man with a large square face and bushy black eyebrows of the John L. Lewis type. His hair has a wave, which I suspect is from one of his Manchu ancestors. He has a high nose ridge and looks like a dark Aryan more than a Mongolian. His voice is pleasing and his argument is forceful and logical. His earnestness is convincing. His enthusiasm is contagious. He is completely unpretentious. In his conversation he is direct and almost blunt. He said to the ambassador two or three times: "You cannot understand the actual conditions here because you have a totally different background." His translator always smoothed off the sharper point but Chou speaks and understands quite a little English so he often interrupts his interpreter and blurts out what he thinks should be said in the way he thinks it should be said.[31]

Ronning adds to the scene in his memoir:

Our general [Odlum] was on his favourite subject—urging the Communists to amalgamate the Red Armies with the Nationalist Armies and trust the people of China to decide the issue as to which party should govern China. Odlum in turn asked me to repeat Chou's reply and the conversation became more spirited as well as more controversial. I could not help understanding Chou's point of view that no political party in China had the ghost of a chance against Chiang's totalitarian government without an army.[32]

Ronning also met important members of the Nationalist government, but he offers no assessments of their dedication to their cause. He had dinner on 24 February with General Ho Ying-ching (He Yinchin), "famous and notorious...who is feared more than anyone in China unless it should be the Generalissimo."[33] They swapped hunting stories. He also visited "the notorious Dr. H.H. Kung,"[34] the former finance minister and brother-in-law to Chiang,[35] in his palatial home. After waiting in the first residence, he was escorted to the second one, "which was even more luxuriously furnished than the first." He was received in an upstairs living room.

It was all done in blue with a cozy charcoal fireplace. A servant brought in tea. Dr. Kung came in dressed in a long satin fur robe with a blak [sic] "*ma kwa*"...One could not help but be impressed by his amiable personality. Most of his conversation seemed to be in explanation of why he was no longer in the thick of things.[36]

Later, Ronning was the only foreigner invited to a farewell banquet in late April for General Feng Yu-Hsiang, the "Christian General," who remembered Ronning from their meeting in Peking in 1923. At Chiang Kai-shek's suggestion, the sixty-three-year-old general was about to leave for the United States to study hydroelectric projects. During the evening, Ronning invited Feng to extend his visit to include Canada, particularly the Peace River country in Alberta. "Old General Feng is a very interesting man with a powerful influence over his audience when he speaks. He speaks simply and directly without any ostentation. He dresses plainly and is admired for his sincerity by all Chinese."[37] Because of his popularity, Chiang Kai-shek wanted him out of China.

All these April dinners in Chungking took place after Ronning's first trip to Nanking in preparation to move the Canadian Embassy. Whether it was the accumulated fatigue from the long, arduous journey from Canada, the difficult living conditions, or the depressing Chungking winter, six weeks after his arrival, Ronning was sick in bed for a week with a bout of bronchitis and had to postpone his trip to Nanking.[38] It was nearly a month later, on 2 February, Chinese New Year, when he finally arrived in Nanking, flying in on a cargo plane, along with the embassy jeep. Bill Bostock, the military attaché who had been in the city for three weeks, met him and with the jeep took them to their temporary quarters in the old British Embassy, which had been left empty since the British closed it in 1936. To Ronning, arriving in Nanking was:

> Like coming out of a prison of eternal mists into the freedom of the clear, blue skies. You cannot imagine what a grand and glorious feeling it was to step out of the plane into brilliantly dazzling sunlight, to realize again that there really was a sun and that it could shine and that it was warm and bright.[39]

Bostock and Ronning were in Nanking to search for property for the Canadian Embassy and housing for its staff. Finding space was not an easy task because much of the better housing was already spoken for, or had been damaged by the Japanese. Nanking still had a large number of Japanese soldiers wandering its streets six months after the war's end. Indeed, the KMT retained several important Japanese civil and military men as advisors in the war against the Communists, as well as an undetermined number of technicians and combat personnel. Among them was General Yasuji Okamura, who was commander of all Japanese troops in China on V-J day and was later convicted of war crimes. He was released by special order of Chiang Kai-shek, who used him as a special advisor. Okamura was the first to introduce forced prostitution ("comfort women") in Japanese occupied areas and was suspected of being responsible for programs involving atrocities and genocide.[40]

The continued presence of Japanese soldiers was not the only strange aspect of Nanking that Ronning saw. One day, atop Purple Mountain, where he had gone with some Americans to view the site of a plane crash, they discovered, close by in a blockhouse, four prisoners with their hands tied behind their backs with wire. On inquiry, Ronning was told they were Communist spies being held without trial.

It was very distressing to go down the mountain leaving behind four men being tortured in medieval barbarity with little hope of eventually receiving justice. It was by accident that they were discovered by foreigners. I am certain it is one of the aspects of Chinese life that the Government is most anxious to hide from foreigners. I have not forgotten and will make use of the first opportunity I get to rub it in to some [of] the complacent officials.[41]

After a long and tedious search, lasting a month and involving negotiations with the DEA, the city of Nanking, and the Chinese military headquarters, Ronning and Bostock found a suitable location for the embassy and ambassador's residence in the house that had been the foreign minister's of the puppet government. With Odlum's permission, they raised the Canadian flag over the ambassador's residence on 7 March 1946. Ronning and Bostock had already moved in on 1 March, and, two weeks later, they held an official housewarming/opening reception, although Ambassador Odlum remained in Chungking. Nanking was still a political backwater compared to Chungking. Writing on 30 March, Ronning drew the contrast:

To the Canadian Embassy [in Chungking] came men of all shades of political opinion. In the atmosphere, which prevails there, these men and women seemed to drop their habitual defensive shells. They discussed in the frankest and friendliest manner the policies about which many of them had deep convictions....In Nanking, however, one got a feeling of political isolation, which extended beyond the foreign community to Government offices....This attitude changed over night when the Generalissimo arrived upon

Embassy staff on floor of new embassy, Nanking, 1946. Ambassador Odlum far left, Ronning far right. [Sau W. Cheung private collection]

the scene. Nanking became a buzzing hive of activity very suddenly, only to subside with a great sigh of relief upon the departure of the great man.[42]

Ronning flew back to Chungking on 4 April to make preparations for Odlum's departure for Nanking on 23 April. Because most of Chungking and all of the embassies were on the move to Nanking, the preparations were hectic, but, by the end of April, Ronning had the embassy to himself in hot and humid Chungking. The old embassy compound was almost serene as Ronning reported to Odlum in early May:

The babies are gone. The babies are gone....I feel certain, General, that if you realized that your Embassy building could really be as tranquil as it was last night, you would have stayed...you might be tempted to return and that would never do.[43]

Odlum used Ronning's 5 May letter as an opportunity to give Ottawa a glimpse of how trying life at the embassy in Chungking had been:

Taken all in all, noise was a principal feature of our life in Chungking; the noises of animals, of fowl and of men, the latter term including women and babies. You will notice after the rest of us came away, the babies disappeared and Ronning waxed eloquent in his ecstasy. It is true that the other noises remained but the silence of the babies was so startling that it drowned out what would otherwise have been deafening overtones and undertones.[44]

It remained for Ronning to oversee the shipping of the contents of the Chungking embassy down the Yangtze through the famous Yangtze Gorges to Nanking. In 1946, as part of Canada's assistance to China, the government of Canada arranged a loan of $12,750,000 to the Ming Sung Company to build, in Canada, nine modern ships for use on the Yangtze.[45] Thus, Oldum directed Ronning to turn to the Ming Sung Shipping Company for the transfer of the embassy goods. After laborious and complex negotiations, requiring appeals to higher authorities in the Chinese government, Ronning selected the S.S. *Ming Pen* to carry him, the staff, servants, goods, and chattels down the mighty Yangtze to their new home in Nanking. He was booked into a superior cabin for the trip, as were an Australian and a Norwegian. Ten days before departure, Ronning went to inspect the ship.

"There she is," said the company man.
"Where," I asked.
He pointed, and I saw a ship whose bow seemed to be reaching to the sky, while her stern hung very low in the water.[46]

Concerned, Ronning expressed doubt that the ship was able to make the trip. He was reassured that all would be well on the day. During the war, the *Ming Pen* had suffered a direct hit from a Japanese bomb on its stern, driving a hole in its bottom and causing the ship to sink. It was refloated and the hole plugged with cement. It was the weight of the cement that caused the stern to ride lower in the water, raising the bow. Ronning was told not to worry because twelve railway locomotives (left over from a never-developed railway) were to be loaded onto the bow, thus balancing the ship.

As well as arranging for the ship, Ronning had to finish up the last bits of business of the embassy, pay farewell visits—some on behalf of the departed ambassador—and attend dinners and international parties. He also knocked down furniture for shipping, answered phones and letters, and received a stream of visitors. Among the visitors were former students of his brother, Talbert, to whom Talbert had delivered letters and pictures from himself and his wife Ella. In speaking of his brother, Ronning told the former students he had been against Talbert going to China because he was "too good." The students agreed: "We have a nick-name for him. Everyone calls him: '*Lao Hao Ren*,' 'Old Good-man.'"[47] Ronning arranged for some of the students to get space on the *Ming Pen*.

Ronning's final days in Chungking were complicated and trying. To make matters worse, he came down with a case of Chungking fever, spending a few days in hospital. He did not tell his parents about the state of his health, but he wrote a full confidential account to his youngest sister Lily (Victoria), who was a nurse.

When I left Canada I was not in too good shape and should have had a good rest before I started but that was impossible if I was to take this position so I started off. The many days of little sleep in an ice cold bomber reduced my resistance and I came down with diarrhea and fever in Calcutta. But I had enough vitality to recover and go on to Chungking. I was determined to get adjusted to the terrible climate there but in January I came down again...When I was able to travel, I went to Nanking. The winter weather [t]here was like a tonic and I gained rapidly. Then back to Chungking with whole responsibility of selling the property and getting several air-lift shipments off besides taking furniture apart and attending to the regular business in a hot humid climate proved too much so I came down with pneumonia.[48]

He was not completely well when he boarded the *Ming Pen* on 21 May 1946. He had rushed to finish all his business to be on board by one o'clock. He had to be carried on board, but departure was delayed because the captain awaited the arrival of Lung Yun (Long Yun), the Yunnan warlord and chairman of Yunnan. Chiang sacked Long, recalling him to Nanking, where he was to be given a nominal position, the equivalent of house arrest. The warlord, being a very important person, commandeered all the best accommodations and absorbed most of the other space for his entourage. Ronning was bundled together with the Australian and the Norwegian, along with their entire luggage, into a small, cramped, airless cabin next to the boiler room. The Rev. James Endicott was also on board in similar accommodations but on the other side of the ship to which the loco-motives blocked access. He and Ronning had little opportunity to talk, although Ronning consulted Endicott on the history of the Yangtze Gorges as they went through them. Odlum liked Endicott personally, but placed no credence in his opinions. Ronning later came to suspect Endicott's views for being too much in harmony with the propaganda of the Communists.[49]

After an exhilarating passage through the gorges, the *Ming Pen* arrived safely in Nanking on 29 May, eight days after leaving Chungking.[50] The journey included a half-day in Hankow where Ronning visited the Lutheran Mission Home and Agency. His assessment of the trip was mixed:

While it was exciting and one of the most unusual trips I have ever had it was also of all the trips I have ever had by far the most grim. I have decided to write to you about it telling some at least of the unsanitary details. They will not make pleasant reading and I must ask you not to let it be published by papers like the Camrose Canadian because I would not dare to paint a true picture for the public but I feel that it is my duty to write about the actual conditions to you....If I never see Chungking again it will still be too soon...If I can help it I shall not visit the place again.[51]

# 6

# Nanking Forever

The end of May 1946 marked six months since Ronning's return to China, during which time he had met numerous leaders on both sides of the Chinese civil tension. The ceasefire General George C. Marshall brokered between the Kuomintang (KMT) and the Communist Party of China (CPC) in mid-January was coming apart. Early in April, Ronning offered his private assessment to his family.

> The situation in China just at present is not too bright. There is a powerful element in the Kuomintang of fascist reactionaries. They will not give up their power without resorting to violence. They fear the result of the recent agreements made between the Government and the Communists and are using their influence to upset everything even if it means civil war. The worst feature of the whole situation is that the Government takes no steps to punish their acts of terrorism against the communists and democratic elements. China has a long hard road ahead. It is only when I compare the progress that has been made since father was out here that I realize what great changes have taken place. One is inclined to be impatient with the apparent slowness with which progress is being made.[1]

At the end of June, the general situation in China was worse.

> China is in turmoil. Pessimism is common. Prices are still soaring.
> Exchange rates with Western money remain low. The cost of living
> here is at least five times as great as in Canada. The political situ-
> ation is complex and perplexing. The present government seems
> unable or unwilling to do anything. Corruption prevails in every
> phase of the national life. Things are very rotten in China. But the
> Chinese people are fine. They are intelligent and some of them are
> patriotic. Eventually they will clean their own house.
>
> There are many fine young men and women in China who are
> determined to make China democratic and put an end to oppres-
> sion and exploitation of human beings. They will win out but the
> struggle will be fierce and there will be many setbacks. I could tell
> you many stories about how the secret police are trying to stamp
> out all opposition to the Government. Their methods are not only
> cruel but stupid and short-sighted. I have heard men in high places
> boast about the success of their underground activities of intrigue
> and bloody murder. Some day I will tell you about some of my
> conversations with them, in their own homes, sitting at sumptu-
> ous feasts or reclining in luxuriously furnished palaces. These
> men do not want to lose their power and will resort to anything
> to retain it. Many of them are admirers of German Nazi methods
> and aspirations.[2]

A welcome diversion from the general political pall came in the
form of a farewell dinner for the British ambassador. With the departure of the ambassador, Odlum became dean of the diplomatic corps
and, thus, it was incumbent upon him to organize the farewell dinner.
In turn, this became the responsibility of Ronning and Bostock. It was
Ronning's first major encounter with protocol. He had been sent to
China without any briefing on the formalities of diplomatic life, but
he was soon to learn. The dinner was set for 7:30 p.m. on 13 June at the
International Club. Bostock and Ronning had to get agreement on the
timing, had to obtain everyone's signature on a farewell scroll, and had

to arrange the seating plan. A member of the French Embassy who knew about such things assisted them as they went from embassy to embassy. All went swimmingly at first, but then

> [w]e were making a tour of all the embassies and legations to get the signatures of the heads of all Foreign Missions in Nanking on a Chinese scroll to be presented to the guest of honour. Our comrade from the USSR insisted, without even consulting his superior, that his Ambassador would never sign below the signature of General George Marshall. His Ambassador was a full-fledged Ambassador representing a major state. The General was only a personal representative of a head of state. The Frenchman, who had accompanied us as a seasoned expert on protocol countered with a long recitation of the occasion in 1852 when the special Representative of the Czar of Russia took precedence over all the ambassadors of the diplomatic corps in Constantinople. He accompanied the memory of this historic fact with graceful flourishes of his previously rubbed hands, completely convincing the Brigadier and your little brother. The comrade, however, brushed the argument aside by stating most emphatically that a Czar was infinitely higher in protocol than a mere president. I wondered why but did not want to revive the controversy. The Frenchman seemed completely subdued and had apparently exhausted his supply of precedents in protocol.[3]

From the outset of his appointment as ambassador, Odlum had an ambition to make Canada important to the Chinese government. It was Odlum who recommended to Mackenzie King that Madame Chiang be invited to address Parliament. However, Canada was, in reality, a bit player, appreciated by the Nationalist government for loans, arms, and aircraft and by the Communists as possibly having some say with the Americans. The arms and aircraft were war surplus that Canada was happy to be rid of, but they caused some friction when they were used in the civil war against the Communists. The Canadian response was that the deals had been made before the civil war had been rejoined.

Chungking, Wuhan, and Nanking are known as China's three ovens, from which foreigners and high-ranking Chinese escaped to mountain resorts. Kuling (Guling), a small town nestled high up in the Lu Mountains, near Kiukiang (Jiujiang) on the Yangtze, was the favourite resort of the Generalissimo and Madame Chiang Kai-shek, where they had a villa called *Mei Lu*. General Marshall stayed in a villa at Kuling during his search for peace and co-operation between the Nationalists and the Communists. On 15-22 August 1946, Ambassador Odlum, dean of the foreign diplomatic corps, accompanied by Ronning, began a week's stay at Kuling on the invitation of the Chiangs.[4] Odlum and Ronning were taken by plane, launch, limo, and sedan chair to Kuling, located 3,500 feet up among towering peaks. Ronning found it beautiful, enchanting, and "[i]n the evening light it has an air of mystery. Luxurious vegetation, splendid trees, rushing mountain torrents, rocks and caves, summer cottages of stone and gothic churches make Kuling a wonderful resort." The Canadians were given a villa and twenty-four hours to rest before their first meeting with the Generalissimo, scheduled for tea on the third afternoon.

At five on 18 August, the president's secretary escorted them to the residence, where, after a few moments, they were brought into the main reception room. The Generalissimo, in uniform, shook their hands and they settled in to talk. Chiang impressed Ronning as youthful and alert but definitely nervous. He tended to repeat himself and appeared to stutter when he spoke.[5] Their discussions were "closely associated with the question of civil war or possible peace in China." And, adds Ronning: "I had no idea when I left Canada less than a year ago that I would have an opportunity to participate in anything like this." Suddenly, Madame Chiang interrupted their discussion to call the Generalissimo away on some urgent matter. She took her husband's place and everyone conversed in English as they took a walk in the garden.

After the walk the Madame sat down with the ambassador and me and talked for nearly an hour. She is rather bitter against the Communists. She flared up and her eyes flashed as she denounced

Poster for Kuling mountain retreat, c. 1930s. [Evans private collection]

them. She resented the stories that had been told about her and the President and what Mrs. Roosevelt was supposed to have said about her carrying her own satin sheets. She did so, she said, because she had eczema.[6]

She invited Odlum and Ronning to a picnic in two days' time. When the time came, they arrived at 6 p.m. only to be told that they were invited a little later to dinner instead. Once again, the Generalissimo greeted them cheerfully, this time out of uniform and wearing a scholar's gown and a felt hat. Ronning, General Odlum, Chiang, and his interpreter sat down for an hour's conversation as arranged for by Madame Chiang.

Just as they were coming to the end of their talk, "the Madame sailed in unannounced. She sang out from the door: 'The chicken cannot wait for affairs of state. It is done to a turn and will get cold.'" The four stood to bow to her but continued their conversation. "In a moment the door opened again and the Madame repeated the warning that the chicken must not get cold." Dinner was at a long table under the trees, where Mrs. George Marshall and Mrs. Petrova, the wife of the Russian ambassador, and their daughter were already waiting. Madame Chiang was trying out a new grill designed in the USA, one adapted to charcoal. The meal began with waffles and Canadian maple syrup, which Odlum brought, followed by fried spring chicken. After supper, they played checkers, with Ronning defeating Madame Chiang but the ambassador losing his last game to the Generalissimo. The evening over, Odlum and Ronning were sent home in sedan chairs. After the evening, Ronning was pessimistic:

My impression is that both the President and his talented wife are determined, if possible, to defeat the Communists and will not come to terms, except on their own. They may, of course, change their minds by force of circumstances. The desire for a peaceful settlement is very strong among all classes in China with the possible exception of certain militarist generals. There is still hope but I must admit that I have less after visiting Kuling.

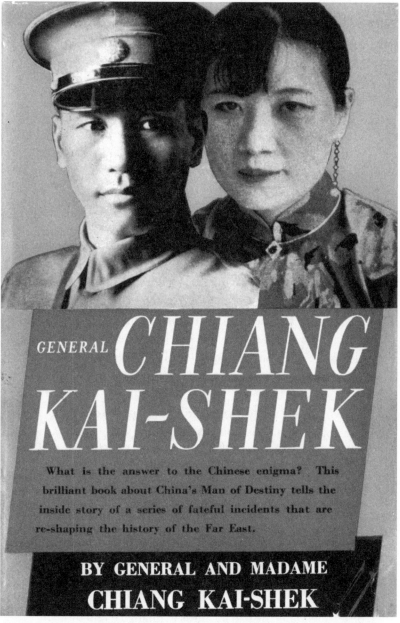

Chiang Kai-shek and Madame Chiang, as pictured on a 1938 book jacket published after the Sian Incident of December 1936. [Evans private collection]

During the week at Kuling:

> We would go for walks with General Marshall and Chiang Kai-shek; sometimes Madame Chiang would walk with Odlum and sometimes with me and we would talk Chinese. Odlum worshipped both of them. One afternoon Chiang sent his son down to Shanghai to carry out the introduction of the new currency. The son had some of the prominent business men of Shanghai shot because they would not turn over their silver and gold for the new currency.

Odlum's and Ronning's final meeting with Chiang was cancelled because of the monetary crisis, and by the early fall 1946, Odlum prepared to return to Canada. Ronning entertained similar plans. After his first six months, the Department of External Affairs (DEA) expressed its satisfaction with his work. He found the work fascinating and engaging, but the DEA had promised him that if he stayed a year, his family would be sent out to join him. The year was nearly over, but little was done about his family. Late in June, he was briefly optimistic that Inga and the four youngest children would soon join him.

> I am trying to get ready for the arrival of Inga and the youngsters. I have not found a house but have high hopes of one. The school problem for Harmon and Kjeryn is going to be difficult but there are a few families with children here now and I hope more are coming. We will have to club together and do something. I remember when we were youngsters in Fancheng, we had only four half days of school a week and look at us now. Maybe we should cut down the number of days we require youngsters to attend school. Meme and Audrey can attend Chingling College and maybe even learn a little Chinese.[7]

A dozen days later, he had business in Shanghai and thought how happy he would be if his family were there: "In a month or two they will be on their way."[8] But his hope was dashed and the reunion delayed. The DEA pleaded lack of transport and suggested that his family delay their trip until three Canadian prefabricated houses arrived in Nanking to accommodate them. Ronning threatened to leave China, but he was triumphant when he received a cable from the department:

> We are taking steps with the Embassy in Washington to provide space to China for Ronning's family. As the war shipping administration allots space, we cannot promise that passage will be available before September 30 but we will do our best.[9]

At last, transport was found and Ronning was told his family would be sailing for China on the *Marine Lynx*. He looked forward to seeing his loved ones by Christmas. Meanwhile, he was attempting to assure a nervous Inga that China had changed since 1927 and conditions were good for foreigners.

> China is much the same, although I see tremendous improvement in the years since I left. Inga is a little afraid that conditions out here are dangerous because she reads in the newspapers about the troubles out here. Remember that only a small proportion of the whole of China is actually involved in fighting. Over four hundred millions are working away at their everyday tasks. The newspapers do not write about them because it is not news. Anyway, both sides in the civil war are friendly to foreigners.[10]

Meanwhile, Ronning was busy. Ambassador Odlum, who had been working on loan agreements and the sale of war surplus materials to the Chinese government, departed Nanking on 15 September. Ronning was made chargé d'affaires, with the responsibility of signing a new Canada-China commercial understanding, acquiring land for a new embassy, and a myriad of other details. Dr. George Patterson, who had served for a time in Chungking under Odlum,[11] was expected to join the embassy from Japan, first as counsellor in Nanking and later as consul-general in Shanghai. He sent packing cases of his

Ronning with Tessie and Katherine Wong in front of embassy, Nanking, c. 1946. [Sau W. Cheung private collection]

possessions to Nanking in advance. Ronning wanted to put them into the ambassador's residence out of the weather, but Odlum, never one to drop a grudge, forbade him to do it, so Patterson's possessions sat outside in the rain until Odlum left. When Dr. Patterson arrived, he moved into a house rented from Pearl Buck.[12]

Late in September, Ronning, as chargé d'affaires, was given a delicious Sunday lunch by Pai Ch'ung-hsi (Bai Chongxi),[13] a Muslim general and chief-of-general-staff and second only to Chiang Kai-shek. It was followed the next evening by an equally delicious dinner provided by the Communists. Ronning summed up what he had learned:

The great general thinks he can defeat the Communists by taking all the key cities which they now occupy and holding the lines of communication....Then he will gradually wipe out the isolated Communists [sic] troops or give them the opportunity of joining the National Army.

Whereas, the Communists

are determined to withstand to the last man and say that the Generalissimo may try but he will never be able [to] wipe them out in spite of American war equipment.

Ronning concluded his account with the simple comment, "Poor China."[14]

Ronning was at odds with Odlum's belief, which was "that as soon as the Generalissimo has demonstrated that he is capable of defeating the Communists in the field, he will show mercy, stop the fighting and set up a democratic government." But, he added, the Generalissimo "has had nearly twenty years to start democratic reforms so it is difficult for me to hope that he will turn from his Fascist ways now."[15]

By mid-December 1946, Ronning's view of the future was gloomier:

The clouds of the last few days are rolling away and all seems well with the physical world but in the society of China things are not so well. Hundreds of thousands of people are cold and hungry. Hundreds of thousands are suffering the horrible ravages of war. Houses are being burned and bodies mutilated. While families grieve for their lost elder sons, the younger boys are being drafted to continue the fight against fellow Chinese. Just now, there seems to be no solution. Peace negotiations have come to a complete standstill and both the Kuomintang and the Communists seem determined to fight it out.

Ronning was an observer at the November meeting of the Chinese National Congress, and, as a guest of the Generalissimo and Madame Chiang, he attended a gala evening of opera starring Mei Lanfan, but his mind was on the long-anticipated arrival in Shanghai of Inga and his children.

At last, the *Marine Lynx* arrived in Shanghai on 30 December. The New Year would be "about the happiest one I have ever had. I have not seen any of the dearest ones for over a year."[16] Fighting a cold, Ronning rushed on board for a joyous reunion on the baggage deck. After one night in the Cathay Hotel (Peace Hotel), where they celebrated the New Year, they were off by train to Nanking and the house Ronning had rented. While the children revelled in the large house and its servants, Ronning took to his bed with his cold. Despite this, the arrival of his family was a desperately needed tonic for the neophyte diplomat. Letters to his parents were filled with family exploits as they discovered Nanking and its surroundings together; comments on the worsening situation in China took second place.

The burdens of running the embassy were lifted from Ronning's shoulders in mid-February when Patterson arrived to take over as chargé d'affaires until the arrival, on 5 May, of Canada's new ambassador, Judge Thomas (Tommy) C. Davis. Like General Odlum, Davis was selected by Prime Minister Mackenzie King, and, like Odlum, Davis had been a judge, a former Liberal politician, and high commissioner to Australia. Prior to his arrival in China, he worked in Ottawa with the director of the Trade Commissioner Service, Department of Trade and Commerce, on a program for advancing initiatives in

China already set in motion by Odlum. The Canadian government had provided a loan to China of $60 million, plus, as previously noted, an export credit guarantee of $12,750,000 to the Ming Sung Shipping Company. Davis was seeking further guarantees for more projects. In his view, there were great opportunities in China, as well as in the newly freed Formosa:[17]

> The present powerful Western influences in China are the USA and the UK I have a feeling that the USA will end up by losing some of its popularity in China. The influence of the UK in the East is on the decline. The name of Canada stands high and we should start to plan to capitalize upon this feeling.
>
> I therefore feel that now is the time to help China to the limit of our ability, so to do and thus lay the foundation for good-will, which I believe will pay out in dividends for many years to come.[18]

In anticipation of greater Canadian engagement in China, the embassy staff was increased, with new secretarial staff and junior officers added. Later, in August 1947, Colonel Freddie Clifford replaced Brigadier Bostock as military attaché. Ronning continued with the job he had begun in the previous year of acquiring land for a new embassy compound. One of the sticking points was the removal of graves from the property, where they had enjoyed excellent feng shui on a hill with views of the city. Removing hundreds of graves was costly and "the old crook who is head of the Association for Burying the Dead"[19] wanted the embassy to pay, not by the coffin but by the number of skulls inside each coffin. Ronning had no faith in the man, and fully expected he would put extra skulls in the coffins in the dead of night. They settled on a per-coffin price. In the end, six acres were cleared and made ready for the three, new, prefabricated houses that had arrived from Canada. In late August 1947, the Ronning family moved into one of them. Ronning was quite pleased:

> Here I sit in a Canadian lumber house in China. With two other similar houses it is on a lovely hill overlooking the city and with

a marvelous view of much of the surrounding country and small mountains and glimpses of the great Yangtze River. We are above the noise and dust of the streets. The gentle breezes blow through the house. It is like a summer resort.[20]

Ambassador Tommy Davis presented his credentials to the Nationalist government on 21 May 1947. Ronning, along with other embassy officers, attended. The ceremony took so long and was so elaborate that Ronning thought the old *kowtow*[21] would have been preferable. Davis turned out to be an easier personality than Odlum, but, although more liberal in outlook, he was at first firmly anti-Communist. In contrast to Odlum, who remained fixed in his opinions, Davis swung from one side to the other, taking "any advice as long as it was convincing."[22] He was also, in Ronning's view, overly concerned with his personal safety. He took cover when the Communists entered Nanking.[23] He arrived in time to see the civil war in China gather momentum and to watch the Nationalist government collapse in the face of rampant corruption and mega-inflation. The longer he stayed and observed the Nationalist government, however, the more his opinion of the Chinese Communists moderated.

Davis continued Odlum's efforts to establish Canada as an important country in the eyes of the Chinese government. The $60 million loan to China was to be used for purchasing, from Canada, decommissioned frigates, war surplus Mosquito bombers, ammunition, and for the building in Canada of a small arms and ammunition plant for China. Canada followed the lead of Britain and the United States in the provision of weapons to China, and, as the civil war heated up, an embargo was from time to time in force. In late May 1947, the US lifted the embargo on the supply of munitions to the Chinese National government. In Ottawa, C.D. Howe, Minister of Reconstruction and Supply, eager to clear the government's warehouses of surplus military equipment, wrote:

I suggest that War Assets Corporation be instructed that the door is open to sale of guns and ammunition, fighter planes, armed frigates and other items of Canadian supply in which the Chinese have indicated an interest.[24]

In addition, Canada and China were engaged in developing an immigration agreement. The Chinese government was unhappy with the policy of Canada, dating back to 1923,[25] that virtually excluded Chinese immigrants from entering Canada. Canada was interested in modifying its previous policy; the question was just how far the modification would go.

Ronning was not closely involved in these matters, but, as the first foreign embassy officer to succeed in completing a land deal in Nanking, he was in demand for his advice. Meanwhile, he monitored the deteriorating situation in China and the vicissitudes of the civil war. His own life was better as he had entered into nearly two full years of domestic life, with his youngest two children in school and his older daughters studying at Nanking University and working part-time at the Canadian Embassy or with the Americans. From a former colleague at the Camrose Lutheran College passing through on her way to a mission, Ronning learned that his brother Talbert was expected to come to Nanking to establish a Lutheran mission. Ronning was skeptical about this plan because Nanking was already full of missionaries of many denominations and sects.

After a quiet family Christmas, the family planned a summer holiday away from the heat of Nanking. Unable to find space at Kuling in 1947, Ronning arranged for six weeks there beginning the third week of August in 1948. After a horrendous boat trip up the Yangtze to Kiujiang, they made it to Kuling, "a mile high and the air is cool and fresh."[26] Kuling was overflowing with missionaries, but, because the Generalissimo and Madame Chiang were not vacationing there, it was calm. Daughters Meme and Audrey arrived later with their boyfriends. Meme was engaged to an American Navy officer, David Westlein. The American ambassador, Rev. John Leighton Stuart, married them in September. Audrey's beau was Seymour Topping, a dynamic newspaper correspondent for Associated Press, and later for the *New York Times*. They married in Camrose on 10 November

1949 when Ronning was still in Nanking, and Topping assigned to Hong Kong.

Kuling was Ronning's first holiday for two years and it was to be his last for nearly three years more. Early in November 1948, the Communist forces threatened Nanking and Shanghai. There was talk of the Nationalist government moving to Canton, abandoning Nanking. Strangely, the Canadian Cabinet did not regard the situation to be serious enough to interrupt deliveries to China of arms and equipment, already underway in accordance with the loan and export guarantees, although it agreed that no further credits were to be extended to China for purchases in Canada.

Late in November, Ronning's family was ordered back to North America and Ronning intended to leave with them, a plan of which Inga heartily approved.[27] The Department of External Affairs, however, asked him to stay on for a few weeks more while the situation in Nanking was clarified. Inga's objection dissolved when Ronning extracted a promise from the DEA that later he would be posted to Norway. "You see, my wife thought me just as expendable as did the Department."[28] On 23 November 1948, Inga and the children left Nanking on a flight to Tokyo, and Meme, along with her husband, left for the United States. Ronning was in bed ill and could not go to the airport to see them off. Once again, he was on his own in Nanking

# The Coming of the People's Republic of China

Seymour Topping of the Associated Press, and Ronning's future son-in-law, described Nanking in January 1949 as

> cowering in hopelessness and despair as it waited for the Communists. Chiang Kai-shek had decided to retire, saying he would yield the government to Vice President Li Tsung-jen (Li Zhongren). On Christmas Eve, the Generalissimo had driven in his black Cadillac to the "Song of Victory" church, an official residence converted by Madame Chiang into a place of worship for Christians in the government, and there, near the Sun Yat-sen Mausoleum, he sang carols in his native Chekiang accent. The next morning, he told his subordinates that he would announce his resignation on New Year's Day. There was reason enough for him to go.[1]

For Chiang Kai-shek, the world was not unfolding as it should. He was losing the military battles, and, because of the corruption in his government and its inability to beat back hyperinflation, he was losing popular favour. The well-to-do, his natural allies, turned against him as they lost their savings through the government's currency reforms and manipulations. By stepping aside, Chiang was solving none of these problems.

Ronning's family had left Nanking by plane for Japan on 23 November,[2] leaving him depressed, low in energy, and suffering from hay fever. By late January, however, he was nearly back to normal and willing to share his observations once again with his parents.

[The Communists] are virtually in a position to march in here almost any day now. They may, on the other hand delay taking this city and Shanghai until they have driven south and annihilated the remaining forces who have withdrawn south of the Yangtze.

Since November when the family left for Japan, developments have been so rapid that Nanking has been in a perpetual state of excitement. The struggle between individuals behind the scenes during the period of the collapse of a corrupt and decadent regime has been most interesting to watch. I shall never forget the words of the young teachers [sic] from Fancheng who had accompanied Chiang Kai-shek on the Northern Expedition whom I met in Hankow in 1927 when he said: "Our military leader has become China's Napoleon. He has sold out the Revolution." I have now seen the exit of "Napoleon." He sold out the Revolution but he did not kill it. It has gained such momentum today that nothing in the world can stop it. Even if the whole American Army tried the job (thank heaven there is no chance of them trying) they could only postpone it. The Chinese peasants are on the march and they are led by the most courageous, intelligent, politically and militarily sagacious, ambitious and ruthless men in China.[3]

Through wholesale corruption in his government, runaway hyper-inflation, and his own poor military decisions, Chiang paved the way for the Communists, who, in contrast, appeared to be patriotic, honourable, reformers intent on cleansing China of its misery. Some of Chiang's demoralized generals joined with the People's Liberation Army, whose members had a sterling reputation for honesty and respect for the ordinary people. Having taken the northeast (Manchuria) and much of China north of the Yangtze by early 1949, the Communists were poised to chase the Nationalists south, and eventually off the mainland to Taiwan by the end of the year. This turn of events came as a shock to the majority of North Americans who had feasted on a steady diet of wartime propaganda portraying Chiang as a valiant and heroic ally, standing shoulder to shoulder with America in the war against Japan, and leading a democratic republic whose symbol in America was Soong May-ling, the Methodist, American-educated wife of the Generalissimo.

In January 1949, the Nationalist government remained in Nanking while advising foreign governments that their representatives should follow it to Canton if and when the time came. In anticipation of the transition, the Canadian Embassy stored rice and silver dollars and repaired an old Japanese bomb shelter in case the city was shelled. Sikh guards and police guarded the embassy day and night. Some diplomats from other embassies, notably the Soviet Union's, fled to Canton in unseemly haste. After they left, when it appeared that the Communists might attack Canton first, there was "a lot of merriment in Nanking diplomatic circles" at their expense.[4] Meanwhile, those who stayed waited to see just what the Nationalist government would do.

Already, in November 1948, Ottawa had advised Ambassador Tommy Davis to follow the British and American ambassadors when the Nationalist government evacuated Nanking. Davis was to take the military attaché with him, leaving Ronning and Mr. Maybee in Nanking,[5] and Dr. George Patterson at the consulate in Shanghai, to handle the affairs of some five hundred Canadians who planned to remain under the Communists. By mid-January, however, the Americans were not prepared to commit themselves to move until firmer information was available.[6] In the end, the British, American, and Canadian embassies were among those that stayed in Nanking to meet the Communist arrivals.

Ronning tried to regain his health. He went hunting for pheasants, teal, mallard, and snipe and once a week he rode a difficult horse

Chiang Kai-shek had left behind. Always the optimist, he hoped that his daughter Meme would come through Shanghai soon on her way from San Francisco to join her husband in Manila. Moreover, although he now expected to be in China for another year, he anticipated his wife Inga and three of their children would rejoin him in the fall, before they all went to Norway in the spring. More realistically, he was relieved that his brother Talbert had not come to Nanking.[7] Like most observers, Ronning did not know exactly what to expect from the Communists, but they could not be as bad as the Nationalists. No one could predict just how completely different the new regime would turn out to be.

In late April 1949, Ronning witnessed the Nationalists' hasty and disorderly withdrawal from Nanking, the looting that accompanied it, and the restoration of order under the Communists that followed. His candid descriptions have never before been published.

Early Saturday morning, April 23rd, the number-one police guards had disappeared and [after] that looting had commenced. The whole police force had been ordered to evacuate the city together with the departing garrison troops. On my way to the chancery after breakfast I saw hundreds of men, women and children streaming into and out of the new houses built by the Chinese Government for the American Advisory Group Officers. The looters were having a gay time laughing and chatting as they carried away doors, windows, flooring and lumber as well as all the fixtures including steam radiators and electrical wall switches. Children lugged screen windows, women carried cubbboards [sic] and men stuggled [sic] with bathtubs that had been torn loose from their moorings. There was great merriment and laughter.

At ten o'clock I went down Lin San Street past the National Assembly Hall to the inner airfield. Looting was at is maximum. If a tornado had hit that part of the city it could not have covered the street with a greater disarray of the contents of dwelling houses, offices and garages. Like ants the whole populace swarmed over the loot—tugging, pulling, politely dividing and carrying away tremendous burdens, all in the best of good humour. Evacuating columns

of troops marching out of the city paid no attention to the looters
in spite of having to make frequent detours around piles of miscel-
laneous loot. Departing troops seemed interested only in means of
transportation and seized passing jeeps and bicycles.

The looting [of government offices] had started early in the
morning when the officials themselves rolled up the carpets and
rushed off with the more valuable equipment. Employees then
carted off the better furniture, after which the populace came
in and wrenched loose all fixtures and tore out the lumber. One
of our chauffers [sic] remarked: "this is the day Nanking's poor
people have waited for to turn summersaults." We saw a young
woman who had removed her clothing to wrap up the loot she was
blushingly carrying off. A rickshaw boy, whom we know, said he
refrained from looting for the first few hours but upon learning it
was not dangerous decided to get his share. He collected enough
fuel for a year, two bathtubs and some automobile tires.

The disaster which overtook his worship the mayor of Nanking
in his attempted flight was typical of the last efforts of many officials
of the former regime to salvage something for themselves out of
the wreckage which their own corrupt practices had created. The
mayor did not take the seat assigned to him on the aircraft carrying
high-ranking local officials. Instead he went to the local bank handling municipal funds and drew out in gold yuan the total amount
of the staff payroll for the month in addition to several wooden
cases of silver dollar reserves. By the time the cases were packed the
aircraft had gone and the mayor started out for Hangchow with his
chauffer [sic] and two bodyguards in an automobile. The next day the
guards turned on him administering a beating to his worship which
resulted in broken limbs and his return to Nanking. He is now
incarcerated in an Executive Yuan residence awaiting trial by the
"people's court" which will be set up by the Communists to whom
Nanking was surrendered so easily by the former rotten regime.[8]

Two days later, Ronning joined Seymour Topping on the city wall
to watch the Communist troops march into Nanking.

The soldiers were orderly and disciplined and were greeted by welcome posters and school children singing new songs of praise. The
first Communist troops into Nanking most certainly did not march
as conquerors of the capital of the enemy against whom they had
fought for years but came in single file, giving rather the impression
that it was all a part of the 'day's work.' They were burned and tired.
They showed the effects of long, forced marches. They were not
smart or snappy. Their clothes were rather shabby and their light
rubber soled shoes worn.[9]

Relations between the diplomatic community and the new
Communist rulers of Nanking were disciplined and proper, with all con-
versations recorded by note takers. The person assigned by the Chinese
Communists to handle affairs in Nanking was a former student leader at
the Harvard-Yenching Institute in Peking when John Leighton Stuart,
the American ambassador, was president. Because of this link, Mao sent
Huang Hua to Nanking. Although a fluent speaker of English, Huang, a
Communist under party discipline, spoke only Chinese in public.

There was no automatic honouring of previous diplomatic privileges. Foreign representatives, when interviewed by Huang, became
aware of the depth of antiforeign—particularly anti-imperialist—
feeling of the new rulers. Ronning's relations with the Foreign
Nationals Bureau of the Nanking Military Control Commission were
as an individual and not as a foreign representative. A key problem
for foreign representatives was re-establishing lines of communications and reconnecting telephones and overseas telegraph contacts.
On issues such as these, the new authorities were reasonable, but not
on matters of diplomatic privilege. Americans hoped the old con-
nection between their ambassador and Huang Hua might lead to a
breakthrough in relations with the Communists, particularly when
Mao issued an invitation for Stuart to go to Peking. But before the
invitation was accepted, Mao made it clear in a public statement that
the Communists would have no dealings with imperialists. Stuart
left China on 2 August 1949. Twelve days later, the United States
announced it was retaining its relations with the Nationalist regime.

In April, when Nanking was "liberated," foreign governments began to evacuate embassy staff. Among those who remained, Ronning was the only one fluent in Chinese. He became known as "Ambassador at large." In June, when he went to Shanghai, he found the person in charge there was Chang Hanfu, a Chinese friend with whom he had flown over the "hump"[10] and had known well in Chungking. As a result, he was given access denied to others. He gained permission for Inga and the children to come in the fall.[11] While taking afternoon tea with Dr. Patterson in the garden of the Shanghai consulate, he observed Canadian mosquito bombers, flown by Nationalist pilots, bomb and strafe Shanghai. Meanwhile, Ottawa considered the situation of its embassy in Nanking. The Chinese Communists had not yet formed a government, but, along with Britain and the United States, Canada gave its ambassador permission to leave Nanking when he saw fit.

> After the return of the Ambassador, it is envisaged that Mr. C.A. Ronning, First Secretary, would become Chargé d'Affaires, of the Embassy. In this capacity Mr. Ronning would have no official relations with the Communist authorities.[12]

There would be no rush to recognize the new government until it was formed.

At the end of August, Ambassador Davis left, along with a number of other foreigners, aboard the S.S. *General Gordon*. Prior to his departure, he met with Huang Hua, accompanied by Ronning. Davis described their talk as "unofficial, personal and most friendly."[13] Huang said he anticipated the creation of a government in the reasonable future and that it would welcome recognition on the basis of friendship, equality, and withdrawal of recognition from the Nationalists.

> He then turned to Canada and recognition. He said hitherto we had been unfriendly and had intervened in the civil war and Chinese internal affairs and were supplying arms and planes to the Nationalists. He suggested we would in some manner have to

indicate change of attitude from hostile to friendly and I noted a slight trace of suggestion that we should have to acknowledge our wrongs and seek forgiveness and recognition.[14]

Meanwhile, the Nationalist ambassador in Ottawa raised concerns over the fact that Davis was leaving Nanking but no senior official would be following the Nationalist government to Canton. He felt that there was no need to retain a person each in Shanghai and in Nanking.[15] But, within a month, in Peiping (Peking) on 1 October 1949, Mao Tsetung proclaimed the creation of the People's Republic of China. In his words, "The Chinese People have stood up!" On 3 October in Nanking, Huang Hua called what remained of the diplomatic community together to make a similar announcement. For the first time, a Chinese official addressed the corps in Chinese and not in English. Moreover, although he was fluent in English, Huang did not interpret his own words. The diplomats were stunned. (Later, Ronning said he was thrilled to hear a Chinese with the confidence to do such a thing.) Keith Officer, the Australian ambassador, broke the silence with a request in English that Ronning, the only Chinese speaker among the group, be allowed to interpret Huang's words. Huang agreed and, thereafter, Ronning became the conduit for special requests from the diplomats.[16] Huang remembered the incident.

I summoned all the members of the former diplomatic corps still in Nanking to a meeting. I made known to them our principles governing the establishment of diplomatic relations, and the concrete policies regarding the treatment of former embassy staff and diplomatic personages in Nanking. I also answered their questions. Some foreigners were quite nervous, as it was the first time for them to have any contact with officials of the CPC Military Control Commission. The Canadian chargé d'affaires ad interim, Chester Ronning, who was born in Fancheng, Hubei Province, translated my words into English. As the entire audience was now clear about the Chinese authorities' policies, the atmosphere in the hall became more relaxed.[17]

On behalf of the absent Davis, Ronning received a telegram from Chou En-lai, along with the text of a broadcast statement by Mao Tse-tung, inviting foreign states to recognize the new government.[18] Ottawa now concentrated on the question of recognition of the People's Republic and abandoned any idea of following the retreating Nationalist regime. Both Ambassador Tommy Davis, back in Canada, and Ronning from Nanking urged Ottawa to recognize the new government as quickly as possible. Ronning saw only disadvantages in delay. Ottawa, however, delayed. The Canadian Minister for External Affairs Lester Pearson, no stranger to Chinese matters, believed the new government should be recognized, but he was not certain of the timing. In Parliament, the Co-operative Commonwealth Federation (CCF) (Ronning's old party) urged recognition, while the Conservatives (the official opposition) were against it. Questions of how completely the new government was in control of China, and of how independent it was of the Soviet Union, hung in the air. At this time, the opinion of the United States was not considered to be a major factor. By the end of the year, Cabinet had twice taken a decision in principle to recognize China, but declined to set a date for action.[19] External Affairs monitored the recognition efforts initiated by Britain and India and was anxious to see what Washington planned to do. A decision on timing was put off until Pearson returned from a January 1950 Commonwealth meeting at Colombo, Sri Lanka. At the meeting, Pearson spoke to Nehru and the British and gained more confidence in favour of recognition. Ronning, in Nanking, was alerted to await a telephone call from Pearson from Hong Kong on his way back to Canada. The call did not get through. According to Ronning, in anticipation of word from Pearson, "The Dept went so far as to advise me to rent a house in Peking in January 1950. At the end of January I was supposed to move to Peking."[20]

In December 1949, Mao Tse-tung travelled to Moscow to meet with Stalin. He stayed there until February when he and Stalin signed a Treaty of Alliance and Mutual Assistance. Despite this, Ronning maintained that relations between Moscow and Peking would never be firm. He harkened back to his conversations with Tung Pi-wu on their flight into Chungking in November 1945. Tung told Ronning, a fellow son of Hupei province, that the Chinese Communists could never place their trust in Stalin, although Ronning warned Ottawa at the end of December 1949 that relations between Peking and Moscow were warming more rapidly than he expected.[21]

In Ottawa, in February 1950, action still had not been taken. Pearson outlined the pros and cons of recognition in a memo for the Cabinet. The pros: the Communist government had fulfilled all of the requirements for de jure recognition; the new government and the Soviet Union had points of conflict that recognition by Western governments might help to increase, both to the advantage of democratic elements in China and to the benefit of Western commerce; recognition would improve the bargaining power of the Chinese in their dealings with the Soviet Union, thus nonrecognition would benefit the Soviets; previous experience of not recognizing the Soviet Union after World War I had proven negative; "Canadian recognition would probably make it easier for the United States Government to follow suit in due course, which it inevitably must do";[22] if others recognize the Chinese government and the Chinese Communists are represented in international bodies, it would be embarrassing for Canada; nonrecognition could cause difficulties for Canadians (missionaries and businessmen) remaining in China; recognition might enable Canada to recoup losses from the Nationalist government's default on its sixty million dollar loan.

The arguments against recognition were almost as numerous. The cons: China as a Communist state is a potential enemy and should not be assisted morally or materially; the US has yet to recognize China due to public opinion and Congressional pressure; it is not clear that the Communist government is willing to undertake international obligations; Britain and India encountered difficulties when they tried to establish relations; the Nationalist government is still representing China in the UN and other bodies; recognition would mean the acceptance of Communist diplomats and consular officials who would exert influence upon Canadian Chinese; parts of Canadian public opinion might take recognition of the Communist regime as approval

of it, and Canadian public opinion is heavily influenced by American
views against recognition; negotiations to solve the default on the loan
extended by Canadian banks to the Ming Sung Company would be
strengthened if accomplished before recognition.[23]

The memo was subsequently forwarded with a recommendation
for recognition, but Pearson, because of divided opinions among his
advisors,[24] and his own doubts about a Cabinet majority, continued
to delay the implementation of the Cabinet decision to recognize.
Ronning remained on tenterhooks in Nanking awaiting instructions.
The bombing of Nanking by Nationalist planes was getting to him.
On 23 February 1950, he wrote home: "When you stand for months at
the receiving end of bombs falling from aircraft sent by a corrupt and
discredited regime and see the wanton destruction of life and property
long after the civil war has ended on the mainland, you pray daily that
the support which continued recognition gives to that regime will be
withdrawn."[25]

In early March, Ronning was devastated by news of the death of his
father. He received permission to return home, but the exiting process
was too complex and time-absorbing to enable him to return in time
for the funeral. He stayed on, hoping to accomplish what he was there
for: the recognition of China. He was

> completely frustrated and perplexed. I could not possibly get out in
> time so I have to resign myself to remaining here where I have vir-
> tually been a prisoner within the walls of this city for months and
> months....My plans for the next few months all depend upon deci-
> sions reached in Ottawa. It is impossible for me to get away now
> before recognition. I will have to stay to perform the task, which the
> Government has assigned to me of negotiating the establishment
> of diplomatic relations and supervising the move north. Then I will
> be free to return.[26]

But Ronning continued to wait. He later described the indecision
in Ottawa as "they hummed and hawed and gurgled ice water until the
Korean War broke out."[27] In April, the air war over Nanking ended with

the arrival of MiG fighters from the USSR, after nearly ten months of daily bombing raids. Still confined within the walls of Nanking, but in buildings with air conditioning, Ronning busied himself with new hobbies: collecting snuff bottles and jade. He was particularly proud of one piece, a jade Han dynasty mortuary pig that he hoped to leave to his children and grandchildren one day. He continued to press Ottawa for instructions. He was trading on the goodwill he had developed with Chou En-lai and other Communist leaders, but his assurances that recognition negotiations were imminent were wearing thin. Ottawa's view of Ronning's position was different:

> Ronning was becoming importunate. Although he was fluent in Chinese and had many lines of contact to the new regime, he was making no progress with the communist officials on urgent matters of supplies and the security of Canadian citizens. His pleas, however, were less influential with the cabinet than were those of T.C. Davis, who was a politician and former colleague of the government and therefore considered more practical.[28]

At last, in yet another effort by Pearson to make recognition more palatable to his colleagues in Cabinet, Ronning was asked to explore informally China's response to a Canadian position. That position, in essence, was to seek assurance, in advance from China, that Canada would not be faced with the difficulties that Britain and India had experienced. China responded that it would be acceptable for Ronning to come to Peking to discuss recognition as long as Canada indicated formally its intention to seek recognition. Essentially, Peking was saying it could not guarantee in advance the conditions of something that had not yet been proposed, but they envisaged no obstacles. Ottawa and Ronning interpreted the Chinese response differently. Ronning found the response acceptable, arguing that it placed no barrier in the way of the original plan, which was for him to go to Peking, and, should the informal talks reach a satisfactory conclusion, to offer a note of recognition. Ottawa, however, hesitated again, looking on the Chinese response as a counterproposal. Ronning was left to wait for further instructions. He was convinced that an oral commitment from him to the Chinese would enable the informal recognition talks to go forward. Meanwhile, the anti-Communist feeling in the United States began to surge, powered by McCarthyism, the China Lobby, and the search for those who "Lost China."[29]

In June, police raided the Canadian Embassy twice. On the first occasion, Ronning was asked to give a written account of his life since he was eighteen. The fact that his life included time as a missionary, an intelligence officer, and a diplomat probably sparked the second raid when police came to search for spying equipment such as radio transmitters and other devices. It was a clear indication that the embassy was tolerated but had no real diplomatic status. The consulate in Shanghai was not touched. In anticipation of positive instruction from Ottawa, Ronning asked friends in Peking to rent him a house and reported to the DEA that the delay was leaving him considerably embarrassed.

In expectation of a favourable cabinet decision late in June two draft telegrams of instruction to Ronning were prepared in External Affairs. Ronning was to "deliver a confidential oral message to the head of the Foreign Nationals Bureau in Nanking stating that 'the Canadian Government is prepared to announce recognition of the Central Government of the People's Republic of China if and when a satisfactory agreement has been reached on the establishment of diplomatic relations, and the Canadian Government is willing to instruct you to proceed to Peking to negotiate such agreement.'" However, Ronning was not to proceed to Peking until he had told Ottawa of Peking's reply to his oral message. This information was to be passed confidentially to Commonwealth governments, and also the US, France, the Netherlands, Belgium, and Italy, giving them advance notice of Canada's decision.[30]

The telegrams were prepared and sent to the Minister of External Affairs on Friday, 23 June 1950, but they were never sent to Ronning

because on Sunday, 25 June North Korea invaded South Korea.
As a result, Ottawa advised Ronning of a further delay in seeking
recognition. Ronning cancelled the house in Peking as Canada's
diplomatic efforts became focused on the UN and efforts to settle the
Korean problem.

From previous conversations with Chou En-lai, Ronning warned
that China was determined to protect the power stations on the Yalu
River and had no intention of letting UN forces advance on the Yalu.[31]
But General Douglas MacArthur, in command of the UN forces, was
not impressed with the Yalu, and Chiang Kai-shek, in Taiwan, looked
to the Korean War as an opportunity to retake the mainland. As the
Cold War grew colder, the Atlantic nations had come together in 1949
to form NATO, the North Atlantic Treaty Organization, for mutual
defence, and some were calling Korea another Munich. China entered
the Korean War in October 1950, putting recognition almost out of
reach, and when the United Nations declared China an aggressor on 1
February 1951, the game was over.[32] The opponents of recognition had
the big excuse they were looking for: the Communist world could not
be trusted. Better to confine China behind a bamboo fence than invite
it into your front yard. Canada, after all, was contributing troops to the
UN forces fighting Chinese volunteers in Korea. Canada's attempts to
recognize China went unachieved for two more decades.

Canada's failure to act within the first months of the Communist
victory can be seen as the result of many factors. First, had Canada
acted on its own, it would have been the first and only country in
North America to do so. But Canada, and its Department of External
Affairs, still lacked experience in Asian diplomacy. It took its cues
from London and Washington, which, in this case, were divided.
While initially America appeared concerned but not yet set against
Canada recognizing the new government in Peking, that mood dis-
sipated by early 1950. Second, the DEA was woefully ill-equipped to
understand the situation in China. Ronning did, but he was very much
a newcomer to the department and not well known to the core group
that had teethed on Atlantic- (NATO-) centred issues and the fledg-
ling United Nations Organization where the question of who was to

represent China was yet to be resolved. Although Canada established an embassy in Japan in 1929, and one in China in 1942, it was far from looking upon itself as a Pacific nation.

In the recognition debate, the two ambassadors to serve in China were on opposite sides. General Odlum clung to his admiration of Chiang Kai-shek, while Tommy Davis envisioned great economic opportunities for Canada inside the People's Republic of China. Yet, no one knew China and the current situation quite like Ronning, but he was far away. As a consequence, his voice was muted and even discounted by those who found some of his reporting unsound. Third, the Liberal government was divided with members of the Cabinet having different reasons for opposing recognition, such as the Communist threat to the Christian world; the unnecessary strain on US-Canada relations for the sake of a pitiful economic stake in China; and the disruptive effect recognition would have on the very pro-Nationalist Canadian Chinese community and on general public opinion that was susceptible to influences from the United States. Fourth, as the Cold War deepened, Canada preferred to seek solutions to global conflicts through the United Nations and as a reliable American ally rather than to be viewed by Washington as one of uncertain virtue. America, after all, was Canada's ultimate protector, while China, not at all.

Ronning stayed on in China, becoming Ottawa's window on events there, monitoring China's attitude toward the Korean conflict. During this time, Peking launched a series of reforms and campaigns designed to end hyperinflation, wipe out common diseases, introduce basic preventive measures in health, and to combat corruption, waste, and bureaucracy. It continued with the land reform, which had accompanied its sweep to victory. The DEA was dubious about Ronning's reports on the social and economic changes introduced by the Communists, fearing he was succumbing to propaganda. But, as Ronning later wrote,

Westerners with no actual experience of what China was like before the People's Republic cannot possibly understand what the early reforms meant to the masses and why the peasants, especially the younger ones, were willing not only to accept but to support the changes that were begun before 1951.[33]

For Under-Secretary of State for External Affairs Arnold Heeney, such events in China were perhaps difficult to imagine. Early in July 1950, while not ruling out recognition, Heeney raised questions about Ronning's mental health and wondered whether he should be brought home.[34] But Ronning remained in Nanking, along with Jim Staines, an administrative officer, and local staff, keeping the embassy going, still hoping for recognition. In mid-July, after eighteen months of confinement to the city, Ronning and Staines were allowed to visit surrounding areas. "It is like being let out of prison," Ronning remarked.[35] And he looked forward to a trip to Shanghai to see an old friend, Dr. K.M. Panikkar, who was India's ambassador to Peking and had presented his credentials to Mao in May. On 13 October 1950, twelve days before China sent People's Volunteers into Korea, Ronning anticipated an early truce, and he looked forward to Inga joining him for Christmas. Hopes dashed, six weeks later he took a driving test, his first in China, because Liao, the embassy driver, was too old to meet the new regulations. After a thorough physical examination—"My height was so great that their measuring apparatus was not high enough"—Ronning answered questions on driving rules and regulation before taking the road test: steering a jeep through the crowded streets of Nanking. He passed, but only one in five Frenchmen did. The next day, curio dealers with whom he dealt came to ask if he had been arrested because he was seen in an official jeep with Communist officials.[36]

As 1950 drew to a close, Ronning's situation made headlines in the *Camrose Canadian*. In a front-page story, his diplomatic career was put in a nutshell.

Ottawa Dispatch Says That Chester Ronning Stuck in China with Pre-Fab Houses
OTTAWA, Nov. 23—Communist China's aggressive moves have thrown a dark new cloud over Canadian Chester Ronning's strange five-year diplomatic mission on the banks of the Yangtze.

Now it's more doubtful than ever when he'll finally get home.

Mr. Ronning, a 56-year-old former Camrose, Alta., school-teacher, is holding down $200,000 worth of pre-fabricated real estate deep within Communist territory.

He lives in Nanking among the three portable buildings Canada shipped out a few years ago because there was no alternative accommodation for ambassador T.C. Davis and his staff.

He has no official status because Nanking is the capital of nothing and because Canada doesn't recognize the government that rules there. He hasn't been home in five years, hasn't seen his family in two or more, has seen Mr. Davis and his other colleagues vanish homeward one by one until he is left with one subordinate clerk H.L. Staines of Victoria, to share his vigil.

There are now two Chinese capitals, the Reds' Peiping (Beijing), the Nationalists' Formosa. Mr. Ronning remains in the ex-Nationalist capital of Nanking and ignores them both partly because somebody has to watch that real estate—in that sense he's a prisoner of experiment—and partly because the whole Chinese question remains up in the air here.

REGULAR CONTACT
External Affairs headquarters hears from him regularly by mail and wire. The official word is that his services are "extremely valu-able" and that "this is not an appropriate time to bring him out." It is doubtful that a replacement could be sent to Nanking if he were withdrawn.

Until Chinese intervention in Korea, it appeared to be largely a matter of time before Canada recognized the Reds—and ended Mr. Ronning's vigil. Now recognition may be far away and his future is under a bigger cloud than ever.

Some day, officials say, it will all work out and he will be moved and so, they hope, will the prefabricated buildings.

Mr. Ronning joined external affairs in 1945 after serving in two wars and teaching at Camrose and in China. His family was evacuated to Canada along with other women and children at the mission in 1948, and is believed to be in Toronto. [This is obviously in error, as all local people know Mrs. Ronning and family are making their home in Camrose].

He speaks Chinese fluently. In the past few years, he's had lots of practice.[37]

In January 1951, Ottawa requested Ronning to close the embassy. He lowered the flag on 26 February, one week short of five years after it was raised.[38] He prepared to return to Canada, having not set foot outside China for over five years, and he was overdue for leave.

8

# A Long Way to Norway

Closing down the Canadian Embassy in 1951 was a bit of a Ronning specialty, as he had done it once before in Chungking, but leaving China was to be more problematic. As for the embassy, Ronning and Staines first reduced the size of the compound by taking a bamboo fence that surrounded the rented former chancery and ambassador's residence and placing it around the three Canadian-owned prefabricated buildings and some smaller brick ones in order to prevent individuals from sneaking in at night. Once the fence went down around the chancery,[1] local people began removing grass, shrubs, and trees—anything that could be dried for use as fuel. They then broke through the bamboo fence and began to remove the vegetation from around the prefabricated buildings and from the garden, which Ronning regarded as one of the most beautiful in Nanking. The crowd withdrew at Ronning's request, but he and Staines remained to watch a new fence put in place. At dusk, some ne'er-do-wells began to dismantle the old bamboo fence, while one or two others started on the new fence. With the assistance of neighbours, the intruders were fought off, but Staines and Ronning remained on guard all night.

Embassy staff on closure of embassy, Nanking, 1951. Ronning is second from left. [Sau W. Cheung private collection]

In the morning, the custodian prepared a written report for the authorities, along with a request for police protection, particularly at night. Ronning took the report and request to the chief of the Foreign Nationals Bureau. To his amazement and great annoyance, he was accused of inciting a riot the day before at the embassy. He lost his temper, protesting, after he calmed down, the absurdity of the accusation. Why would he want to start a riot at his own embassy? He was in contact with Chou En-lai on the question of Canada's recognition of China, and he (Ronning) had rented a house in Peking in preparation for that. Despite the Korean War, it was only a matter of time before he concluded the negotiations. He would report the previous night's events at the embassy directly to Chou, unless the foolish charge was dropped and the bureau provided police protection for the embassy. In the end, the bureau chief agreed. The embassy compound was ringed with police and soldiers by the time Ronning returned.[2]

In Chungking, Ronning had simply packed up the embassy goods and chattels to move them to Nanking. This time was different: the embassy, once closed, was going nowhere. Goods had to be packed up and some things disposed of. He engaged Mr. Chen, a scholar and embassy translator, as caretaker of the buildings until they were sold or moved to Peking (assuming recognition). When making an inventory, Chen and Ronning came across a packing case containing a collection of oracle bones accumulated by Dr. James Mellon Menzies, a scholarly Canadian missionary who had served in Anyang, Honan. The bones (tortoise shells, shoulder blades of cattle) were used for divination during the Shang dynasty and contained the earliest form of Chinese writing. Popularly called "dragon bones," they were ground up by local apothecaries for medicine. Menzies collected from ones he found in apothecary shops. It seemed the collection had been left with Ambassador Davis for safekeeping until it could be sent to the University of Toronto.[3]

Because of the value and significance of the collection, Chen refused to take care of the embassy. The new government was hypersensitive to China's heritage and how much had already been lost to foreigners. Anyone caught with the bones would be in serious trouble. Through an intermediary, and hoping for anonymity, Ronning passed the collection to the Nanking National Museum. This was to no avail, for a few days later he was visited by police who asked to see his antiques and a list of all the gifts he had given to others since he arrived in China. Thinking the matter of the bones had been solved earlier, it was only when he was called in for more questioning by police that he realized that they were looking for forty bones that had gone missing. Once it was clear he knew nothing about them, Ronning was let go. Once again, he assumed the matter of the bones was settled.

Arranging for Staines and himself to exit China was the next problem. The morning of the day they were to leave by rail for Shanghai,
he and Staines went down to have their baggage cleared by customs.
A search of their goods took up the whole morning, with some of
Ronning's snuff bottles and a few of Staines's name chops removed
for assessment by the head of the National Museum.[4] When the head
arrived, he took one look at the materials and loudly criticized the customs officers for troubling him with items that were clearly not over
three years old and bits of junk sold to unwary tourists. At Shanghai,
their luggage was searched again but without incident. Another day's
train travel took them to Canton where they and their luggage were
thoroughly searched. The officers were surly and they removed some
items. On top of this, Ronning learned for the first time he had to have
a license to take out his gold ring and gold-rimmed glasses. Previously,
the only license required was for the export of his shotgun.

At 6 a.m. the next day, Staines and Ronning started for Hong Kong.
They reached Shenzhen, a small border station, but were hauled out of
the line of people waiting to cross into Hong Kong and interrogated.
They were required to strip and were subjected to a full body cavity
search. Ronning realized again they were looking for oracle bones. He
explained to the unusually polite officers he had given the bones to the
National Museum and that they would find them there. His search-
ers apologized, saying that one of the officials who had searched them
before had been accused of being lax and they were only doing their
job. They wished him a safe journey and escorted the two Canadians
to the border gate through which they passed to a train that had been
kept waiting for them. The British guards held the train a little longer, in
order to offer Ronning and Staines some hot coffee. It was 3 March 1951.

Once in Hong Kong at the Gloucester Hotel, Ronning took to
his bed with a cold "and also to think things over. I did not want my
personal inconveniences to prejudice my analysis of the tremendous
changes that had begun to take place in China."[5] He was cautioned by
telegram from External Affairs not to say too much. "You will be subject of great interest and probably closely questioned. Please confine
your statements to press to platitudes until you have seen us."[6] After

a trip to Vietnam to visit Audrey, Seymour Topping, and his granddaughter, Susan, Ronning left for Canada by plane from Hong Kong at
midnight on 24 May. In Tokyo, he stayed briefly with Arthur Menzies,
the Canadian ambassador and son of the oracle bone collector, to
whom he expressed "special distress over the stringent body search
by Chinese Communist border guards before he was allowed to cross
the border to Hong Kong."[7] He then boarded a ship for San Francisco,
where Inga and the family met him, having driven down from
Camrose. Another traumatic absence from his family was at last over.

Ronning expressed his feelings on leaving China in a letter to his
family:

> This will be the fourth time I have left China, and each time has
> been more or less associated with the most important events in
> China's recent history.
>
> The first time was just as the Boxer Rebellion was breaking
> out. The second was prior to the revolution that established the
> Republic. The third was at the climax of the "Great Revolution."
> The fourth is during the period when the new People's Republic is
> in conflict with the United Nations in Korea. The dates: 1899, 1907,
> 1927, and 1951. It has just occurred to me that each stay here has
> been six years—nearly a quarter of a century altogether.
>
> ...I leave here with a heavy heart, because I have not been able to
> accomplish that for which I have been working and waiting all this
> time—recognition of the real Government of China.[8]

It is sometimes assumed that had Canada recognized Peking
in a timely way, as Ronning suggested, he would have been named
ambassador. While one will never know for certain what would have
happened, it is unlikely that Ronning would have been appointed
other than as chargé d'affaires while Ottawa decided on a new
high-profile ambassador. Naming Ronning ambassador at this
time would have been unusual for a number of reasons. First, he
had not been in the diplomatic service very long and he had been in
charge of the embassy in Nanking only briefly and under unusual

circumstances—between Chinese governments. Second, the first two Canadian ambassadors to China were political appointees, former provincial Liberal Party ministers who had been broken into diplomacy by a first posting as high commissioner to Australia. Ronning's political experience was with the wrong party, the Co-operative Commonwealth Federation (CCF), which would not qualify him for any special preferment from Prime Minister Mackenzie King. Third, reasons one and two taken together added up to a recently appointed diplomat of actual junior rank with no experience other than in China and without the right political clout.

Fourth, appointing someone as Canada's first ambassador who was closer to the premier of China than he was to the prime minister of Canada was problematic. Given how External Affairs functioned in those days, the new ambassador to China (assuming recognition) would have been either a senior member of the diplomatic corps or yet another Liberal friend of the government. No doubt, Ronning, after suitable leave, might have been promoted to counsellor and sent back to support the new ambassador. But even this would fly in the face of DEA policy/practice, which was to avoid overspecialization. In this case, Ronning would have had to serve elsewhere outside Asia before returning to China. He most certainly would have eventually become ambassador to China, but a little later in his career. Of course, one will never know.

If Ronning had sailed home with visions of Oslo in his mind, he was in for a surprise. He could find no one at External Affairs in Ottawa who remembered promising him a posting to Norway. It was validation of the old Norwegian saying: "If someone goes so far as to make a promise, you can't expect him to keep it too!"[9] Instead, he was appointed head of the American and Far Eastern Division of the Department of External Affairs. In 1952, the division was divided into two parts, with Ronning heading the Far Eastern part. In this position, he suggested that the department seek "non-Caucasian" recruits for posts in Asia.

[T]he response at first was guardedly positive, but reservations soon intervened. One objection was that such employees would be

"specialists," not provided for in the department's personnel policies; another was that limitations on the opportunities for minority
candidates would prevent them from enjoying "the normal and harmonious career in the Service from Third Secretary upwards." The
conclusion was that although applicants should not be discouraged, there should be no special inducements. While the possibility
remained of "the engagement as Head of Mission of a non-Caucasian Canadian of pre-eminent standing," no action followed.[10]

Ronning was destined to serve the rest of his time in the department, which was the same as when he was recruited—overwhelmingly
white and male. In 1953, one of those white males, Arthur E.
Blanchette, fresh from a posting in Mexico, suddenly found himself
in the Far Eastern Division. He wrote this charming appreciation of
Ronning's style:

> Monday morning, I duly reported to the Head of Division: Chester
> Ronning. I did not know it at the time, but I was extraordinarily
> lucky. He was one of the most outstanding men under whom I
> would have the good fortune of serving: knowledgeable, kindly,
> approachable, friendly, helpful.
>
> I remember to this day how, not long after my arrival in the
> Division, he handled my first memorandum to the Minister. He
> must have noticed that I was nervous when I brought it in to him
> for consideration: "Arthur, read it to me." I proceeded to do so with
> some trepidation. He listened intently and said: "Arthur, that's fine.
> Give it to me." And he signed it then and there. He had won a friend
> for life.
>
> ...My service with him remains embedded in my mind as one of
> the happiest periods of my professional life.[11]

In 1953, Ronning was sent to the United Nations as part of the
Canadian delegation when Minister for External Affairs Lester
Pearson was president of the UN General Assembly and involved in
the negotiations to bring a halt to the fighting in Korea. During this

period, Ronning developed a lifelong admiration for Pearson. It was his opinion that Pearson, who was given the Nobel Peace Prize following the settlement of the Suez Crisis of 1957, deserved it more for his work on Korea, a view shared by Escott Reid, a senior Canadian diplomat who was very influential in formulating Canada's approaches to the UN and NATO.[12]

Ronning's major strength was that he understood the Chinese point of view and was able to advise accordingly. In Ottawa, he was in a better position to continue to argue for the recognition of China, but opinions within and without the department remained divided on the timing and wisdom of such an initiative. Meanwhile, he heard of the fallout after the closing of the Nanking embassy. The local Chinese staff was called in by the authorities and questioned repeatedly. Chen, the caretaker, was compelled to denounce Ronning as someone who only gave up the oracle bones when he realized he could not get them out of the country. Tessie Wong, receptionist and secretary, was encouraged to denounce Ronning in the press as an imperialist whose countrymen were killing Chinese soldiers in Korea. She refused, even after many sessions of hard questioning, before she was assigned to a newspaper reading group that met four or five evenings a week to study the official line of the government.[13] Odlum, and particularly Ronning, made continuous efforts to help her leave China, but without success.

Ronning remained in contact with his friend Dr. K.M. Panikkar, the Indian ambassador in Peking, who wrote him a personal and confidential letter in June 1951, outlining Chinese views on the continued impasse in Korea. During the course of the conflict, the Americans had moved their fleet into the Taiwan Straits. It was a sore point with the Chinese government. Panikkar outlined their attitude:

The Chinese position as they have been explaining to me continually is that there can be no peace as long as America thinks that she has divine mandate to decide the affairs of East Asia. As a leading official said the other day, "If the Americans think that Formosa is necessary for their defence, does it not stand to reason that Hawaii is necessary for the protection of China!" The basic fact is that China now has to be treated as a Great Power and not merely as an area of interest.

...The prejudice and blindness of some people in high authority at a certain time have led us into this tragedy. Eighteen months ago China could have been handled fairly satisfactorily, though the West would have had to give up its pretensions of being the moral guardians of Asia.

...I am satisfied about one thing. Even the occupation of half of China, if this were possible, will not bring this regime to its knees.[14]

Ronning shared Panikkar's letter with General Odlum, who was then serving in Ankara as Canadian ambassador to Turkey. Odlum maintained contact with a number of the high-level members of the discredited Nationalist regime, so his response was perhaps predictable.

I know Panikar [*sic*] and I am acquainted with his psychological background. He has a bias towards the left and a disdain of the West. Moreover, he is supremely conscious of "Asia."

...In this particular case, I think he has analyzed the situations in Korea and China very well indeed—with one proviso. If the people of China as a whole are really slowly and steadily moving behind the Mao Tse-tung (Mao Zedong) government, then Panikar's analysis will probably hold good.[15]

Ronning went to Washington, DC, in July 1952 where he called on Leighton Stuart, the former American ambassador in Nanking. Stuart had suffered a stroke soon after his return to the United States in 1949 and was still recovering. They had a long conversation during which Stuart indicated "his belief that there would be gradual modification of American policy to China. He was certain that the policy would become more realistic and would face the realities."[16] But no effort was made by Canada to recognize China while Ronning was in Ottawa on the Far Eastern desk. Moreover, Canada-US relations regarding China were muddied by the charges levelled by Rev. James Endicott that the Americans had resorted to germ warfare in Korea.

At the UN, Canada worked with India to find a solution to the negotiations at Panmunjom, leading to an armistice or truce. Indeed, Ronning's work formed an essential part of Canada's diplomatic efforts directed toward containing the Korean conflict and toward urging the United States to restrain other ambitions that its policy-makers and generals might have vis-à-vis China. Ronning was later to write,

> In my view Canada's performance in the General Assembly of 1952 and in subsequent negotiations, principally with the United States, to get an armistice in Korea in 1953, illustrates how a middle power can be effective in dealing with international crises which otherwise could lead to world war.[17]

This view, however, has been challenged by scholars such as Dennis Stairs, who feel that Ronning exaggerated the importance of Canadian diplomacy in reaching the armistice.[18] But Ronning, having so closely followed the twists and turns of the negotiations, observing Pearson's role in them, might be forgiven for not noticing the woods for the trees. Reg Whitaker and Gary Marcuse also chide Ronning for his view.

> Canadian diplomat Chester Ronning later wrote that "the President of the United States finally accepted the Canadian view and ordered the American representatives at Panmunjom to offer armistice terms as endorsed by the UN." As flattering as this might be to Canadian pride, it is rather a self-serving statement for which there is little evidence in the historical record.[19]

During his three years in Ottawa,[20] Ronning resumed normal family life and caught up on his overdue leaves, although some of them had to be cut short for meetings of the UN. Along with the unfinished business from the embassy in Nanking involving former

staff members, there was the question of some of his personal possessions left behind and which he hoped to retrieve. He continued
to correspond with General Odlum and Tommy Davis, his former
ambassadors, and to visit Consul-General George Patterson in
Boston. It was while Ronning was chatting with Patterson in his home
in late December 1953 that the former Shanghai consul died of a heart
attack at age sixty-six.[21]

On 21 January 1954, Ronning received his long-promised reward:
appointment as Canadian Minister to Norway and Iceland. He prepared to leave from New York on 10 April with Inga and their three
youngest children aboard the *Oslo Fiord*, bound for the land of their
ancestors. Then, a surprising thing happened. While they were en
route, Ottawa asked Ronning to forego Oslo in order to serve under
Pearson as the deputy head of the Canadian delegation to the Korean
Peace Conference opening soon in Geneva, where Canada expected
to play an active role. A conference on Indochina was to follow, but
Canada was only to observe. Clearly, Ronning was being typecast,
never to be free of Asia in a department that discouraged specializa-
tion. Alarmed by the request, he replied with a plea to save his marriage,
which, he argued, depended upon his going to Norway. He promised to
be in Geneva for the conference opening on Monday, 26 April 1954.

Ronning planned to present his credentials to King Haakon VII
(a constitutional monarch)[22] as soon as he arrived in Oslo. Then, after
making his excuses, he would leave for Switzerland. But that was too
simple. In the mid-Atlantic, he learned of a death in the Norwegian
royal family: it would be weeks before the king could receive new
heads of diplomatic missions. Once again, Ronning's ingenuity came
to the rescue. He arrived in Norway on Easter Monday, 19 April, in
time to attend the funeral on Friday in Oslo. There, he pleaded his special circumstances to the king's secretary.

I asked if I could possibly present my credentials so I could be in
Geneva on Sunday. On Saturday I was taken to see the King, driven
by a man who used to drive the horses on the royal carriage and was
driving a car for the first time. I came to the door of the palace and

the man said, "You are two minutes late; hurry up because the king is always on time." We hurried to the next post and we were told we were one minute early. I went to the next place and there was a man who pointed me upstairs. I started climbing the stairs, but I was blinded by the sun and was not sure where to go. Then I heard the command. [I had taken some Norwegian drill when I was a student at the Camrose Lutheran College from an instructor who mixed his English and Norwegian.] "Stand on your bones and tighten you fists." I knew it was a command for soldiers, and I heard them presenting arms. I was told to hurry, "Remember you have to leave in fifteen minutes, because he is in mourning." I was ushered in and introduced. We sat down and talked. I spoke in Norwegian and he spoke Danish, but we switched into English when we could not understand each other. It took one hour. I was motioned to leave, but the King said not to pay any attention.[23]

Ronning flew to Geneva on Sunday, 25 April. On arrival, he was mistaken for the Danish foreign minister and was presented with flowers. The Korean conference that opened a day later ended on 15 June in a stalemate. The Indochina conference, at which Canada was only an observer, began after a short break and continued late into July when a peace agreement was reached including International Control Commissions (ICCs) to monitor it. In the view of John Holmes, senior member of the Canadian delegation, "Of all the important peace-making documents of our time none was so badly drafted and curiously drawn as the so-called 'Geneva Settlement' of 1954." However, it seemed not to concern Canada at all, but to the great surprise of Holmes,[24] who had already left Geneva, Canada was proposed, along with Poland, as members of the ICCs, under the chairmanship of India.

Ronning was very active during the Korean conference. China had a large delegation of 150 members led by Chou En-lai. They "rented the large Villa Montefleuri at Versoix, surrounded by a spacious garden and vineyards. Chou had carpets and antiques brought out from China, and two of Peking's best chefs for the parties he planned to give."[25] The Chinese sincerely hoped for a peace agreement. Ronning

chatted often with Chou and other members of the Chinese delegation, which included Huang Hua, Chang Hanfu, and Wang Ping-nan,
all friends from Chungking and Nanking. This annoyed the American
delegations because they were strictly forbidden to talk with the
Chinese. One day during a crucial phase in the Geneva negotiations,
Chou En-lai was seen to engage Ronning "in earnest conversation
in front of all the newsmen at the Palais." The newsmen rushed up to
John Holmes, another Canadian diplomat,

> to confirm their views that Chester and Chou were settling the
> division of Vietnam, which was the crucial issue of the time, and
> refused to believe that I was ignorant of the subject under discus-
> sion. When I later told Chester that he had stopped the world's
> presses, he said, "Oh we were having an interesting talk about the
> dialect in the Northern Province of Hupei."[26]

Ronning took the opportunity to introduce Lester Pearson to Chou.
It was when Chou was talking to Pearson in a side room off the
conference hall that John Foster Dulles, the American Secretary of
State, appeared in the doorway. Chou extended his hand, but Dulles
turned on his heel and left. Whether or not it was intended as a snub
to Chou, it was seen as one by those who observed the scene. One of
the observers was Ronning, who referred to the incident frequently
thereafter. In later years, he would say that Dulles shook his fist,[27] or
that he looked daggers at Chou, but none of the other accounts of the
incident mention this. Pearson recalled the incident without men-
tioning Dulles at all:

> the Americans wished neither politically nor socially to recog-
> nize the Chinese delegation. At the first tea break there was some
> fraternization among the delegations. The Chinese, however, were
> off by themselves. Not even the Russians were with them, though
> at the time there was no breech between them. They looked rather
> sad, isolated. Chester Ronning, who knew them all from his days
> at our Embassy in China in the late 1940s, said: "Come, let's go

over. I want to introduce you to Chou Enlai who's a friend, and some others." I agreed, and the Chinese seemed very grateful that somebody recognized they were there. I had a pleasant talk with Chou Enlai, in the course of which he invited me to the great villa they had taken for the conference (we were staying in the old Hotel de la Paix). My later call on him was greeted by the Americans with consternation. They did not like it at all. And General Bedell-Smith, who was the American delegate, let me know that I was letting the side down badly by such normal fraternization. He felt it was wrong to let the Chinese feel they had any friends at all in the Western camp....Incidentally, as a small footnote to history, when I left to go back to Ottawa, Chou Enlai sent me a beautiful book of Chinese brush-paintings on rice paper; it has remained one of my most cherished possessions.[28]

Seymour Topping records that Ronning rushed forward to shake Chou's hand to save the Chinese premier the embarrassment of appearing to have made a miscalculation. No matter what, the incident provided a topic of conversation when the two met nearly two decades later.[29]

Later, during the Indochina conference, Ronning was able to intervene successfully with Wang Ping-nan during a luncheon discussion on recognition to get Canadian missionaries released from custody in China and allowed out of the country.[30] He also, through direct conversations with Chou En-lai, achieved the release of Squadron Leader A.R. MacKenzie, a Canadian pilot training with the USAF, who was shot down over North Korea but whose name did not appear on the prisoner exchange lists as arranged under the armistice. It took some time to locate MacKenzie, and his release was consequently delayed until December 1954. During the delay, Ronning had to caution MacKenzie's family not to take money from the press for their story and thus jeopardize his release. The release of MacKenzie and of the missionaries was due primarily to Ronning's connections,[31] and emphasized the need for Canada and China to recognize each other.

Ronning was also very friendly with the Indian delegation. Its leader, Krishna Menon, said later, "I used Ronning, or rather, Ronning used me."[32] Ronning's relations with the United States delegation were not as friendly. In fact, the American delegation was suspicious of him because of his relations with the Chinese delegation.[33] As the Korean conference moved to its stalemate and adjournment in mid-June 1954, Ronning, as acting head of the Canadian delegation, issued a statement, taking to task the attitudes of the Communist states represented there, which questioned the right of the United Nations to intervene in Korea. He also criticized a resolution put forward by Molotov, the Soviet representative. He concluded:

Mr. Molotov wants us to talk about broad principles which sound easy and attractive and to leave the difficult details till later. This, however, is a method of approach, which could have disastrous results. I am sure that if Mr. Vyshinsky were here he could supply a good Russian proverb explaining what happens to carts when they are put before horses. However attractive it might be to reach agreement at this point—and no one is more anxious to reach genuine agreement than we are—nevertheless, we believe that in the long-run it will be better if we squarely face the facts of our disagreement and acknowledge them than to delude ourselves with false hopes and lead the people of the world to believe that there is agreement when there is no agreement.[34]

Ronning's high profile at the Geneva meetings was most likely a factor in Chou suggesting Canada as a member of the International Control Commissions for Indochina; the United States could scarcely object.[35]

Shortly after the conclusion of the Korean conference, Pearson referred in a speech to the danger of not recognizing China:

From information my officers gathered and which I gathered—and I pause for a moment to pay tribute to the capable officers who assisted me at Geneva—I am satisfied the view is widely held that non-recognition and non-admission [to the UN] of China is certainly not only standing in the way of the lessening of international tension—it is tending to keep up international tension, thus endangering world peace.[36]

But, less than a year later, John Foster Dulles visited Ottawa and outlined to Cabinet the American thinking on the Chinese:

At the moment, Asia was the area which gave him and the members of the U.S. administration the most concern. The situation created by the attitude of the Chinese Communists could only be described as grave. He had always felt, in his dealings with the Russians, that they were ruthless and coldly calculating and, consequently, were not likely to push their actions to the point, which might bring war. They reasoned well. He did not feel the same way about the Chinese Communists. He thought this was partly due to temperament and to the fact that they were riding the crest of their first revolutionary wave, during which they had already secured what they regarded as victories over the west. They interpreted the results in Korea as a victory because they measured the change from the time they intervened. Then there was the victory over the French in Indo-China, climaxed at Dien Bien Phu. Now, with the withdrawal of the Nationalists from some of the coastal islands they were pushing towards Formosa. Both their propaganda and what information it was possible to secure from other countries indicated strongly that peaceful overtures would only be met with contemptuous rebuffs.[37]

From Geneva, Ronning returned to begin his life in Norway and Iceland. On 24 June 1955, Queen Elizabeth and Prince Philip arrived in Oslo on the newly christened royal yacht *Britannia* for a three-day state visit. Ronning and Inga were very much involved hosting a tea party on behalf of Canada in the flower-bedecked reception room of the Holmenkollen hotel, high on the mountainside above Oslo. Ronning suggested to the Queen that she take the opportunity to enjoy the view from the ski jump a few minutes from the hotel, while Inga

Inga Ronning presented to Queen Elizabeth, Oslo, June 1955. [Ronning/Cassady photo collection]

briefed Prince Philip on her children and grandchildren. When the Queen left, she took Ronning's advice without informing her entourage, resulting in cars going in opposite directions. That evening, as the Ronnings were taking their leave after King Haakon's state dinner, Prince Philip called out across the crowded room: "Say, Mr. Ronning, that was a jolly good tea we had this afternoon!" The next day, at a garden party given by the British ambassador, the Queen told Ronning she had indeed enjoyed the view, but she enjoyed more the sight of the cars going in the wrong direction. The royal visit involved a full round of visits, a gala performance of *Peer Gynt*, receptions, tree plantings, and a short farewell voyage down the Oslo Fiord on the *Britannia*. Four days later, on 30 June 1955, the Canadian government announced it was raising the status of its diplomatic mission in Norway to that of embassy. Chester Alvin Ronning, who two decades earlier addressed the Alberta Legislature as its first Norwegian Canadian member, became Canada's very first ambassador to Norway in time to host a Dominion Day reception.[38]

At the time, Norway's population was less than four and a half million, while Iceland's was around 150,000. Both countries were founding members of NATO, and there were few, if any, tensions in their relations with Canada. Ronning easily related to the democratic stance of Norway's governing Labour Party. He and Inga mixed well with Norwegian society, including King Haakon VII. They also met Canadians visiting Norway. One of them was a peripatetic Quebec student named Pierre Elliot Trudeau, who had been twice to China and discussed his views with Ronning. There was also time for the Ronnings to visit the home areas of their forebears and to learn first-hand why the Rorems left an otherwise idyllic spot, because, as Chester observed, "You can't eat scenery."[39] Above all, it was a splendid time for Inga, who had sacrificed a great deal for Chester's diplomatic career.

One Sunday, Ronning stood in for the British ambassador at St. Edmund's Anglican English Church in Oslo when King Haakon came for an annual ceremony. Ronning was to receive and send off the king. By convention, the congregation could not leave the church until the king drove off at the end of the service. In Ronning's words:

My wife and I stood on either side of the King and for the first time
my wife admitted that I was taller than the King. When the service
was over I conducted him out to the front steps, but his car was not
there. I offered him my car. He said, "Don't worry, if you don't mind
waiting." I said, "No." Because, it was an opportunity to have a talk,
which we did, but his car did not come. Eventually it showed up; he
got in and left. That evening he gave a dinner for Haile Selasse to
which all ambassadors were invited. The King came round to greet
me. "I am sorry I kept you waiting at the church. It was the preacher's fault, he did not preach long enough."[40]

Norway had good relations with China. It recognized the new
government in 1950, but it was not until 5 October 1954 that each
country opened a legation in the other's capital. In March 1956, while
at the Norwegian Foreign Ministry, Ronning bumped into Halvaard
Lange, the Foreign Minister, just back from UN meetings in New
York. Lange took the opportunity to express his regret that Ronning
would be leaving Oslo to take up the position of Canadian ambassador to China. In New York, Lange had run into Lester Pearson,
who told him of the Canadian plan to recognize China. This came
as a surprise to Ronning, but any excitement he might have felt was
short-lived, however, when he learned what had happened. Prime
Minister Louis St. Laurent and External Affairs Minister Pearson
had gone to White Sulphur Springs, West Virginia, to inform
President Dwight Eisenhower of the Canadian plan. They went to
see the president because they feared Secretary of State John Foster
Dulles was too emotional on the subject. To their shocked surprise,
Eisenhower created a scene, condemning the Canadian proposal
to recognize the "Chinese Communists whose hands were drip-
ping with the blood of Americans killed in Korea."[41] The Canadian
initiative was stillborn. Even the *Camrose Canadian*, whose pages
gave positive support to Ronning and his diplomatic career, firmly
endorsed Eisenhower's position. In an editorial on 4 April 1956, the
*Canadian* cautioned,

Red China has a lot of internal housecleaning to do before decent people can be expected to accept her on equal terms, and it is not becoming for British and Canadian spokesmen to belittle the Eisenhower viewpoint till this housecleaning is done.

Perhaps the diplomatic highlight of Ronning's ambassadorship was the visit of Lester Pearson to Iceland on 24–26 September 1956, on his way back from a NATO committee meeting in Paris. At the time, Iceland was in a fisheries dispute with England and the majority in the newly elected parliament was from the People's Alliance Party, which had a number of pro-communist members. Because the Americans retained a military base at Keflavik, there was fear that Iceland might become anti-American, more pro-Soviet, and ultimately threaten to withdraw from NATO. Pearson's visit was a success and a timely reminder of the importance of NATO and Iceland's role in it.[42] It was a tribute to the high regard in which Pearson held Ronning that he undertook the visit despite pressing engagements elsewhere. In fact, Pearson arrived without local money and relied on Ronning for a loan of 550 Kroner, which he later paid back with a personal cheque for $34.50 and the unused balance of the loan.

But the Department of External Affairs could not indulge Ronning in his Nordic roots for long; Canada could ill afford to let his Asian expertise lie fallow. In February 1957, only three years after his appointment to Oslo, Ronning was assigned to the more demanding position of high commissioner to India.[43] Not only were Canada–India relations more complex but also a crisis was festering in Southeast Asia, which Canada monitored as a member of the International Control Commissions for Indochina under India's chairmanship. Summing up his time in Norway, Ronning joked that he often wondered why Canada needed an ambassador to Norway because the countries were so similar. Nonetheless, he was very happy to have been called to do the job as a token for his long service in China. During his time as ambassador, he grew to appreciate the life of Norwegians and Icelanders, who placed less emphasis on business than on living.[44]

Ronning with Mr. and Mrs. Lester B. Pearson, Iceland, September 1956. [Ronning/
Cassady photo collection]

# Delhi, Nehru, and Dief

From the sparkling fiords and cool, bottle-green landscapes of
Norway, Ronning made his way to the hot, dusty city of New Delhi,
India. He arrived in May 1957, the hottest month of the year, with aver-
age temperatures of 42°C, to take over the position that Escott Reid
had made his own. Reid, eleven years Ronning's junior, had followed
a more traditional career path. A Rhodes Scholar and a member of
the Co-operative Commonwealth Federation (CCF), he joined the
Department of External Affairs (DEA) in 1939 when he was thirty-four
after several years as the secretary general of the Canadian Institute
for International Affairs (CIIA). He was in at the beginning of the
United Nations and NATO and used his formidable intellect to help
shape these institutions and Canadian foreign policy. Some scholars
see him, like Ronning, as a major left-wing influence on Canadian foreign policy. He established an enviable rapport with Jawaharlal Nehru
during the first decade of Indian independence.

Following World War II, and particularly after it gained inde-
pendence in 1947, Canada worked closely with India as a fellow
Commonwealth country on many international issues, such as the
Korean War armistice, the 1957 Suez Crisis, and the Colombo Plan

for co-operative economic and social development in Southeast Asia. Nehru and Pearson worked well together on international problems, and relations between the two countries were harmonious. In 1956, Canada delivered a nuclear reactor to India, years before international nuclear control treaties. Escott Reid had left Delhi, having set in motion a program of assistance to India that included Canadian-built small aircraft (Dakotas, Caribous, and Otters) and further nuclear upgrades. Ronning represented Canada as these materials arrived.

Life in Delhi required some adjustment on Ronning's part. Three years as an ambassador had accustomed him and Inga to the rounds of meetings, receptions, dinners, and galas that mark the life of a high-level diplomat. To be sure, every ambassador has support staff and allowances to ease the round of engagements, but entry into a new post is a particularly hectic time. In addition to establishing the vital links with the national government and its agencies, there are courtesy calls, getting-to-know-you receptions, and dinners involving contemporaries in other embassies. Ronning was faced with all this in a rapidly developing city of two and a half million during days of searing heat and high humidity—hotter conditions than those he experienced in Nanking and Chungking. It was little wonder Inga delayed her arrival in New Delhi until the slightly cooler days of September.

Ronning took up his position the same year Nehru and the Congress Party were re-elected with a large majority, but the shine was beginning to go off Nehru's leadership. His well-founded reputation as an outstanding international leader and peacemaker was intact, but fighting and corruption inside the Congress Party were wearing him down. In 1959, his daughter, Indira Gandhi, was elected president of the Congress Party, something he did not approve of. And later he came into conflict with her on policies, finding her tough to the point of being ruthless. Nehru's foreign policy began to fray. He was criticized for the forceful occupation and annexation of the Portuguese enclave of Goa in 1961. The brief Sino-Indian border war of 1962 left the Indian military humiliated, the Defence Minister Krishna Menon looking for a new job, and Nehru seeking military assistance from America. Elections the same year (1962) saw the Congress majority greatly reduced. Nehru died on 27 May 1964 after months of declining health. Ronning had left Delhi two weeks earlier.[1]

Ronning already had many friends among Indian government ministers and its diplomatic corps, and he soon found that, like his predecessor, he hit it off with Nehru, developing a high regard for him, but perhaps not so high as for Chou En-lai.

> Our relations with India were very good particularly during Mr. Nehru's time. I regard him as one of the most capable international figures that I have known during the course of my service representing Canada abroad. I don't think he did as much for India as Chou has done for China, but his hands were tied because of the differences between the two countries. I fear Mr. Nehru did not fully comprehend that the peasants of India were its greatest drawback because of their attitude and aspects of their religions. In some respects the peasants of China and India were quite similar in that the landlords had great power over them in both countries. Chou went first to the main problem, but Nehru was not quite aware of the power of the peasants and their degradation. The peasants of India, for example, would fall on their faces when the Maharaja went through the country. The Chinese did not worship the Chinese landlords but they feared them. Nehru had not appreciated the situation of the peasants in India, as did Chou in China. Nehru thought that by modernizing India he would solve the problem. Nehru and Chou were both intellectuals and they had a great knowledge of the differences between the East and the West.[2]

Nehru regularly invited Ronning and Inga to lunch with him and, early on, with his daughter Indira. At the lunches,

> Nehru and I did all the talking. (My wife did all the talking at home and I did the talking in public.) Indira said nothing either. Nehru was very important internationally and because Canada and India were tied together in the Commonwealth. Nehru had studied in England and was impressed with aspects of England, although he

Ronning and Prime Minister Pandit Jawaharlal Nehru, New Delhi, 1957. [Ronning/ Cassady photo collection]

had his differences with them. He revealed himself in these conversations we had which he continued even if we were in large gatherings. He would take me for a walk, sometimes with my wife, but she had had enough talking at the lunches. I had a very high regard for him and we agreed on most policies. We did not see eye to eye on differences between India and China, but he was more anxious to retain good relations with China. He liked Chou very much, but his daughter took a rigid anti-Chinese, anti-Communist position, one not even held by top military men.[3]

Three main aspects of Canada–India bilateral relations drew Ronning's attention during his time as high commissioner: aid, atomic power, and a visit by the prime minister of Canada, the Rt. Hon. John George Diefenbaker. Ronning preferred to call Canadian aid to India an investment. He realized the great importance of India to Canada economically and he trumpeted Canadian contributions to India's infrastructure in the fields of hydroelectric power generation, atomic power, building construction, and education. Ronning's own agenda was to emphasize education as much as possible, but a major part of his time involved the International Control Commissions (ICCs) set up by the Geneva conference of 1954 for Vietnam, Cambodia, and Laos. As mentioned in the previous chapter, India chaired the commissions. Canada and Poland were the other members. Ronning worked mainly with M.J. Desai, the expert on Indochina in the Indian foreign office. Vietnam drew the most attention and was the largest file in the high commission office, but Laos was the problem that interrupted Ronning's stay in New Delhi.

Prime Minister Diefenbaker's visit came near the beginning of Ronning's term as high commissioner. Diefenbaker was first elected with a minority government on 21 June 1957, but, the following year, he became the first Progressive Conservative leader since 1930 to win a majority. He became prime minister the month after Ronning took up his position in New Delhi, and he came to visit India seventeen months later. New Delhi was one stop on a grand world tour by the prime minister that included the UK, France, Germany, Italy, the

Vatican, Pakistan, India, Sri Lanka, Malaya, Singapore, Indonesia,
New Zealand, and Australia, and which left a trail of exhausted diplomats in its wake. Diefenbaker's disdain for diplomats as privileged
prima donnas was well known. Also, he was not in favour of the recognition of China. Ronning resolved not to mention China at all during
the visit. Diefenbaker had already met Nehru at a Commonwealth
conference and held him in high regard. In his memoirs, he says,

> I will always think of Pandit Nehru as a transplanted Englishman
> who, while living in something of a metaphysical world, neverthe-
> less was one of the great realists, capable of achieving his objectives
> with courage and determination, a Harrovian to the end.[4]

In a meeting with Nehru on 26 November 1958, Diefenbaker outlined the gist of John Foster Dulles's remarks on American foreign
policy made at face-to-face meetings earlier in the year in Ottawa.
Dulles adamantly supported a policy of nonrecognition of China.
Nehru surprised Diefenbaker with his opinion that the American
policy very much suited China, enabling it to put pressure on the
Chinese people to accept the new reforms.[5] At this point, Nehru
made reference to Ronning. Diefenbaker, in his account of the discussion, makes no mention of Ronning, but R. Basil Robinson, the
DEA official seconded to the prime minister's office, remembers the
conversation a little differently. "In the course of his remarks Nehru
paid a graceful tribute to Chester Ronning...by drawing him into
the conversation as an acknowledged expert in Chinese affairs."[6]
Ronning's report of the meeting, drafted by Robinson, leaves out
Nehru's direct reference to him, but a separate confidential note to
Norman Robertson in Ottawa does, along with interesting addi-
tional information. After conversing with Nehru, Diefenbaker asked
Ronning to talk to him about China.

> I replied that before making my comment I should inform him that
> I thought the American policy in the Far East, as far as Communist
> China was concerned, was extremely dangerous because, in my

Prime Minister John Diefenbaker, Pandit Nehru, and Ronning, New Delhi, November 1958. [Ronning/Cassady photo collection]

opinion, it was based on a wrong analysis of what had happened in China before and after 1949. Mr. Diefenbaker asked me to explain...I said it would take me at least fifteen or twenty minutes.... Mr. Diefenbaker told me to fire away. I did.[7]

Ronning explained that the American view of the Chinese Communist Party as a creature of Moscow was completely false, because the Chinese party had rejected Moscow orthodoxy decades earlier when it accepted Mao's leadership. The American policy of trying to support the Chinese people against the Communist government because it represented a foreign power was based on a "completely fallacious" analysis.[8] Ronning then made reference to his own experiences in China, and even after an hour of debate, Diefenbaker urged him to continue.

Ronning referred to Eisenhower's treatment of Prime Minister St. Laurent and Lester Pearson in 1956, when they told him of Canada's intention to recognize China. "At this point, Mr. Diefenbaker asked me if I was sure that the President had taken this attitude in 1956.... Are you sure that it is not something you have heard this year which you have confused with something else you heard in 1956?" Ronning confirmed the facts on the way to the airport the next day. Diefenbaker told him the information was important because "Mr. Eisenhower had made the same statement during the summer of 1958 and that, if anything, he had stated his position in even stronger terms."[9] Combined with the 1956 information,

> it indicated that Mr. Eisenhower's attitude and United States policy, instead of becoming more flexible, was becoming more rigid. This he said would be a factor in the decision he would have to make regarding Canada's position. Mr. Diefenbaker did not explain to me exactly what he had in mind.[10]

Diefenbaker was referring to conversations in Ottawa in July 1958, when he and his Minister for External Affairs Sydney Smith[11] met with President Eisenhower and John Foster Dulles. In his memoirs, Diefenbaker glosses over the president's reaction:

We were chatting about matters in general and not really agreeing on anything, as Dulles was in a rather obstructive mood. Without warning Sydney Smith suggested that public opinion in Canada was getting more and more interested in some form of normalization in our relations with Communist China, particularly in the field of trade. He went on to suggest that perhaps the time had come to accord the Peking regime formal recognition and to admit China to her seat in the United Nations. This put President Eisenhower into a temper and he replied that public opinion in the United States was so dead set against this, he could not see the day when recognition would become possible.

Further, in Eisenhower's opinion, it would mean America's withdrawal from the United Nations and the removal of its headquarters from American soil.[12]

Basil Robinson, however, describes the meeting this way: Diefenbaker saw

the indignant reaction of the president and Dulles to a remark made (half in jest) by Sidney Smith to the effect that Canada ought to recognize the Chinese communist regime. On hearing this Eisenhower pounded his fist on the desk and shouted that the day Canada recognized the Peking regime he would kick the United Nations out of the United States. The point was not pursued.[13]

The two attempts (1953 and 1958) to raise with President Eisenhower the question of recognition of China ended in presidential tantrums. Canada's failure to proceed effectively put an end to any hopes Ronning might have had of becoming ambassador to China. He knew nothing of either attempt until afterwards, but each failed effort put his chances of representing Canada in China further and further out of reach.

A highlight of Diefenbaker's visit to India was a tiger hunt, which, along with other arrangements for his visit, greatly pleased the Canadian prime minister. As his later public references show,

Diefenbaker found in Ronning a diplomat he could trust, even though they were poles apart on the question of China. Ronning, too, was honoured with a tiger hunt, killing five, plus two leopards, to the relief of the local peasants on whom the big cats preyed.[14] Ronning became a popular and a well-respected figure in India.[15] A school named after him recognized his dedication to education. Despite his popularity and success, Ronning was not satisfied with Canada–India relations. In a report to External Affairs in May 1960, three years after he took up his position, he provided Ottawa with a realistic assessment of Canada–India relations.

> I would stress at the outset that generally speaking Canadian–Indian relations are cordial. The picture of Canada in the minds of the Indian public is, for the most part, however, rather hazy. Canada is about as far away from India as it is possible to be on this earth and, since Canada does not have the international stature or resources of the USA or the USSR, the Indian public is not moved to consider either the similarities or the differences, which exist between the two countries. On this plane, therefore, while relations are friendly it is a friendship based on ignorance rather than knowledge.
>
> I see no prospect of any sudden strengthening of our relations with India. These relations are, in both cases, important preoccupations,–and these preoccupations are not likely to change in the near future. Yet India remains the most important uncommitted nation in the world and by far the most important democracy in Asia. All thoughtful people recognize what an enormous amount depends on the future of this country. This has certainly been clearly recognized in Ottawa for a long time. But as I have attempted to point out, such diplomatic efforts on our part will be more useful if they proceed from a basis of realism rather than from wishful thinking. There are no grounds whatever for complacency in the field of Canadian–Indian relations.[16]

One aspect of Canada–India relations that became controversial a decade after Ronning left Delhi involved atomic reactors. The first

reactor, know as CIRUS (Canada India Research Utility Services),
was built in the late 1950s near Bombay (Mumbai) as a Canada-India
joint venture funded under the Colombo Plan. The second reactor,
known as Laughing Buddha, was built in two phases in the 1960s
at Ranapratapsagar, financed by a loan given to India by Canada.
Ronning was involved in negotiating safeguard agreements for the
two reactors. In each agreement India declared that the reactor would
be used for peaceful purposes only, and the Indian government passed
the Atomic Energy Act in 1962 to provide for controls to make sure
that atomic energy was used only for peaceful purposes. Later, Indira
Ghandi grew anxious as China tested an atomic bomb in 1964 and
Pakistan began to pursue an atomic weapons program in 1972. In May
1974, India conducted an underground test of an atomic weapon,
throwing Canada-India relations into disarray.

In 1961, Ronning was taken away from Delhi and assigned to be
the acting head of the Canadian delegation to the Geneva conference
on Laos, which lasted until the early months of 1962. Counsellor A.C.
Campbell was acting high commissioner when India's army occupied the Portuguese enclave of Goa on 17–19 December 1961.[17] The
Laos conference in Geneva was called to stabilize the situation in that
country. Originally, the Laos ICC was to carry on its work of supervis-
ing the peace until such time as the competing political parties agreed
on a stable government. The party on the right was supported by the
United States and the one on the left by the USSR. In between were
the neutralists. In 1958, the Laotian government requested termi-
nation of the ICC, but instead its work was suspended pending the
outcome of elections. In 1960, a neutralist coup followed by a rightist
countercoup led to fighting among the parties and the threat of civil
war. Prime Minister Nehru called for the ICC to be reactivated, and
Prince Norodom Sihanouk of Cambodia called for an international
conference on Laos. President John F. Kennedy, newly elected, was
persuaded that a neutral Laos would be the best solution, and later, in
June 1961, received Nikita Khrushchev's support for the idea.

Fourteen countries sent delegations to Geneva in May 1961 to begin
meetings on Laos. The ICC for Laos was reactivated the same month

after the warring parties agreed to a ceasefire. Foreign ministers headed their delegations at the opening sessions before leaving their subordinates to do the difficult work. Howard Greene was the Canadian Minister for Foreign Affairs, with Ronning as deputy and acting head. Chen Yi, China's foreign minister, headed a delegation that included Wang Ping-nan, Chiao Kuan-hua, Chang Hanfu, Gong Peng, and Gong Puseng, all of them friends of Ronning. Andrei Gromyko, Soviet Foreign Minister, and a Deputy, Georgi Pushkin, led the Soviet group; Dean Rusk, and, later, Averell Harriman represented the United States; Prince Sihanouk attended for Cambodia; along with representatives from North and South Vietnam, Thailand, and, of course, Laos. Britain was represented by Malcolm MacDonald and Sir Alec Douglas-Home, British Foreign Secretary, who co-chaired the opening session on 16 May with Andrei Gromyko. Representatives of France and Poland also took part in the meetings. As was his habit, Ronning spent a great deal of time with the Chinese and Vietnamese delegations.

The conference did not start well, with arguments over seating arrangements. This was reminiscent of the 1954 conference on Korea, when John Foster Dulles manoeuvred so that China would not have a front row seat. In 1961, the main question was who represented Laos. In the end, representatives from each faction were seated. Ronning spent time with Dean Rusk, whom he found set in his anti-Red ways. He was greatly relieved when Averell Harriman arrived and was willing to meet casually with Chinese and North Vietnamese delegates. Later, Harriman commented on his great respect for Ronning and his work during the conference.[18] John Kenneth Galbraith, the recently appointed American ambassador to India, also attended. He describes in his journal entry, dated 29 July 1961 how he was brought up to speed on the Laos situation:

Shortly after I arrived the proceedings began. The British with great politeness and urbanity denounced the Russians. The Russians then denounced the British and Americans. The North Vietnamese joined the Russians, and the South Vietnamese came down on the side of the Americans. The Indians and the Burmese remained silent, having the day before, being neutral, denounced everybody. The meeting lasted only two hours. Short meetings are a great aid to the peace, for otherwise the denunciations are longer.

It is Harriman's decision not to participate in billingsgate and recrimination. This is a tremendous innovation in modern diplomacy. (I learned that he was forbidden by the State Department to communicate with the Chinese. I sent an indignant letter to the President on the subject, and this ridiculous bar was removed.)...

I talked to the conference staff and acquired a good deal of additional information. Then I had a brief nap, watched the rain over the Lake, bought a large supply of sleeping pills—they are available here without prescription since suicide is a human right—and dined pleasantly with Malcolm Macdonald, Harriman, Chester Ronning, and two or three others. The discussion was extensively, but not exclusively, on Laos. I was beginning to feel pretty well in control of the problem.[19]

During the first weeks, the various interested parties set out their positions in a series of plenary sessions. Eventually, the conference got down to detail. It was agreed that the reactivated ICC should monitor the ceasefire, but physical conditions were such that helicopters were essential if the commissioners were to do their job. More than anyone else, and on behalf of Canada, Ronning continued to press the need for helicopters. He was called "Mr. Helicopter" thereafter. The conference was expected to last three months, but it was still in session ten months later when the participants finalized an agreement to neutralize Laos. The conference then adjourned until the Laotians formed a government. In July 1962, fourteen months after they originally met, conference members signed a final agreement.

The Laos conference played havoc with the continuity of Ronning's term as high commissioner to India. He returned to New Delhi in March 1962, expecting that his term would soon be over. Ronning and Inga represented Canada well in India, but the summer heat of New Delhi bothered both of them, draining their energy. Inga was absent as much as possible during the May–September period. Early in May

1959, with the temperature already 42°C, they left for two months' home leave in Canada, where Inga was scheduled to have her gall bladder removed. Because she did not recover quickly, they stayed close to home in Camrose, returning to Delhi in August, but during the next months, Inga suffered from jaundice and intestinal problems. She returned to Canada in June 1960 and remained there until October. The next spring, they left Delhi for two months' leave in South Africa with daughter Meme and son-in-law David, after which they moved to Geneva for the Laos conference opening in May 1961. They stayed in Geneva until the conference recessed the following March. They then returned to Delhi, expecting to leave there for good in June 1962, but the Department of External Affairs asked Ronning to remain until May 1964. As Ronning wrote Odlum, 10 June 1961, "after much heart-searching Inga and I finally agreed."

In mid-June 1962, with Delhi already blisteringly hot, they left for two months' home leave in the US and Canada. They planned to fly to Geneva, pick up their car, drive to LeHavre, and load the car and themselves onto the S.S. *United States* to arrive in New York on 27 June. After New York, on their way to Camrose and Valhalla, they planned to visit family in Washington, Nova Scotia, Ottawa, Chicago, and Minneapolis, but, as in the past, Ronning's best-laid plans "*gang aft agley*."[20] No sooner had they arrived in New York than he learned he was needed back in Geneva to sign the final agreement on Laos. Effectively, he was left with the month of August for abbreviated travel. Returning to New Delhi in September, Inga and Chester began a debate on where they might retire: Camrose, California, or Edmonton. But autumn in India was far from calm.

October 1962 saw world attention focused on Cuba and the Missile Crisis that pitted President John F. Kennedy against Nikita Khrushchev in a deadly game of chicken involving the potential use of atomic weapons. As the contest of wills reached its climax and Soviet missiles were being withdrawn from Cuba, China, on 20 October, invaded India. China disapproved of India giving asylum to the Dalai Lama when he fled from Tibet in 1959, and, under Nehru's "Forward Policy," India had set up military posts in border areas under dispute with China. The two countries had failed to reach an agreement on the border between them. Some sections were in genuine doubt, while others, drawn by the British in the previous century, were unacceptable to the Chinese.

China's invasion caught India off guard. Nehru was dejected because he believed he had control of the situation, and he was disillusioned with Chou En-lai who he thought had abandoned previous commitments to settle international disputes peacefully. Ronning was caught in an awkward place. He admired both leaders, but personally, he was sympathetic to the Chinese position. He found Indira Gandhi's response to China to be too hard line and emotional. At the same time, because of his good relations with the leaders on both sides, he was in a unique position to work behind the scenes to help diffuse the tension over the Aksai Chin region on the borders of Kashmir.[21] Galbraith described a conversation with Ronning on the subject.

> This afternoon I visited Chester Ronning, the Canadian High Commissioner and an old China hand. He shares my view that the Chinese objectives are limited and we need not be concerned about their descending into the Indian plain. He thinks the Chinese can defend a claim to the Aksai Chin Plateau in Ladakh—they occupied it for two years before the Indians seem to have discovered they were there....
>
> Krishna Menon, whom I have not seen for many weeks, has been in touch with Ronning on arms—he is evidently still very reluctant to talk with us. When Ronning saw Menon last Friday, the latter talked about a ten-year war and implied that the Chinese might head for Madras. Ronning had seen Menon today and found him somewhat more calm.[22]

These were the days of Canada "the helpful fixer," when our diplomats got involved in settling disputes that were not core to Canada's main interests.[23] Previously, Canada had supplied India with a number of planes,[24] some of which were now being used to drop food and clothing to Indian soldiers cut off from supplies. The Chinese made no objection to Canadian planes being used to drop food and did not regard Canada as an aggressor.[25] Canada and India were fellow members of the Commonwealth, but, on the other hand, Canada had begun a series of lucrative grain deals with China. Initially, the Canadian government accepted the Indian version of events and sent aid (see note 17). It did not heed, however, calls from some Canadians to divert to India wheat destined for China. By the time the war was over, many Canadians had begun to see the Chinese side of the matter.[26] One month after they invaded, the Chinese withdrew.

The Chinese invasion greatly damaged Nehru's reputation as an international statesman and India's foreign policy took a more hawkish turn. In addition, Nehru's health began to fail and, as mentioned previously in the chapter, he was ill during Ronning's final months as high commissioner. Indira Gandhi then asserted her power. Ronning recalled later that he met with her only once and that he found her less easy to deal with. She missed a farewell lunch for him in early May 1964 as he prepared to leave India, sending him a typed note of apology and best wishes. Roland Michener, another distinguished Albertan, replaced Ronning as high commissioner.[27]

India had taken a toll on the Ronnings' health. After leaving India, Chester and Inga retired to their little white house in Camrose, close to their oldest daughter Sylvia (Cassady) and her family. They purchased an organ to refresh the skills Chester had acquired in Minnesota in 1922 and resumed their hobbies of sculpting, carving, and painting. Inga was well known for her painting and Chester for his sculptures.

Ronning's entirely unplanned and unexpected entry into diplomacy had led to a remarkable twenty-year career, but his retirement was not to be quiet. He received invitations to speak on international issues, particularly Vietnam and China, at conferences and public meetings. These proved to be the opening shots of his campaign to deal with unfinished business: the recognition of China and its seating at the UN, and finding peace in Vietnam. Minister for External Affairs Paul Martin marked Ronning's retirement with a letter full of praise for his accomplishments, but, as it turned out, official retirement was not the end of his diplomatic career. Within two years, he was asked to undertake a special mission: his diplomatic grand finale.

# A Smallbridge Too Far

During the latter half of the nineteenth century, France established
a colonial empire in Southeast Asia known as French Indochina. It
included the countries now known as Cambodia, Laos, and Vietnam.
Japan occupied the area during World War II, although Vichy France
continued to administer the region. France attempted to reassert its
full control following the war, but it ran into resistance from independence groups. The situation deteriorated and, in 1954, an international
conference to establish peace in Indochina met in Geneva. At the
same time, the French suffered a spectacular military defeat at the
hands of the Viet Minh in North Vietnam at Dien Bien Phu.

As a result of the conference, France bade farewell to its Asian
empire and its component parts were free to establish their own
governments in a process overseen by International Control
Commissions (ICCs). Canada, an observer at the conference, was
chosen, along with Poland and India (the latter being the chair), to
staff each of the ICCs. The agreement on Vietnam became the most
difficult to enforce. It called for elections to bring about the peaceful
reunification of the North and the South, but the elections were never
held, leaving the North and the South locked in an armed struggle for

dominance. The 17th parallel became the front line of the Cold War
in Asia. The Communist Viet Minh under Ho Chi Minh ran North
Vietnam, with its capital in Hanoi. The USSR and China supported
it. South Vietnam, with its capital in Saigon, was run by the restored
monarch, Emperor Bao Dai, and his Prime Minister, Ngo Dinh Diem.
The United States and a number of its allies supported it. Diem, however, refused to hold elections as prescribed by the Geneva agreement,
and, in 1956, he declared the Republic of South Vietnam and selected
an administration dominated by Catholics.

Beginning in the mid-1950s, the administration of President
Dwight Eisenhower began to supply "advisors" to the government of
South Vietnam. Their numbers increased under President John F.
Kennedy in order to assist the Saigon government in its fight against
a growing insurgency led by a group called Viet Cong. The Kennedy
administration further involved the United States in the politics of
South Vietnam, which involved assassinations and coups. President
Lyndon Johnson expanded American military involvement, making
the growing war his own. Following a controversial incident in the
Gulf of Tonkin on 4 August 1964, the United States Congress gave
Johnson the authority to pursue a direct war against North Vietnam.
He ordered the bombing of the North and increased the number
of American military personnel in South Vietnam. While putting
increased pressure on the North, he invited other countries to offer
assistance in bringing about peace. The major conceptual disagreement was that Hanoi saw the war as a civil war and anticolonial, while
Washington looked upon it as an invasion of the democratic South
by the communist North, which had to be stopped lest the rest of
Southeast Asia fall to communism.

In a speech at Temple University in Philadelphia on 2 April 1965,
Prime Minister Lester Pearson, over the strong objections of Paul
Martin, Minister for External Affairs, called for a halt to the bombing of North Vietnam. His words were moderately phrased, but the
damage was extraordinary. Canada had earlier refused to send troops
to Vietnam, so American officials considered that criticism from the
prime minister was totally unacceptable when delivered inside the

United States,[1] no matter how mild it was. President Johnson, enraged, summoned Pearson to Camp David for lunch, where he fulminated against the Canadian leader, using the extremely foul language for which he was famous. It is said he accused the prime minister of entering his home and "pissing on my rug."[2] Contributing to his rage was the fact that many American draft dodgers were receiving asylum in Canada.

Undeterred by the chill in Canada–US relations following Pearson's speech, Paul Martin searched for a Canadian initiative to bring North Vietnam and the United States to a peace table. Previously, in 1964, he agreed to let Blair Seaborn, Canadian member of the ICC, carry messages from the United States to the government of the North. Seaborn made two trips, but the strategy backfired, giving Canada a diplomatic black eye, when the United States referred to Seaborn as one of their agents. As hostility to the war grew in Canada, and more Americans who opposed the war and/or wished to avoid the compulsory draft for military service took refuge in Canada, Martin looked for another angle of approach to the Vietnam problem.

Convinced that the road to peace in Vietnam passed through Peking, Martin conceived of a mission to Peking and Hanoi, with Ronning the ideal candidate to undertake it. Once again, the Department of External Affairs (DEA) sought to exploit Ronning's social democratic views and his friendships with Asian leaders—in this case Chou En-lai, Chen Yi, and Ho Chi Minh. Moreover, Ronning understood the background to the crisis. If he proved willing, Ronning would undertake the mission code named "Smallbridge."

Beginning on 24 December 1965, and for thirty-seven days thereafter, the United States halted bombing of the North. In January 1966, during the halt, Ho Chi Minh wrote the member countries of the ICC asking them to urge the United States to halt the bombing permanently and to seek peace. Appended to the letter were four points upon which North Vietnam insisted for peace. In sum, they called for the complete withdrawal of all outside military forces and a return to the 1954 Geneva agreements. Delivering Prime Minister Pearson's reply to Ho Chi Minh was a reason for Smallbridge to go to

Hanoi, while publicly the mission was described as an inspection trip of Canadian ICC units in Saigon and Hanoi.[3]

In retrospect, it is easy to see how unlikely it would have been for Smallbridge to succeed, but, at the time, it seemed worth a try. Martin's hunch was that Ronning could find common ground between the two parties. But, for all his pluses, Ronning also had negatives. His good relations with Chinese and Vietnamese leaders were offset by his poor relations with American policy-makers. American animosity went back to the Geneva conference on Korea in 1954 and was reinforced at the conference on Laos in 1961-62, when Ronning's friendly chats with the Asian communist leaders and officials caused American diplomats to "see Red." Moreover, prior to his retirement, Ronning was critical in private of American policy on China and Southeast Asia, and since retirement, had gone public. Although he had a friend in Averell Harriman, President Kennedy's representative on the Laos conference, Dean Rusk, now the Secretary of State under President Johnson, wrote Ronning off as a communist and perpetual missionary. Ronning had the potential to be distrusted by both sides.

Summoned from Camrose to Ottawa by Martin, Ronning proved open to the proposal, although he was aware that many Canadian diplomats who served on the ICC for Vietnam favoured the American position. They did not see the fighting between the North and South as a civil war but as an insurgency in the South sponsored by the North. Ronning's view was that the United States was at fault because it failed to follow through on the Geneva agreement to hold elections. He was not prepared to be, or be seen to be, an agent for America. At his initial briefing at External Affairs,

> The Under Secretary for External Affairs invited all the interested officers in this subject and he gave me instructions on what I should say. I sat quietly until he finished his "long song and dance." His instructions were similar to those given previously to Seaborn. I said, "I am not prepared to accept any of the instructions you have given. You go back to Mr. Pearson and say I am not available." The Under Secretary said, "No, no, Paul Martin needs you." I said, "If

that is the case, I know Mike Pearson's attitude and I support that, and I will accept any advice he gives, but not along the lines of instructions you have given. Unless you arrange this I will not go."[4]

As a result, although Pearson had reservations about the wisdom of the mission, Ronning received instructions more to his liking. He objected to the original ones because they put him in the position of supporting one side, when his objective was to find middle ground between two opposing views. Ronning went to Washington to gain American support for Smallbridge, but William Bundy, Assistant Secretary of State, with whom he met, communicated to the president and the Secretary of State Dean Rusk his lack of enthusiasm for the venture. Charles Ritchie, Canada's ambassador in Washington, sat in on the meetings and, in his view,

> There was total noncommunication, and Ronning was very general and impressionistic in his presentation, which really was based on the inevitable triumph of peasant risings, you know rather reminiscent of Mao Tse-tung—"the fish in the water" and all that sort of thing—and this didn't go down naturally at all well. But, or of course, his knowledge of the situation and his experience and his sincerity were very valuable and should have been given an objective assessment without prejudice and taken into account, but I don't think they were.[5]

Afterward, Ronning left for Vietnam, stopping in Hong Kong where he stayed with Audrey and Seymour Topping without telling them what he was really about. Martin thought Ronning should try to go to Peking on his way to Hanoi to meet with Chou En-lai and Chen Yi, but the Chinese politely rejected the idea. Ronning thought a visit to Peking was a bad idea and he later denied it was ever proposed. On the other hand, Martin in his memoirs says the Chinese rejected the visit because of the Cultural Revolution, and because Canada was too closely linked to the United States. Further, in interviews with Peter Stursberg, Martin implied that Ronning himself contacted Chou and Chen Yi from Hong Kong, only to be told no.[6] Andrew Preston, however, indicates that the official record shows there was a Canadian government contact with Peking from Hong Kong at the time, but not by Ronning.[7] Little matter the details, it appears the Americans were suspicious of Ronning for being too close to China and the Chinese rejected Ronning for being too close to the Americans.

Ronning left Hong Kong for Saigon on 5 March 1966, accompanied by a skeptical Victor C. Moore, the Canadian member of the ICC and Seaborn's replacement. After pro forma meetings with South Vietnamese leaders and Henry Cabot Lodge, the American ambassador, Ronning and Moore flew via Vientiane to Hanoi, where they stayed from 11 to 17 March. Ronning's purpose, as he later said, was "to find an agreement between America and the North Vietnamese." After a warm welcome, he was put in "a very satisfactory hotel," after which he strove to find some basis for an understanding:

> I never worked so hard in my life visiting various branches of the government until I got up to Pham Van Dong. (I was also an old friend of Ho Chi Minh.[8]) I planned to talk to Pham on the basis that the US broke the Geneva agreement and not Vietnam. He said to me: "You can tell the Americans that we are willing to make peace with them on one condition, and one condition only, that they stop the bombing of North Vietnam. It has nothing to do with the war in South Vietnam we can talk about that later. We will come to the peace table and we will name the place once the Americans stop the bombing."[9]

Ronning was elated. He thought he had achieved a breakthrough, a simple first step that would lead to greater things. He clarified further with Pham that the four points were negotiable.

Paul Martin, however, gives a slightly different description of what took place:

> Ronning had a two-hour interview with Pham Van Dong on 11 March. The prime minister said that his sole condition for

commencing negotiations was a cessation of all military activity against the North. If the Americans made a declaration to this effect, then (subject to further indirect talks, via Canada) negotiation could begin. Pham then emphasized that he did not wish to use Canada formally as a channel of communication. The hesitation underlying his offer was evident. He had promised to hand Ronning an *aide memoire* before his departure, but his advisors had given him second thoughts, and the offer was not put in writing. The suggestion that the North Vietnamese would be willing to talk while the war in the South went on, on condition that the Americans stopped bombing the North, was apparently too sensitive to risk to paper, but Ronning left Hanoi believing that he had achieved a major concession.[10]

Moore, who sat in on the talks, thought Ronning performed brilliantly and lost his original skepticism. But, like an outsider intervening in a domestic dispute, Ronning perhaps undervalued the pent-up suspicions on each side.

Ronning returned first to Hong Kong and then went on to Ottawa, where

> I reported to Mike Pearson and though I did not support the party he led, he was the person I admired most in Canada. When I gave him the report he said it was a more interesting analysis than he had received from External Affairs. He was in favour of accepting Pham's proposition.[11]

But when Ronning reported his findings to Washington on 21 March 1966, he faced a wall of doubt and suspicion, along with questions relating to details he had not addressed. His breakthrough was dismissed as nothing new or substantial because the Americans were certain that, ultimately, the North Vietnamese would not budge from their previously stated four points. Washington thought the proposal to be unworthy of a reply. At best, it was regarded as a well-meaning effort, which had to be tolerated for the sake of Canada–US relations.

Martin, however, insisted that Ronning should have something to return to Hanoi with, if only to keep open a Canadian channel to North Vietnam. After a long delay, he was told that if Ronning returned to Hanoi, he should seek clarification of the original offer and advise the North Vietnamese to communicate directly through Rangoon in future.[12]

Ronning's second visit set for June was already dead before he arrived. He reached Hong Kong to find that reports were circulating, saying the United States was willing to stop bombing if the North stopped assisting the Viet Cong in the South. In Warsaw, where the United States and China held periodic meetings, the Americans informed the Chinese of their proposal that they knew would be passed on to Hanoi. Moreover, the United States was already interested in operation "Marigold," an effort to communicate with North Vietnam through the Polish member of the ICC.

According to Paul Martin, Ronning waited in Hong Kong once again for word of a possible trip to Peking. Ronning, on the other hand, protested:

> I did not intend ever to go via China to Vietnam. If there were any suggestion that I should do that, I knew nothing about that whatever. I did not phone Chou Enlai from Hong Kong and I didn't have any conversation with the Chinese. None whatever.[13]

It was against his better judgement that he left Hong Kong for Hanoi.

He was greeted with more flowers and better accommodations, but he did not see Prime Minister Pham. He met with foreign office officials and foreign minister Nguyen Duy Trinh during the week of 14–18 June and received rude and rough treatment during their discussions. Hanoi's reply "was an outright refusal even to consider such an abject, impossible, condition." "I went home."[14]

Home, in this case, was Ottawa, where, once again, he reported to Pearson and to Paul Martin, who invited William Bundy of the American State Department to Canada to pick over the entrails of Ronning's second visit. After their meetings, lasting seven hours into

the evening of 21 June 1966, Bundy returned to Washington, leaving
Ronning with pangs of conscience.

> I began to wonder if my [first] report had encouraged the
> Americans to think that Hanoi had made these concessions
> because the bombing was really hurting them and that Washington
> therefore became all the more determined that bombing would be
> pursued relentlessly until North Vietnam was crushed.[15]

He was correct: the Americans had scheduled increased bombing
raids on the North beginning the next day, 22 June, but bad weather
delayed them to the 29th.

Ronning's missions were but another phase in a multiphased
attempt by Paul Martin to influence the diplomacy of the Vietnam
War. The missions were also but one in a series of peace-feelers duly
noted by the Americans as they sought to win the conflict. The introduction to the official State Department documents on Vietnam for
1966, published later, puts them in American perspective.

> Throughout 1966, while pursuing the war in Vietnam, the admin-
> istration continued concurrent diplomatic efforts to precipitate
> peace negotiations. Washington attempted peace initiatives during
> 1966 indirectly through Hanoi's patron, the Soviet Union, and
> through other third parties and directly to Hanoi through public
> pleas for discussions. In March, Pham Van Dong, Premier of the
> Democratic Republic of Vietnam, suggested to retired Canadian
> diplomat Chester Ronning that bilateral talks might begin if the
> bombing ended. But the U.S. Government insisted upon recipro-
> cal action from Hanoi before it terminated the air attacks. When
> Ronning returned to Hanoi in June, the North Vietnamese refused
> to countenance the preconditions. The next month, however, Jean
> Sainteny, an emissary sent to North Vietnam by French President
> Charles de Gaulle, found the politburo possibly willing to termi-
> nate its southward infiltration in exchange for a complete bombing
> cessation by the United States.[16]

A raw insight into the American attitude toward Ronning is found in a telegram to Washington from Oscar Vance Armstrong, American consul in Hong Kong, following a meeting with Ronning after his first mission in March 1966.

> Ronning characterized results of his mission by quoting old Chinese saying: He had "travelled ten thousand miles to present a feather." He said he is more pessimistic about long-range Vietnamese problem than before his trip....Ronning commented to me that he did not disabuse North Vietnamese leaders of their estimates of increased US military action. Instead, he tried to impress upon them that US could bring vastly greater military power to bear than could the French in 1950's, and that therefore there was no chance of history repeating itself (as they seemed to believe)....Ronning found that as a Canadian he was treated better than the British who support American position fully, but was made politely aware that Canada was little more than American satellite. However, Pham Van Dong was appreciative of Pearson's public statement of regret over resumption of bombing in North.
> Ronning found his several hours of talks with Hanoi leaders very wearing and frustrating....He got the impression he was object of a team effort at wearing him down...Some were talks also scheduled in early morning with scarcely fifteen minutes notice, apparently to keep him off balance.[17]

Armstrong conveys none of the sense of optimism of Ronning in his belief he had scored a breakthrough with Pham. Understandably, Ronning held back until he was debriefed in Ottawa, but Armstrong's telegram prejudiced his results in the eyes of the already prejudiced State Department, even before he arrived back in Ottawa.

Bromley Smith of the National Security Council forwarded Armstrong's telegram to President Johnson on the evening of 16 March 1966. His short note speaks volumes. Clearly, Washington looked on the missions as a learning exercise for Canadians who doubted American policy:

Mr. President:

The hardest information we have gotten from Hanoi in some time is contained in the attached cable reporting the views of Chester Ronning, a retired Canadian Foreign Service Officer with life-long personal connections with China.

His report to Prime Minister Pearson will be helpful in destroying illusions still held by some in Ottawa.

Bromley Smith[18]

Later, the *Pentagon Papers*[19] revealed that Dean Rusk and President Johnson, from the beginning, did not take Ronning's missions seriously.

Ronning returned to Camrose; he would soon be seventy-two, having spent the last twenty-one years of his life as a diplomat. He said he was never given any instructions on how to be a diplomat, although he was well inoculated. No surprise, perhaps, when Lester Pearson, arguably Canada's greatest diplomat, believed that "Practically anyone can get into it and become an Ambassador."[20] But, one would hasten to add, to rise to the level of a Ronning took special talent.

In August 1966, Ronning and Paul Martin spoke at a conference on international affairs held in Banff, Alberta. Ronning's missions had been front-page news across Canada during the spring as Canadians hoped for their success. In late summer, Ronning was still smarting from the treatment he had received from the US State Department. Technically, his lips were sealed and he did not raise the subject in his formal presentation, but he gave vent to his feelings during the informal receptions. It was an opportunity to observe the master of diplomacy in action. He spoke to every one of the participants individually, divulging, for their ears only, the reason why his missions had failed. Each person left the room carrying a secret, which each thought to be his alone, told to him in confidence by Chester Ronning. Later, when details of the missions became the subject of broader discussion, he was able to turn to friends and say, "I knew that. Chester Ronning told me in confidence some time ago."[21]

In a speech at the University of Calgary,[22] seventeen months after he left Hanoi on his second mission, Ronning outlined what, in his view, had to be done to end the Vietnam conflict. "I suggest," he said, "that the issues in Asia are not democracy versus totalitarianism, free enterprise versus communism, or any other of the cold war clichés. The issue of today and tomorrow is the haves versus the have-nots. That issue can be solved only by intelligent economic measures not by war." He then outlined a number of steps to end the Vietnam conflict and avoid any thoughts of inevitable war with China. The first was to end the bombing, followed by direct talks between the belligerents to agree on an overall ceasefire. Third, was a decision on the dynamics of a preliminary peace conference.

> Finally, a conference attended by the four delegations engaged in the fighting plus delegations from the great powers and other powers concerned such as the members of the international commission, would draw up an agreement guaranteeing the sovereignty, independence and territorial integrity of Vietnam and its neutrality, if that is the desire of the Vietnamese themselves. Internal matters must be left to the decision of the people of Vietnam without foreign intervention.

Ronning's advice was not taken, and the war carried on with immense destruction, loss of life, and attendant misery, until 27 January 1973, when talks in Paris between Henry Kissinger and Le Duc Tho called for a ceasefire, an end to the fighting, and the peaceful reunification of Vietnam under an agreement supervised by an international commission. Little more than two years later, the North Vietnamese forces of Ho Chi Minh entered Saigon, taking control of the whole country.

No one knows what would have happened had the United States taken Ronning's 1966 missions seriously, but at least two key policymakers later stated that they wished they had. In his memoir, *On the Front Lines of the Cold War*, Seymour Topping recounts an incident after Ronning had passed away:

Audrey and I happened to meet Bill Bundy at a reception...He told us he had felt guilty for a long time about how he had dealt with Ronning and handled his report when he met with him that June night in Ottawa. He said he should have given more weight to the proposal that Ronning had brought back from Hanoi. He had wanted to apologize to Ronning, but since that was not possible, he was glad that he could at least express his regrets to Audrey.[23]

In his book, *In Retrospect*, Robert McNamara, the former US Secretary of Defense under Lyndon Johnson, and super-hawk on Vietnam, states: "In retrospect, we were mistaken in not having Ronning at least probe the meaning of Pham Van Dong's words more deeply."[24] Much too late did hubris give way to common sense.

# Unfinished Business

Now a private citizen, Ronning was free to engage in the debates over Vietnam and the questions of the recognition of China and its seating in the UN. He was outspoken on all of these issues. His missions to Hanoi had raised his profile to even higher international levels. The missions had failed, but Ronning was willing to talk about them, and how he believed the US had sabotaged his efforts. He turned a diplomatic defeat into a public relations victory. Students at Canadian and American universities courted him. He took part in teach-ins and debates. Through television and radio interviews, he reached the broader public. Invited to Geneva for Pacem in Terris II,[1] 9–14 July 1967, he advocated a permanent international peacekeeping force for the UN. He and Inga combined their trip to Geneva with visits to Oslo, Paris, and London. It was their last major trip together, for Inga passed away in Camrose on 27 October 1967.

Following the death of his beloved Inga Marie, Ronning returned, almost obsessively, to finishing the tasks of China and Vietnam, perhaps as a way of dealing with his grief. While still in government service, he was not alone among Department of External Affairs (DEA) diplomats in thinking that Canada should recognize China and challenge Washington to do the same, but it was Ronning—the late-harvested diplomat—who appeared to take the issue most personally. He never missed a chance to discuss China and he never lost sight of "the fallacious analysis" upon which American policy was based. Even his posting to Norway in 1954 provided opportunities because Norway had recognized China. Moreover, it was from Oslo that he attended the Geneva conferences on Korea and Indochina that had enabled him to renew his contacts with Chou En-lai and other Chinese diplomats. Oslo was not an exile from China matters. Then, Ronning's final posting to India landed him in the thick of Asian diplomacy.

An engaging, loquacious man, of optimism and good humour, Ronning was able to charm people like Mike Pearson, Paul Martin, Chou En-lai, Averell Harriman, John Kenneth Galbraith, and even John Diefenbaker. Ronning and Nehru admired each other, but he could not win over—not that he tried much—John Foster Dulles or Dean Rusk, who saw him as an emotional preacher who was pro-peasant revolutions. He brought hope to those in Canada who advocated recognition of the People's Republic of China, while to its opponents he was "a Communist" and "a China lover," blind to the real threat. While his views were often unpopular, particularly in the United States, Ronning had an impact through his son-in-law Seymour Topping, a key figure writing for the *New York Times*. Topping was with Ronning in Nanking in April 1949 when the People's Liberation Army took that city, and later he covered the 1954 and the 1961–62 Geneva conferences.[2]

By 1964, when Ronning retired from the DEA, the tide of public opinion in Canada had begun to run in favour of recognizing Peking. While opinion in Quebec remained negative, reflecting the influence of Rome, in western Canada the grain sales to China, beginning in 1960, prodded the question: If they are good enough to trade with, why don't we recognize them? Even the sensational reporting, in the latter half of the 1960s, of the sensational events of the Cultural Revolution did not destroy the predominant view that Chiang Kai-shek was not, and was not likely ever again to be, the ruler of China. The frustration for Ronning was that the step was not taken; the main hold-up was the United States, which was repeating in Vietnam the mistakes it had made in China. The fact that Peking was in charge of China, apart from Taiwan, was inescapable.

Ronning threw himself into the battle of the campus teach-ins to add his weight to the general urge to point out to the American administration the error of its ways. His peace missions to Vietnam made him even more sought after as a speaker; he became the darling of late 1960s campus activists. He spoke at universities and colleges on both sides of the US-Canada border. They gave him a lofty platform from which to continue his education of the North American public on the China issue. The story of his life was told in a variety of forms in newspapers throughout North America, with some reports in the United States emphasizing that he was really of American origin, giving him greater credibility as a critic. Senator William Fulbright approached him looking for angles of attack on the Vietnam issue, and he was embraced (figuratively) by John Diefenbaker, who, judging from his words uttered in Parliament, looked upon Ronning as a dove of peace that might be dispatched from time to time, if only old "Noah" Pearson could see things more clearly. Thus, Ronning, a socialist, previously sheathed in the neutral armour of a diplomat, was given a platform by the Liberal Cabinet, and was applauded by the Conservative opposition. He became a catalyst for Canadian anti-American feeling over the Vietnam War. In return, he used the opportunity to direct attention to the real issue behind it all, the correct perception of China.[3]

Ronning made his views on China clear at Banff in the late summer of 1965. It was a message he would repeat in the next half-dozen years.

It disturbs me therefore to see that we continue year after year to support an Asian policy which was based on a fallacious analysis of developments, particularly in China. To deal effectively with the problems of the Far East we must have an understanding of the causes, which produced the present situation in Asia, and our policies must be based on correct analyses of historical facts, not fantasies.[4]

In the fall of 1966, Ronning set out on an exhausting speaking tour, giving public lectures at the University of Alberta,[5] addressing teach-ins at Toronto and McGill, and speaking at the University of Calgary and to United Nations associations, foreign relations groups, and service clubs from Montreal to Victoria. In January 1968, he gave the convocation address at St. Olaf College, Northfield, Minnesota, arguing for an independent Chinese policy for the United States, free of Vietnam. He prefaced his remarks with the comment that he was "speaking as a Canadian about a situation that is at least partially Canada's affair...My hopes are for a new Western policy of co-existence with China."[6] In July that year, he took his message to the annual Couchiching conference on current issues, at Geneva Park on the shores of Lake Couchiching in Ontario. Whether he sat on a platform with Senator Edward Kennedy or stood before the Camrose Lions Club, he treated every listener as a possible convert. He felt that the issue of China was too important and that it had been left too long in the hands of an elite of policy-makers.

Ronning addressed thousands of people during these years, but he had a wide audience as well through the press. Articles relating to Vietnam, but ultimately to China, appeared in newspapers throughout North America. Moreover, he was well received by reporters and columnists on both sides of the border. Charles Lynch, a senior columnist for the Southam News chain in Canada, called him the most remarkable man in the DEA, and remained a loyal supporter throughout the years.[7] To John R. Walker, a commentator and columnist on foreign affairs, Ronning was the Canadian government's "best old China Hand," and Frederick Nossal, who had served as a correspondent in Peking, noted that Ronning was "one of the few Canadian career diplomats who has come out openly to support recognition of Peking."[8] In the *Washington Post*, David Kraslow said that Ronning was "considered one of the ablest Asia hands in the Western World."[9] Back in Alberta, the *Edmonton Journal* dubbed Ronning "this quiet Albertan" and followed his progress with admiration.[10]

Ronning's extraordinary activity generally brought favourable editorial comment and good press coverage. He was a newsmaker,

Ronning addressing convocation, University of Alberta, May 1965. [Ronning/Cassady photo collection]

but it would be wrong to imply that he was universally liked and that his message was always accepted. John Kettle, who had earlier asked the question, "Is Canada helping Red China to conquer the world?" attacked Ronning and others in an article in *Canada Month* entitled, "The Great Canada–Red China Love-fest."[11] Back in Camrose, he received letters denouncing him as a communist, but these were small voices compared to the general acclaim he received. Late in 1967, the *Montreal Star* endorsed his views as those of a man "not driven by blind emotionalism."[12]

In the spring of 1968, Pierre Elliot Trudeau, the new Liberal prime minister of Canada, declared that the recognition of China was on his agenda. Clearly, Ronning was in harmony with the thinking of the new leader. Audiences now asked him to be more precise. What was to happen to Taiwan? The Ronning solution was for Canada to recognize only those parts of China over which the government in Peking had control. Taiwan, he said, was a question that would be settled in the fullness of time.[13] His efforts helped to alert Canadians to a change in Canada's policy toward China. His arguments carried a great deal of weight with Trudeau and with his foreign policy advisor, Ivan Head, a fellow Albertan, with whom Ronning talked about China policy during their frequent meetings in Alberta, and when Ronning visited Ottawa. On 13 October 1970, in the midst of a major crisis in the province of Quebec, Minister for External Affairs Mitchell Sharp announced that Canada and China had exchanged instruments of mutual recognition. Ronning was ecstatic.[14] The business left undone in June 1950 was finally completed. He had no hope of being ambassador, but he could now return to the land of his birth to be greeted by Premier Chou En-lai as an old friend. Moreover, Canada had taken the step before the United States.

Ronning welcomed his friend Huang Hua as the first ambassador of China to Canada. Shortly thereafter, on 25 October 1971, when China was at last seated in the United Nations, Ronning phoned Huang in Ottawa to congratulate him. Huang was appointed that November to the United Nations as the People's Republic of China's first representative. Chang Wen-chin,[15] another old friend of Ronning's, replaced Hua in Ottawa.

Huang Hua offered this assessment of the background to recognition:

Looking back, it is not difficult to see how much courage and resolution Trudeau had in putting forward this idea against the international backdrop of that time, which showed he was far-sighted.

Then he turned to those who deserve some credit as well.

In the course of promoting the establishment of diplomatic relations, some other Canadians also made contributions, such as
Foreign Minister Sharp, senior former diplomats Chester Ronning
and James Endicott [sic],[16] as well as some Canadian-Chinese and
overseas Chinese residing in Canada, and other personages from
different walks of life.

He next explained his relations with Ronning:

I was most familiar with Ronning. In April 1949, while I was working in the foreign affairs office in Nanking he was the Westerner I
was in touch with most frequently....[H]e has a deep affection for
the Chinese people.[17]

With Canada's recognition of China, one might think Ronning
was content, but this would be failing to take into account his
American dimension. There remained the question of American
recognition of China, not to mention peace in Vietnam. Ronning
was regarded by some senior Americans outside the government,
like Averell Harriman and John Kenneth Galbraith, as a wise head on
Asian policy. He had already played a role in undermining the foundations of Cold War policy. In March 1969, the National Committee
on United States–China Relations sponsored a first national conference on "The United States and China: The Next Decade." Held in
New York City, it attracted some 2,500 people. Ronning was one of
the three Canadian contributors.[18] The conference took place when
the new Richard Nixon administration was relaxing restrictions on

trade and communications with China. After reminding the audience that the United States had never used troops to interfere in China's internal affairs, Ronning called for the US to begin trade with the People's Republic of China in nonstrategic goods and to welcome its correspondents.

Ronning regularly answered the call to comment on events in Indochina, making speech after speech, advocating ways of finding peace for Vietnam. He condemned the American bombing of Cambodia in May 1970 and he could be counted on for comments on the progress of the war throughout that year.[19] In February 1971, he "loosed another blast at United States policy toward Communist China," as he testified before the Canadian Senate Committee on Foreign Affairs.[20] Early in 1971, he was news in the United States, courtesy of the *New York Times*, not to mention in Canada where Ronning's opinions and pictures spread from coast to coast, particularly in the *Globe and Mail*, which had its own correspondent in Peking. In April, he returned to China at the invitation of Premier Chou En-lai. It was a joyous homecoming and his impressions and observations received wide circulation in the Canadian and American press.

In addition, a film, *A Journey Forward*, was made of his trip for showing on Canadian television.[21] The event was newsworthy in itself: Ronning, the old China Hand, who had made the recognition of China his own personal crusade, was going home. Moreover, it was a chance to glimpse the People's Republic of China in what appeared to be a period of post-Cultural Revolution calm. It was more than a Canadian story. Audrey (Ronning) Topping accompanied her father, becoming one of the first American reporters to have access to Communist China. Ronning's interviews with Chou En-lai became an Audrey Topping exclusive in words and photos. As a bonus, Seymour Topping, an old China Hand in his own right, received a visa on behalf of the *New York Times*. Moreover, in June 1971, the *New York Times* began to publish the *Pentagon Papers*,[22] in which Ronning's missions to Hanoi received renewed attention. Then came the drama of Henry Kissinger's arrival in Peking in July to explore the possibilities of a visit to China by President Nixon.

Critics of America's China policy were dangerously close to becoming the establishment.[23]

In June and July 1971, amid the publicity and flurry of stories about his impressions of the new China, Ronning was given space for two stories in the *New York Times*: "China's 700 Million Are on the Way" and "After Mao What?"[24] Following the release of the film of his trip in October 1971, he appeared once again in the *New York Times*, this time with a picture–Ronning at the feet of a huge white statue of Chairman Mao.[25] In January 1972, as President Nixon prepared for his February trip to Peking for an historic meeting with Mao Tse-tung, Ronning's article, "Understanding Chou Enlai," appeared in the *Boston Sunday Globe*.[26]

Ronning's impact upon American thinking is very difficult–if not impossible–to assess, but, for an outsider, his views received great attention. In March 1973, he was called as a witness for the defence in the trial of Daniel Ellsberg and Anthony Russo for leaking the *Pentagon Papers*. Ronning told the jammed Los Angeles courtroom that his missions to Hanoi were no longer secret by the time the *Pentagon Papers* were leaked in 1971, but he took time to describe the purpose and outcome of his trips to Hanoi and how a State Department leak had severely damaged his chances of success. His testimony was splashed across the front pages of papers throughout the United States.[27] He was now being pressed to write his memoirs, a task he undertook with some reluctance but in the hope it would lead to a better understanding of China.[28] His old friend, Alfred Knopf, published them in 1974. Ronning's *A Memoir of China in Revolution* was the only book on China policy by a Canadian to be published in the United States during this period.

Following the Shanghai communiqué of 28 February 1972 at the end of Nixon's visit to China, Ronning became less and less a critic of America's China policy and more and more an advocate for the new China. His message was made more compelling by his ability to compare the old China with the new. His lectures drew large crowds. His audiences were mainly sympathetic, but, because the North American thirst for China was being slaked by others with differing perspectives, his view was increasingly looked upon as too rosy. Among his harsher critics were his fellow Albertans. Late in November 1974, he spoke at the University of Alberta following a film on China, *The East Is Red*, which praised the Communist revolution and its accomplishments. Wrote one local reporter:

> In the audience, the most conservative could not shake the uneasiness wrought by the made-in-China film. Not one of them would stand a chance in a hand-to-hand showdown with the terrible tykes, harbingers of a "yellow peril" if there ever was one.[29]

The publication of his *Memoir of China* in 1974 only brought Ronning more criticism. "A hodge podge from Ronning," said Charles Taylor, a former Peking correspondent for the *Globe and Mail*, while Peter Worthington in the *Toronto Sun* called it "a frivolous book...of rather mundane anecdotes and trivia."[30] Dean Emeritus E.H. Soward of the University of British Columbia in the *Vancouver Sun* was kinder, and John Kiely of the *Kitchener-Waterloo Record* was generally favourable but advised readers to skip the Korea sections.[31] Christopher Young in the *Ottawa Citizen* called Ronning "Canada's most eminent China-watcher and China-lover." Young found little excuse for Ronning, "suggesting that freedom of religion exists in today's China, or for the implication that the typical worker's family has a flush toilet."[32] An anonymous reviewer in the *Meunster Prairie Messenger* made the perceptive observation that the book revealed two Chester Ronnings: the historian and the nostalgic grey-haired grandfather.[33] Alberta reviewers were more demanding. Steve Hume of the *Edmonton Journal* set out the standard by which he judged Ronning:

> Diplomats as the instruments by which governments communicate, are at times a paradoxical union of elegant and harsh and nitty-gritty reality; of the polished actor and the cool efficient analyst; of the elaborate ruse and the blunt ultimatum...Far from being the impartial observer, [Ronning] has long been a participant in a love-affair.[34]

Brian Brennan of the *Calgary Herald* wanted something more substantial:

> [I]nstead of providing us with the literary equivalent of a 15-course feast at the Pan Hsi Restaurant, Kwangchow, Dr. Ronning has served us something akin to the luncheon special at Joe Wong's Fine Eats. An hour after reading the book one is left with a distinct feeling of unfulfilment.[35]

Ronning's memoir fared generally better abroad. In Britain, Richard Harris gave it a serious review in the *China Quarterly*. In the United States, however, R.F. Swanson in the *New York Times* dismissed it in a three-book review as "one of those 'contributions to a better understanding' volumes," after telling his readers: "The fact is, Canada is not of overwhelming importance in the scheme of things, except to Canadians." Ronning's anti-Americanism and his "ideological blinders" put off another reviewer. R.M. Seaton in the *Coffeyville Journal* observed:

> Ronning remembers running barefoot during many happy days in the mountains with Chinese boys who herded cattle—"We enjoyed squishing fresh green cow dung between our toes to flatten it out for quick drying"—I think a little of that stuff may have seeped into the pages of this book.

Others, however, from the *Washington Post* to the *Los Angeles Times*, to the *Fresno Bee*, were more sympathetic, characterizing Ronning as understanding rather than high-handed, and saw in his career an American might-have-been. Several reviewers made the point that a Ronning could not have escaped the McCarthyite backlash in the United States.[36]

Ronning's *Memoir of China* was compiled mainly in New York, Hong Kong, and Camrose while he was involved in a round of lectures, travel, and interviews. As a speaker, he had the engaging habit of tantalizing his audiences with hints of secrets yet to be revealed.

Many Canadians looked forward to the book, some in the hope that those ultimate revelations would provide some further evidence to advance a favourite argument either for or against the formulation, direction, and execution of Canadian foreign policy. For them, it was a disappointment. It raised more questions about the recollections of the author than it settled outstanding problems. The book made more sense, however, within the American context. Published in the United States, it carried Ronning's familiar message to the American public, where it did have an impact. He made it clear that his purpose was to further the understanding of China, and his view was that the United States had the greater need.

One cannot deny that Ronning's views about the new China were overly enthusiastic. This was partly because his standard for comparison was the China of the 1920s and the late 1940s and partly because of the euphoria he experienced on returning home after such a long absence. He often confused the ideal, described to him by Chou En-lai and others, with the broader, harsher reality. Indeed, as a guest of the premier of China, he travelled under special circumstances, and, wherever he went, the word that he was a special guest of the highest order preceded him. He was honest in reporting what he saw, but what he saw did not apply generally, and was often unique or experimental. Moreover, he was predisposed to the system that the Communist Party had developed.

As a social democrat who knew the hopelessness of the old system in China, Ronning was thrilled to see what had been achieved. He attributed most of the major changes to the efforts of Chou En-lai than to those of Mao Tse-tung. Nevertheless, one should not dismiss Ronning's views of the new China as naive. He was familiar enough with the personalities and qualifications of the Chinese leadership to be aware of the intraparty struggles, and he had experienced some of the system's sharp edges. If he erred in being too positive, it might have been to overcome what he knew to be the negative picture that remained popular in North America. Others who went to China during the initial honeymoon period of Canada–China and US–China relations reinforced many of Ronning's views. There was so much to discover and most generalizations could not be thoroughly tested.

Including the Hanoi missions, his trips to China, the *Pentagon Papers*, his lectures, articles in newspapers, television specials, and his book, Ronning was before the North American public for nearly a decade—a rigorous retirement for someone who gave up active diplomatic service at age seventy. It was the finale of a career that had become inextricably entwined with one issue: the recognition of the People's Republic of China as an independent regime based in Peking. For him, the issue went beyond Canada's acceptance of his view to the greater need for the United States, the home of so much of his family, to recognize the error of its ways. He pursued the China question with a singleness of purpose that at times appeared similar to his father's zeal for spreading the gospel. Like Christian in *The Pilgrim's Progress*, a book he admired greatly, he bore a burden—the recognition of China. It was with noticeable relief and joy that he greeted American recognition of China in January 1979 and laid his burden down.[37]

According to Liao Dong, Rev. James G. Endicott, in an interview with him, recalled a conversation with Ronning in the early 1950s in which Ronning said, "you work from the outside and I will work from the inside" for the recognition of China.[38] Yet, it was only when Ronning worked outside that he achieved the results he wanted, but, even outside, he bore the presumed stamp of approval from the DEA. He would sometimes tell audiences that unlike diplomats from other countries, Canadian envoys had complete freedom to express their opinions to their home government, regardless of whether it was in line with official political thinking of the party in government. However, it is unlikely that his listeners believed he was straying too far from official thinking. He was not only seen to have the support of the Liberal Cabinet in 1966, but, when it was later rumoured that he had lost its support because he had been too outspoken, John Diefenbaker rushed to his rescue.[39]

12

# Returning Home

Ronning's second mission to Hanoi took place one month after the
first stirrings of the Cultural Revolution in Peking on 16 May 1966.
During the next two years, the movement spread throughout China
with a great destructive attack on Chinese tradition and with devastating impact upon intellectuals and party leaders. At the University of
Calgary, on 15 November 1967, in a major speech entitled "Is the West
Drifting to Inevitable War with China?" Ronning warned his audience of the real possibility of a broadening of the Vietnam War into a
wider nuclear conflict. Then he expressed his views on the politics of
China and the Cultural Revolution, which was in its second year. He
acknowledged the serious outbreaks of violence in China involving
rampaging Red Guards, teenagers encouraged by Mao to make revolution and to destroy old traditions.

> The total destruction of property and loss of life has, however,
> perhaps not been greater than that experienced during similar
> disturbances in some highly developed nations of the West...The
> conclusion that China is in the throes of a civil war is based, I fear,
> on wishful thinking.

He went on to explain that schools were closed at times for students to work in order to counter the old tradition of the scholar-officials who never undertook manual labour.

> Tendencies amongst educated Chinese to revert to anything remotely reminiscent of these aspects of old traditions are classed by today's revolutionaries as counterrevolutionary. Schools are therefore periodically closed. Students are sent out to work with the peasants on the soil, to factories to experience life with industrial laborers, and to the ranks of the Red Guards to obtain para-military training.

Further, he said:

> What makes sense to the Chinese may be ridiculous for those who have less knowledge of how reactionary the old order was in China and how determined modern Chinese leaders are to eradicate the tenacious old tendencies, including the corruption which brought down the former Nationalist regime.

Then he added:

> There have been colossal mistakes in the trial-and-error efforts to industrialize China, and it may be that similar mistakes are being experienced in the feverish tempo of the Cultural Revolution movement. The Chinese, however, are capable of absorbing even disastrous results of such experiments.

Turning to the topic of his lecture and the possibility of the Vietnam War spreading, he commented:

> I have learned from my conversation with many influential Chinese, during the past few years, that they are certain China will sooner or later be involved in a war with the United States....The

十

涼山在前进

Cultural Revolution (1966–76) poster stressing modernization in the countryside.
[Evans private collection]

certainty in the minds of the Chinese that they will be involved is
the chief cause for the urgency to keep up the tempo of the revolution to unify and strengthen the nation for the anticipated struggle.

Casting his mind back to the Korean War and the Chinese entry into
that conflict in 1950, he said that, at that time,

The Chinese welcomed war with the U.S. even if it would mean
aerial bombardment of China. Today they are more cautious
because they are uncertain of Russian support.[1]

Ronning returned to China with members of his family four times
in the fourteen years that remained to him, in 1971, 1973, 1975, and,
finally, in 1983. Each time he visited places he had not seen before, as
well as those with which he was familiar. The first two visits were on
the invitation of Chou En-lai. Ronning had hoped to return to China
at the time of recognition in late 1970, but his trip was delayed. He had
defended the idealism of the changes proposed at the outset of the
Cultural Revolution in 1966 and he did not give much weight to the
sensational reports about it. In his *Memoir of China*, he gave his reasons for wanting to go back to China.

> I suppose everyone is nostalgic about his place of birth. It was
> twenty years since I had closed the Canadian Embassy in Nanking,
> forty-four years since I had been in Fancheng. There was, how-
> ever, a much more important reason for wanting to revisit China.
> I wanted to find out for myself what truth there was in some of the
> reports of newspapermen and China-watchers. Had the Chinese
> really all been regimented and were they hopelessly brainwashed?
> Had they completely lost their sense of humour? Could they no
> longer laugh? Did they never have fun? Did they have no differ-
> ences? Did they all look alike, talk alike, walk alike, dress alike,
> and think alike? Were they colourless and drab and uninterest-
> ing? Had they become a race of faceless robots controlled by
> ruthless masters?[2]

In general, the timing for the trip appeared good. The most destructive phase of the Cultural Revolution (1966–68) was over and the Red
Guards, Mao's young heroes, were ordered to make revolution in the
far frontiers of China. The Communist Party met in the spring of
1969 and declared the Great Revolution for the Establishment of a
Proletarian Culture to be over. Further, it enshrined in its constitution
that Lin Piao (Biao), the Defence Minister, was to be Mao's chosen
successor. China appeared to be stable once again.

Ronning arrived in China in mid-April 1971, around the time
the new Canadian Embassy opened in Peking under Ambassador

Ralph Collins, whom Ronning knew as a child in 1922 in Peking. Accompanied by two of his daughters, Audrey (Topping) and Sylvia (Cassady), Ronning explored the Canton region, making his way north to Peking prior to visiting Fancheng. His party arrived in the capital on May Day and they were invited to have tea with Chou En-lai later that afternoon. Chou's "eyes sparkled as he grasped my father's hand, and welcomed him back to China," wrote Audrey, who captured the reunion in words and in award-winning photos.

> The Premier and Dad, whom Chou often referred to as his *lao pengyou* (old friend) reminisced about their various meetings in former days. Then Dad said that if his *lao pengyou* would come to Canada, he would personally cook Chou a Chinese meal there.[3]

Chou chided Ronning for retiring from the Canadian diplomatic service, and when Ronning countered that he had retired at age seventy, five years beyond the mandatory age of retirement, Chou commented that he was seventy-three and saw no reason to retire. He thought he and Ronning should be treated as exceptions. Later, he took Ronning to the top of Tiananmen to view the fireworks and to introduce him to Mao Tse-tung, who, Ronning later commented, had a very limp handshake. Later, Ronning told his daughters that he "had been wild with excitement, not only at the fireworks display but also at the sight of the hundreds of thousands of people in Tiananmen Square. In them, he said, he could feel the presence of a new power."[4]

Four days later, Chou invited Ronning and his daughters to dinner at the Great Hall. Also present were Ronning's friends from the diplomatic corps: Huang Hua, Chang Wen-chin (Zhang Wenjin), and Chiao Kuan-hua (Qiao Guanhua). What follows is part of Audrey's description of the evening:

> The Premier escorted us to a scrumptious-looking round table set with blue and white porcelain, ivory chopsticks, three wineglasses at each place and an exotic display of sliced ancient eggs, spiced chicken, bean curd and other cold dishes.

Tea with Chou En-lai, Beijing, May 1971. [Ronning/Cassady photo collection]

He turned to Dad. "Now, there will be no protocol," he said. "We will sit according to the old Chinese custom where the honored guests sit opposite the host. These younger people don't remember the gracious old customs as we do."

We sat down and Chou raised his glass of Mou-t'ai in a toast. "Let us drink to old friendships," he said. *Moutai* is a white liquor made of sorghum, the waters of the Mou Tai river and fireworks....

Premier Chou looked relaxed, extremely handsome and much younger than his seventy-three years. A beautiful girl in her early twenties with long braids brought in a steaming dish of baby shrimps with king crab meat and Chou said it was from the province of Hubei. Then he introduced Dad to the girl, who was also from Hubei. Chou was delighted when Dad talked to her in her native dialect. He threw his head back and laughed like a little boy who had sprung a pleasant surprise.

Dad and the Premier began to talk about their hometowns, which happen to be in neighboring provinces, and before long they were exchanging old Chinese jokes and riddles. The riddles are asked in rhyming, almost singsong Chinese, and when Dad asks them he sounds like an old Chinese opera singer, which is much funnier than the riddle itself. Qiao Guanhua, the vice-foreign minister, a tall, charming man Dad had known for years, laughed so hard I began to worry. In English the riddles lose their wit, but here is an example of one Dad asked: "What is a golden ax with a silver handle?"

Everyone pondered and repeated the riddle. The Premier of China assumed a look of mock concern as if he were solving a great world problem. He conferred with his top advisers and darted glances at the gray-haired foreigner who sat grinning across the table.

Then they gave up. "What is it?" asked Chou.

"A bean sprout!" roared Dad, filling the room with fiendish laughter.

"Now here's another," he said gleefully, and sang out: "there was an old man of eighty-eight whose whiskers grew in before his teeth. What is it?"

More pondering. This was a very serious question. Finally Huang Hua looked triumphant,

"Corn on the cob!" he said victoriously.

"Right," said Dad. "Good for you!" But he looked disappointed. Meanwhile something was brewing in Chou Enlai's corner.

"All right now," Chou said, looking like Charlie Chan. "I'll give you one: What is green and red and lies between two slabs of white jade?"

The more Dad puzzled the brighter Chou became. Sylvia tried to come to Dad's rescue.

"A lettuce and tomato sandwich," she volunteered.

Chou shook his head and laughed. "No!" he said, looking pleased as Punch. "It's a stuffed bun."

We raised our glasses in a *kan-pei* (bottoms up) to the winners.

Several delicious courses followed and talk became more serious. Chou Enlai explained the development of the Sino-Soviet
ideological split in intriguing detail while we enthusiastically con-
sumed sugar pea shoots with elephants' ears (black wood fungus),
hot bamboo tipped in chicken fat, steamed rice sticks stuffed with
gingered meat and a dish called Lion's Head in Amber Sauce which
looked suspiciously like my homemade meat balls and gravy but
did not taste like it.

We raved so much about the Eight Heavenly Flavors dessert that
the Premier had the cook write out the ingredients and explain how
to make it...

After dinner the Premier graciously conceded to Sylvia's and
my bourgeois request that he autograph our menus. Later he took
Dad to see the Hubei room, having recalled where it was situated,
and presented him with pictures of it—to remember, he said, this
evening with an old friend. Then Chou wished Dad good luck and
fair weather for his journey back home to Hupei.[5]

Remarkably, the evening meeting took place when the superficial
calm of Chinese politics was about to be broken and the battles of the
Cultural Revolution renewed. The Chinese Communist Party teetered
on the brink of a major crisis, for soon Lin Piao (Biao), Mao's chosen
successor, attempted to seize power in a coup. There were rumours of
a plot named "571," which stood for "May 1971," but was also a homo-
phone for "armed uprising." By later official accounts, Lin had made
a number of attempts to assassinate Mao. When his intrigues were
uncovered in September, Lin, along with his son Lin Li-guo, an air
force officer, fled toward Russia in a military Trident jet that crashed in
Mongolia outside China, killing them both.[6]

Heading south, the Ronning party visited Shihchiachuang
(Shijiazhuang), the city where Norman Bethune is buried, and later
travelled to Fancheng. As previously noted, Ronning's return to his
birthplace was filmed for a television special, *A Journey Forward*. He
looked for his mother's grave but could not find it. Instead, he rededi-
cated the monument commemorating Hannah Rorem, originally

Ronning in front of school started by his mother in Fancheng, May 1971. [Ronning/ Cassady photo collection]

raised by his father, in the Hung wen schoolyard. He was agog with the changes in Fancheng, the new districts and the fine factories. The visit triggered memories of his youth, and he was able to find old timers to share them with. The locals were intrigued by his Hupei accent, and, in one case, an elderly lady was puzzled enough to ask how it was he spoke like a local but looked like a foreigner. Typically, Ronning assured her, "I have spent so much time abroad, I have begun to look like them."[7] After a visit of five weeks, Ronning returned to Canada. His journey to his birthplace received extensive coverage in North American newspapers and on television.

Ronning's trip in the fall of 1973 did not receive as much publicity. Nixon's visit to China in February 1972 had quenched some of the great

American thirst for information on China, and Canadians were growing used to the increasing number of reports from travellers exploring the limited number of places open to foreign tourists. Also, Ronning's travels coincided in part with the state visit of Prime Minister Pierre Trudeau to commemorate the third anniversary of the establishment of Canada–China relations on 13 October 1970. Moreover, his visit coincided with a major struggle within the top ranks of the Chinese Communist Party. Lin Piao's (Lin Biao's) treachery exposed a festering wound, the mark of a rupture between Cultural Revolution zealots, championed by Chiang Ch'ing (Jiang Qing), Mao's wife (later the leader of the infamous Gang of Four), and moderate pragmatic modernizers under Chou En-lai. The split became public after a meeting of the Central Committee in August 1973, with the launch of a campaign to "Criticize Lin Piao and Confucius" (the latter meaning Chou En-lai). Despite this struggle, the affairs of state proceeded as scheduled. Ronning, meanwhile, was content to travel to parts of China he had never seen before, in this case, Inner Mongolia. He wrote:

> The highlight of my trip in 1973 was without doubt a visit to Inner Mongolia, perhaps because the grasslands, where Mongolians ride and round up cattle and horses just like Western cowboys, were so much like the rolling hills of Grande Prairie in Alberta before they became fields of wheat and fescue.[8]

Trudeau was but one in a series of foreign leaders visiting China that summer and fall. Like the others, he met with Mao Tse-tung. In his case, it was on the afternoon of 13 October 1973, the previously mentioned third anniversary of the announcement of recognition. That evening, Trudeau hosted a banquet before preparing to travel south from Peking by late evening train in the company of Chou En-lai and Teng Hsiao-p'ing (commonly spelled today as Deng Xiaoping). Teng, who had served as general secretary to the Communist Party of China's Central Committee, was savagely attacked during the Cultural Revolution and then demoted, but he was brought back by Mao earlier in 1973 to assist Chou with the

Ronning in China, 1973. His Chinese name is to the right. [Evans private collection]

affairs of government. That same evening, Ronning, with his daughter Audrey and his granddaughter, were returning from their visit to Inner Mongolia. Chou En-lai made special arrangements for Trudeau and Ronning to meet at the station. Seymour Topping describes the preparations as told to him by Audrey:

We were back, arriving by train, from a cold two-week tour of Inner Mongolia and dad was wearing a coat lined with goat hair. We were met at the railway station by Chou Enlai and escorted into a guest room where Li Xiannian and Deng Xiaoping were waiting. Chou introduced Deng, a short, pale man of austere demeanor, as his great friend and colleague. We then were invited to take off our coats and pose for pictures. When dad took off his coat, we saw that the white goat hair of the coat's lining had come off on his dark Sun Yat-sen tunic. "Oh!" said Chou, "You can't meet your prime minister looking like that." Then Chou and Deng began brushing off the hair. This was the moment, of course, for Trudeau to walk in and embrace his fellow Canadian. When they parted, Trudeau and the Chinese were covered with goat hair. Everyone laughed so loudly that the security people standing outside the door were alarmed and dashed in.[9]

On this visit, Chou confided in Ronning that his health was not good and that this was likely the last time they would see each other. The state of the premier's health was a closely guarded secret; nonetheless, speculation abounded by the summer of 1974. By then, Chou had entered the Military Hospital 302 and worked from there for his remaining eighteen months of life.

Ronning's trips in 1971 and 1973 formed the basis for most of his controversial descriptions and his comments praising the transformation of modern China, recorded in his 1974 *Memoir of China*. He described the Great Leap Forward and the Commune Movement as successes that helped the country endure three years of bad harvests and natural disasters during 1959–61, without famine, and he discounted those "sheer madness" descriptions of the backyard furnace movement. Yet, by 1974, Chinese critiques of the Great Leap and of the communes were known, including the evidence of famine. Moreover, Chou En-lai himself had ordered the withdrawal of published statistics for the period because they represented objectives rather than actual achievements. It was also known that P'eng Te-huai (Peng Dehuai), the Defence Minister, had challenged Mao with his first-hand investigations of the countryside that showed the great suffering to the peasants caused by Mao's policies. It cost him his job. Ronning's uncritical comments diminished his standing in North America as a China expert.

Ronning returned to China in September 1975 with daughters Audrey and Meme and two grandchildren, intending to make a film on the Yangtze River and its gorges. He spent his formative years beside or near to the river and he wanted to express his feeling for it in a documentary film. It was also shortly after farmers near Sian (Xi'an) stumbled upon terracotta figures marking the third century BCE gravesite of Ch'in Shihuang-ti (Qin Shihuangdi), the first emperor of China. Audrey Topping scooped the world with an article in *National Geographic* on the find. Ronning's party arrived in Peking on 20 September and he requested to see Chou En-lai. His request was denied as were others he made when the group made periodic stops in Peking during the next two months of their travels. Deng Rong, Teng Hsiao-p'ing's daughter, describes Chou's situation at this time.

Zhou went through six major and eight minor operations. His condition deteriorated rapidly in September, as the cancer continued to spread. Wracked by pain, he showed no outward sign. His will was indomitable. Zhou Enlai faced death calmly. He gave orders as a fearless dialectic materialist.

"Don't keep my ashes after I die. Fertilize the fields with them, feed them to the fish."…

Near the end, Zhou's only concerns were the future of the Party and the country, the madness of the Gang of Four, and that truth had not yet prevailed over falsehood. The signs were ominous— the situation was deteriorating, his battle comrades were in great danger. Zhou was very worried.[10]

In November 1975, in Peking at the end of his trip, Ronning attempted again to see Chou. This time, Chou, desperately ill, was willing to see him, and secretly sent someone to escort him to the hospital, but security guards prevented Ronning and Audrey from leaving their hotel. After repeated denials, Ronning became angry and tried to shout his way out only to be stopped by a guard with a bayonet fixed on the end of his gun.[11] Since the summer of 1973, Chou had come under increasing attack from the Gang of Four. Even when he was on his deathbed, they showed him no mercy. Ronning left China without seeing Chou and in considerable doubt as to the future direction of the revolution he had so closely studied, and whose leaders he knew well, but he did not express his worries publicly.

Chou En-lai passed away on 8 January 1976, the beginning of a fateful year for China. Ten days later, Ronning, staying in Scarsdale, New York with the Toppings, expressed his feelings about Chou at the Congregational Church. It was a difficult assignment because Chou and Ronning had been genuinely fond of each other.[12] He talked of their thirty-year friendship and of Chou's accomplishments in transforming the old China. He paid tribute to Chou's wife, Teng Ying-chao (Deng Yingchao), and how important she was to Chou's survival and work. Then he commented on Chou's personal qualities; how he lacked personal ambition and devoted himself to his country. Chou En-lai

> was a warm hospitable and charming host. When members of my family dined with him each time we visited China, he talked to each of us, joked and laughed heartily as if he didn't have a care in the world and stayed up to all hours of the night. One midnight when I suggested that it was time for him to retire, he suddenly asked me if I had visited the Hupei Room in the Great Hall of the People. I had not. He immediately protested: You must see the room of your Province. I was promptly led off to see it. He took his time to talk about every painting and the significance of every piece of sculpture until long past midnight. He was particularly fond of my grandchildren and talked about the importance of young people.

Ronning spoke of Chou as an example to the younger generation in China and how the premier's death dealt a great blow to all the people of China. In Ronning's opinion, Chou was China's greatest statesman of the twentieth century and that "[i]t has become more necessary than ever for our 'one family world' that statesmen should have some of the qualities of Chou Enlai."[13]

After Chou's death, Ronning was kept busy with interviews and lectures on the internal situation in China. He was invited to give the Sproule Lecture at the University of Calgary on 4 March 1976. That evening, standing behind a low lectern and in front of a huge map of China, he addressed an overflow audience on the topic, "Where Is China Going?" He downplayed the idea that China would change following the death of Chou, or even when Mao died. He finished his address and returned to sit on his chair at centre stage. At this point, a student stood up and asked, "But Mr. Ronning, you have not answered the question: where is China going?" Ronning rose, stepped forward, leaned over the lectern, looked directly at the student, and replied with a grin, "I don't know!"[14] He was prescient.

On 30 August 1976, just ten days before Mao died, Ronning was in Gravenhurst, Ontario, to speak at the official opening of a museum of the house where Norman Bethune was born.[15] The house was a regular stop on the itinerary of Chinese official delegations visiting Canada. The Department of External Affairs had purchased it and turned it into a museum honouring Bethune. Ronning had prepared a text for delivery, but the Chinese delegation was late and the sun shone directly in Ronning's eyes when it was time for him to speak. Frustrated, he abandoned his notes and spoke of the Chinese revolution, ending his remarks in Chinese. At the close of the ceremony, he led the Chinese delegation on a tour of the house. Unfortunately, the other guests had picked the food tent clean, leaving little for Ronning and his guests when they exited the house.[16]

In China, 1976, the year of the Dragon, was fraught with change. After Chou's death, Teng Hsiao-p'ing, who was expected to take the premier's place, was demoted and removed from office once again. Mao appointed Hua Kuo-feng (Hua Guofeng), a virtual unknown, to run the country and to be his successor. In July, at Tangshan, near Peking, there was a disastrous earthquake; a traditional sign of a corresponding jolt to come in human affairs. The Gang of Four, led by Chiang Ch'ing, appeared triumphant in the ongoing struggle between the Maoists and the modernizers.[17] On 9 September 1976, when Mao died, they prepared to seize power.

While he was on firm ground in his praise of Chou, Ronning's tribute to Mao after the death of the "Great Helmsman" was problematic. In a widely published article,[18] he wrote:

> The people of China deeply mourn the loss in death of their highly-respected teacher, liberator and Chairman, Mao Zedong. They do not, however, mourn in despair. They have themselves participated enthusiastically in the prodigious efforts required to create a new China. They mourn, therefore, in gratitude to and praise for the first philosopher in the history of China who not only understood them but trusted them despite their illiteracy....For the people of China, Mao's type of socialism is providing an infinitely better life than the poverty, misery, disease, filth, hunger and starvation which characterized the life of the poor before the People's Republic of China was established in 1949. They are, therefore, determined to continue the revolution to modernize China.

He goes on to say that Mao

> deserves the credit for laying the foundation for a new socialist China and for working out a policy especially adapted to the needs of the people and which, therefore, captured the imagination of the masses who participated willingly and enthusiastically in the arduous labour involved. They also shared in reaching decisions regarding immediate objectives and the ways and means of attaining desired results. That was the secret of Mao's successes.
>
> Some Western observers conclude that the astounding achievements in China are possible only under the despotic rule of a totalitarian dictatorship. *Ipso facto*, China is a totalitarian dictatorship and Mao is the ruthless, despotic ruler. How completely and utterly wrong they are.

Later, Ronning agreed that errors, some of them serious, were made through Mao and his colleagues using a trial-and-error method:

The redeeming feature of the trial-and-error method is that errors are anticipated and, therefore, are more easily corrected....Mao Zedong has been falsely accused of wholesale, ruthless, mass executions, especially of landlords, when land was distributed to the peasants. The fact is that in many parts of China landlords were treated with relative benevolence....The numbers executed, however, have been grossly exaggerated.

Mao was severely criticized by foreign observers for the "Great Leap Forward" and the "Great Proletarian Cultural Revolution." Both of them had some bad effects in cities. In the rural areas, on the other hand, they caused no serious disturbances and, in the long run, both have had beneficial results. The Great Leap did raise agricultural production and the Cultural Revolution stopped the tendency of cadres to fall into the trap of becoming mandarins....

All of the secrets of Mao's successes in changing China were dependent on the basic principle of first changing the environment to make it conducive to better social behaviour.

Ronning's words were a gentle whitewashing of Mao at a time when his reputation was greatly damaged by the excesses of the Cultural Revolution (1966–76), which he had launched and directed. Yet, during the few weeks after Mao's death, Ronning was not alone in assuming the revolution, as fostered and fathered by Mao, would continue. Most China watchers bet on a collective leadership to follow Mao,[19] but more dramatic events were to come in late October, even as Ronning spoke before the Camrose Lions Club on the twenty-third. He assured his audience, "There is no possibility of diverting the program of Mao Tse-tung in China."[20] But, in mid-October 1976, Hua Kuo-feng gave orders to arrest the Gang of Four. Huge demonstrations soon took place throughout the country, cheering the fall of the Gang. Not long afterward, Teng Xiao-p'ing returned to power, ultimately to

Ronning and Tessie Wong, Canton (Guangzhou), 1971. [Sau W. Cheung private collection]

launch the reform program first proposed by Chou En-lai as far back as 1964. Although he continued to be honoured, Mao was rigorously criticized, particularly for the Great Leap Forward and the Cultural Revolution. He no longer enjoys the lofty status Ronning attributed to him, but Chou's reputation continues to grow.

Ronning did not live long enough to witness the changes wrought under Teng's leadership. Although Arthur Menzies thought that Ronning "would have supported this trend,"[21] one can only guess at what he would make of the current transformation of China, all set in

Ronning and Ambassador Wang Dong on the steps of his Camrose home, 1978. [Evans private collection]

train by the diminutive man who brushed goat hair off his suit on the night of 13 October 1973.

Back in Alberta, Ronning's home in Camrose became a place of pilgrimage for visitors from China, and a must stop for all Chinese students who came to study at the University of Alberta in Edmonton. Each ambassador to succeed Huang Hua called on Ronning in Camrose. Chang Wen-chin and Wang Dong appeared on the front page of the *Camrose Canadian*, photographed as they said farewell to Ronning on the steps of his house. Ronning, tall, distinguished, with

Ronning with Mayor William Hawrelak, Ministers Horst Schmid, Neil Crawford, and Al Adair of the Alberta government, and members of the Chinese Cultural Society, welcoming Chinese Ambassador Chang Wen-chin, Edmonton, 1974. [Ronning/ Cassady photo collection]

a shock of silver-white hair and sparkling eyes, had an inexhaustible fund of stories about modern China and its leaders. Everyone listened with rapt attention and delight. He recited Chinese rhymes from his childhood, along with sayings from his home province of Hupei. All who visited him knew they had met a great man. In 1967, he was among the first people named an Officer of the newly established Order of Canada. Five years later, he was made a Companion, Canada's highest civilian honour. It was followed a decade later by membership in the newly founded Alberta Order of Excellence, the province's highest civilian honour.

Ronning, greeted on his final trip home to China, Beijing, October 1983. [Ronning/ Cassady photo collection]

Ronning was a special guest at banquets and was much honoured in Canada and in the United States. Ronning was awarded innumerable honourary degrees, among them from the universities of Alberta, Calgary, Lethbridge, Simon Fraser, Waterloo, and, following in the footsteps of his father, from St. Olaf College in Minnesota. With so many doctorates, he was pleased to be called Dr. Ronning. He served on the senate of the University of Alberta, his alma mater, and he gave guest lectures on modern China to students in universities and high schools throughout the province. In 1980, the National Film Board of Canada released a film on his life called *China Mission*, directed by Tom Radford. It was two years in the making and Ronning was completely involved in its preparation. The film begins with scenes from a family reunion at Valhalla.

During the 1970s, Ronning continued to pursue the issue of an exit visa for Tessie Wong, the embassy receptionist and secretary left behind in Nanking in 1951. Tessie had been confined to the Nanking embassy until the building was sold in 1958, after which she was allowed to tend to her sick mother in Canton. Throughout this period, and later during the years of the Cultural Revolution, she was harassed and her home raided. Ronning raised the question of an exit visa for Tessie with Chou En-lai in 1971 and 1973, each time receiving assurance that a visa would be forthcoming, but it was not. He and his daughter Audrey visited her in Canton in 1973, and he raised the issue again in 1975 with Chiao Kuan-hua, and even Teng Xiao-p'ing, only again to be given assurance. Then came the events of 1976 and the demotion of Teng and later the forced retirement of Chiao Kuan-hua.[22] Only when Teng returned to power in 1977 was action taken regarding Tessie's exit visa. Then it was swift. She was given four days to leave the country, eventually reaching Canada and Camrose where she spent some months with Ronning and his family in 1978, before moving to Ottawa to take a job at the library of the Department of External Affairs. Two years later, Ronning gave her a copy of his *Memoir of China*, inscribed:

> To Tessie Wong in admiration for the manner in which she con-
> ducted herself during extremely tough times in China from 1951 to
> 1958. She became a citizen of Canada in 1980 and now works in the
> Library of External Affairs in Ottawa. Good Luck Tessie.[23]

Well into his eighties, Ronning continued to be generous with his time, giving numerous television and radio interviews and agree-ing to be questioned on tape about his political career as part of an oral history project. From May to September 1980, he agreed to be interviewed by me about his life, his views on China, his Hanoi missions, and a host of other topics. He paid his last visit to China in the fall of 1983, just as Teng's reforms began to take root. An old friend, Wang Bingnan (Wang Ping-nan), president of the Chinese

People's Association for Friendship with Foreign Countries (CPAFFC)
invited him and his six children to revisit China. Ronning had three
wishes: to see Fancheng and his mother's tomb; to visit the famous
Dunhuang Caves, and to see the Jiayu Pass at the west end of the
Great Wall. Although concerned over how well their father, whose
memory was not as sharp after a small stroke, could take the rigours
of the trip, Sylvia, Meme, Audrey, Kjeryn, and Alton and his wife
Avril agreed to accompany him. Liu Gengyin, who first met Ronning
at the 1961 Laos conference, and who in 1975 went with Ambassador
Chang Wen-chin to visit him in Camrose, was assigned to travel with
them in China. Liu's description of the visit is touching and worth
quoting in part.[24]

In mid-October 1983, on a fine day of autumn, Ronning arrived at
the Beijing Airport and his two daughters helped him walk down
[from] the plane. I welcomed him there. The old man was very
excited and hugged me immediately when we met, shouting out in
Chinese with his Hubei accent: "Here's back the old Hubei guy!"[25]

I took them to the Friendship Hotel of the CPAFFC and told
Ronning that the house had been used by Chiang Kai-shek before
1949. He was so surprised that without taking a rest he had a look
at every room. The next day, President Wang Bingnan entertained
Ronning and his party at the Great Hall of the People. The last time
they met was in 1961 at the Geneva conference, and after 20 odd
years, reunion was surely delightful for the two old friends. In his
toast, Wang Bingnan said to Ronning, "It is our honour that you
revisit China at such an advanced age of 89." Smiling, he replied, "I
am not sure if it is an honour that you put me up in the house which
used to be the residence of Chiang Kai-shek, your old opponent."
Wang burst into laughter saying, "We make such arrangement
because you are an old friend of the new as well as the old China."
His witty reply aroused laughter among all present.

Ronning numbered his children from one to six and made a roll
call before they set off every morning to see to it that no one was
absent. Then he would shout in Chinese, "March!"

He stayed in Beijing for 3 days mainly to meet his old friends. After that, I accompanied them to visit other cities. As Ronning had wished, we went to Xi'an, Dunhuang, Jiayu Pass, Lanzhou and Bingling Temple. He was very healthy and vigorous all through the trip and he told us many Chinese stories and puzzles.

While visiting the Dunhuang Caves, the old man looked at the ancient sculptures and mural paintings carefully. He told his children the history of the caves and the stories depicted in the murals like a tour guide. The local staff specially carried a seat for the old man in case he needed to take a rest after climbing up and down. But he preferred to see more and only used it for a few minutes.

The journey ended at Ronning's birthplace in Xiangfan of Hubei Province. In 1971 and 1975, he came here to pay respect to his mother at her tomb. This time, he was aware that it could be his last visit, so unlike the days before when he was quite lighthearted he became rather silent. On the day of their arrival in Xiangfan, Ronning led his children to the tomb to pay respect, and thus he realized all his last wishes.

In the evening, the mayor of Xiangfan hosted a grand banquet to celebrate his 90th birthday (his nominal age according to the Chinese traditional way of counting). There were birthday peaches and longevity noodles, specially prepared for the celebration and some of his local acquaintances came to express their congratulations. There were also fireworks making his last visit to China end in a warm and happy atmosphere.

Liu completes his account with a brief outline of Ronning's final year.

After he went back to Camrose, the state of his physical and mental health declined. He could no longer look after himself and soon was sent to a nursing home. On December 31, the last day of 1984, the old man eventually completed his life's journey of 90 years and peacefully left the world.

Chester Alvin Ronning was survived by his six children and their spouses, twenty-four grandchildren, and fourteen great grandchildren, along with his brother, Talbert, and two sisters, Hazel and Victoria. His funeral at Messiah Lutheran Church in Camrose on 4 January 1985 was a celebration of his extraordinary life. Liu Min, chargé d'affaires of the Chinese Embassy in Ottawa, attended with a delegation of Chinese mourners. There were also representatives of the governments of India, Canada, and Alberta. Ronning's brother Talbert, from Chicago, assisted in the service, speaking in Chinese, Norwegian, and English. Seymour Topping, managing editor of the *New York Times* and Ronning's son-in-law, delivered a Greeting, an eloquent eulogy dwelling on Ronning's humanity and his great accomplishments, concluding with "There can be no farewell to Chester for truly he lives in the hearts of the people."[26]

An echo came from China less than two weeks later, when Professor Chen Zuyu, who spent a two-year sabbatical leave at the University of Alberta in 1980–82, wrote of his reaction to Ronning's passing.

I was shocked by the death of Chester Ronning, former Canadian ambassador to China, a faithful and devoted friend of the Chinese people, especially Premier Zhou Enlai.

Five years ago, as a visiting scholar to the University of Alberta...I saw Ronning many times in public activities. Born in the province of Hubei, Ronning was affectionate toward his native land. I remember once at a party welcoming Wang Dong, the visiting Chinese ambassador, he read aloud with perfect Hubei accent: "Fear no heaven, fear no earth; the only thing worrying me is hearing a Hubeilao (fellow from Hubei) speaking Mandarin." The remark was greeted by a burst of laughter.

A year ago, on January 17, I read an article by him in China Daily in which he welcomed premier Zhao Ziyang who was then visiting Canada. He recalled the process of the normalization of diplomatic relationship between the two countries, which he had helped arrange. I could not imagine, only a year later, that time had grabbed a tireless fighter and one of our best Canadian friends.

"Sino-Canadian friendship is what I strive for," Ronning wrote in the China Daily. I am confident that his cause will survive him. The tie between the two great nations established by Premier Zhou, Ronning, and many Chinese and Canadians will grow even stronger with each passing day.[27]

# Taking His Measure

Ronning was the son of avid and devout Lutheran parents. His father, in particular, was zealous in his faith, as was Ronning's older brother Nelius. Ronning, however, made little outward display of his religious beliefs. He attended church regularly, and he lived a Christian life, but Biblical references were noticeably absent from his writings and speeches. In our more than thirty hours of taped interviews, I can find no such references, but he did call on Chinese classics, Confucianism, as well as local Hubei folk sayings and Norwegian ones. He followed an open approach to religion in his administration of Camrose Lutheran College. Tran Van Dinh, a former Vietnamese diplomat, who met Ronning in Washington, DC, in February 1971, described him as "a man of wisdom, filled with compassion and with a penetrating sense of humor." Someone whom "Confucius would have been proud to have...as a disciple," whom "Buddha would have been pleased to count as...a follower," and whom Laozu "would have been happy to have...as a drinking companion."[1]

Ronning was more explicit in his political beliefs, regularly acknowledging the Christian foundations of Western political life. He was a democratic socialist and made no bones about it. He believed that his father was one, too, although his father shied away from the name. Ronning spent the first half of his life in unsettled times, both in China and Canada. Revolution was brewing in China during his childhood and was more overtly evident when he went back to teach at his father's school in the 1920s: his students and fellow teachers were actively participating in the Communist-directed rural uprisings. In his youth in Valhalla, he was taken with the message of the United Farmers of Alberta (UFA), well before it turned to politics and formed a government. When he returned to Canada from China in 1927, he revived his links with the UFA, running successfully in a by-election. He joined in the founding of the Co-operative Commonwealth Federation (CCF) and helped to shape CCF policies, becoming the first leader of its Alberta wing. He campaigned vigorously and with conviction for the party. He firmly believed that the capitalist system was wrong and that no reform could be accomplished until it was abolished and a system of shared responsibilities and a government dedicated to the needs of the ordinary people was established. He connected with the hard-pressed farmers during the Depression. Although Ronning knew some labour union people to be socialists, he regarded unions as part of the capitalist system, created as a reaction to it. Labour unions were out for their individual members, not necessarily for the whole of society. Unfortunately, for Ronning's political career, Albertans succumbed to a radical variation of his message expounded by the Social Credit Party led by William Aberhart.

Ronning stuck to his principles. They not only guided his political career but informed his actions throughout his life. In his eighties, he spoke of how voters in Western democracies continue to elect the wrong people to serve in government, and that so much of what is essential to daily life is in the hands of people who are not elected and are difficult to regulate. Despite this, he remained optimistic that democratic socialism would eventually be realized. In looking back at his time in Alberta politics, he concluded that this experience enabled him to understand the Chinese revolution in a way he could not have done without it.[2] He no doubt recognized echoes of the farmers' movements in Alberta in the peasant-based movements and their struggles in China.

All his life Ronning was a teacher, never missing an opportunity to enlighten his listeners. Never dull, he usually captivated his audience within the first minute of speaking. He possessed great powers of description, both in writing and speaking. As a professional educator, he was open to progressive ideas and experimentation. He demonstrated this during his fifteen years as principal of Camrose Lutheran College, broadening its offerings and increasing its enrollment. He sought to develop a harmonious atmosphere within the college, all the better to promote learning, perhaps most evident in his conducting of the college choir that he took to first-class levels.

Ronning entered the Canadian diplomatic service in an unusual way and not until he was nearly fifty-one. The Department of External Affairs (DEA) needed someone who knew China and the Chinese language. Normally, it would have looked in southern Ontario, among the many Canadian Protestant missionaries who had experience of China, or among businessmen from Ontario or British Columbia with Asian connections. Ronning was not one of these. He was the son of American Norwegian Lutheran missionaries, and his Canadian roots were in the farmland of northern Alberta. Moreover, he was educated at the universities of Alberta and Minnesota,[3] not those of Ontario and England, and his degrees were in education, not history or politics. His wartime intelligence work in Ottawa brought him to the attention of the DEA, which was also interested in his socialist outlook. Once appointed, he adapted quickly, but because he had not spent years working his way up to the rank he held of first secretary, he was less familiar with, and less constrained by, strict protocol. It was part of his nature to respect people, but he was never in awe of position.

Because he had family and family roots in the United States, Ronning was perhaps more familiar with the nature of American power than were most Canadians. In return, American policy-makers distrusted him as they did their own old China Hands, whom they thought had been taken in by Mao and had "Lost China." Ronning's previous history as a leader of the Alberta provincial CCF Party made him suspect to many members of the Canadian Conservative Party as well. In the stereotypes of the Cold War, they considered Ronning to be "pink." In the opinion of Douglas Ross, a historian of Canadian foreign policy toward Vietnam, Ronning was one of a very small group of three who represented left-wing views within the DEA.[4] Ross makes a great deal of the left-right split in DEA/DFAIT (Department of Foreign Affairs and International Trade) over the issue of Vietnam, placing Ronning on the left (which he was).

I disagree with Ross, however, in his view of the split. Canadian diplomats served on the International Control Commissions (ICCs) for Southeast Asia as set up in Geneva in 1954. In fact, a large percentage of the personnel of DEA/DFAIT passed through the commissions. The majority of them, it is said, became persuaded of the American view of the situation in Vietnam. Ronning, who was struggling to be neutral, on his 1966 missions to Hanoi, encountered this pro-American bias when he was being briefed in Ottawa prior to his departure. He had been retired for two years and he was shocked at this attitude. He later relayed this opinion to Douglas Ross in a telephone interview. The split that was evident to Ronning in 1966 was not so predominant earlier on and so it is stretching matters to put Ronning on the left side of a split, which developed when he was really no longer in the department. Moreover, I feel Ross goes too far in his Cold War, right vs. left interpretation of Canadian policy when he projects the left-right split back onto the issue of the recognition of China, when no such split existed. For the majority of the department, the question was one of timing only. But Ross goes further and claims that Ronning's posting to Norway in 1954 was because the right had won out over the left and Ronning was sent into exile. Nothing could be further from the truth. Ronning had requested a posting to Norway and had made it a condition of his accepting a permanent job in DEA/DFAIT. And, even as he got to Norway, he was assigned to the conferences in Geneva on Korea and Southeast Asia. From Norway, he was appointed high commissioner to India. Some exile! His posting to Delhi put him at the heart of things also involving Chinese affairs. In fact, Ronning was one of the few in those days of the DEA whose career hinged on Asia.

It can be argued that in the two decades following the establishment of the People's Republic of China in 1949, Ronning was not only the best informed person on Chinese affairs in the DEA, but, beyond that—in Canada. This was because of the time he spent in China and the quality of his contacts inside the Chinese government. Nonetheless, one foreign diplomat at least was of the opinion that he was undervalued by the DEA. Sir Walter Crocker, Australian high commissioner to India during Ronning's time there, wrote: "His Government made some but not much use of his knowledge. In some respects it distrusted his knowledge because it clashed with their policy or prejudices, or with those of the United States."[5]

It was speculated within the Department of External Affairs that it was Ronning's good relations with Chou En-lai that prompted the invitation for Canada to serve on the ICCs in Indochina.

> Ronning makes no mention of this in his memoirs and seems never to have spoken to anybody in the Department about it. In any event, if he was involved, he has much to answer for! Staffing the Indochina Commissions became the single biggest administrative and personnel problem that the Department had to face during the next 20 years.[6]

Ronning applied the techniques he had learned as a teacher and college principal to the running of an embassy. Trilingual and gregarious, he engaged everyone he met in conversation. Those who worked with him and for him have nothing but warm praise for his empathy and understanding. He applied the same qualities to diplomacy, seeking to solve problems with peace and harmony rather than with acrimony and conflict.

Ronning has been referred to as one of the giants of Canada's golden age of diplomacy.[7] Indeed, he was fortunate to enter the service at the end of the war when Canada's international standing was noteworthy. Canada emerged from the war as an industrial power with a large navy and a tempered, well-trained military. It was committed to the United Nations and was seen as a mover and shaker, both there and in the Commonwealth. Pre-war European empires were coming apart; it was a time when Canadian diplomats could meddle in conflicts that had no direct impact on Canadian interests but which needed fixing in the broad interests of peace. Canadian diplomats were seen, rightly or wrongly, as relatively unbiased. Of course, with the Cold War deepening, Canada was often called an American satellite and even a running dog of imperialism, but this was more rhetoric than a firmly argued proof.

Ronning ran counter to the rhetoric, largely because of his close personal relations with Chou En-lai. Their relationship grew during the five years following the defeat of Japan and the renewal of civil war in China. His understanding of Chinese culture and society formed in his early years as a child and youth in Fancheng, and built upon during his time as a teacher there in the early 1920s, gave him an empathy toward the revolutionary struggle of the Chinese people. This experience harmonized with his time as a social democratic activist in Alberta. It was a factor in his selection by the DEA to serve in Chungking.

Ronning was perhaps predisposed to find the cause of the Chinese Communists more to his liking than that of the Nationalists. His frequent meetings with Chou developed into a genuine friendship and regard, each for the other. This close link with the premier of China did much for Ronning's stature as a diplomat and a China expert, but in the end, it did not produce any major advantage for Canada in its relations with China. In fact, some might argue that it was the Chou-Ronning relationship that caused Canada to be stuck with the ICCs for Southeast Asia—as referred to by Arthur Blanchette above, a costly and thankless task. In the end, it was arguably American interests (such as those of the *New York Times*) and those of his own family that benefitted the most from Ronning's closeness to Chou.

It goes without saying that Canada gained international importance because of its closeness to the United States. It was close but separate. Ronning fitted well within this atmosphere. He felt he was free to talk to anyone and was not shackled by restrictions that sealed the ears and mouths of his American colleagues. His facility with the Chinese language and his China experience made him unique in the Canadian Foreign Service, and his views on Asia were listened to carefully, if not always acted upon. Unfortunately, his strength was a weakness in the opinion of the American State Department. Having purged their own ranks of their seasoned China Hands, Washington, the American centre of diplomacy, greatly needed a Ronning-style perspective, but the blinkers imposed by the Cold War nullified such a possibility.

Ronning was also fortunate to be active at a time before the speed of modern communications circumscribed the activities of the dip-lomats in the field. He was a proactive diplomat who worked to make things happen. His career was centred on Asia and he accumulated enough friends and connections throughout the region to give his opinions gravitas.

Bruce Gilley, in an attempt to delve into the future of Canada–US and Canada–China relations, makes some startling statements regard-ing Ronning's role in their early formulation.

> Beijing has long treated Canada with warm condescension that it usually reserves for weak client states. Norman Bethune, the card-carrying Montreal doctor...resonates in China because he symbolizes this essentially kow-towing tributary ideal. Another Canadian "friend of China," Chester Ronning, Canada's ambassador [*sic*] to China during the Chinese civil war, is shown in a 1980 National Film Board documentary regaling premier Zhou Enlai in Chinese with talk of his fried rice during a 1971 meeting in Beijing.

And later he adds, apropos Canada's approaches to Washington on China policy:

> This policy of quiet remonstrance with Washington over China policy then collapsed under the Maoist romanticism and crude anti-Americanism of Trudeau and Ronning.[8]

Gilley appears to overlook the fact that when Bethune and Ronning were active in China, the Chinese were hardly in a position to be condescending. Indeed, at that time, the Chinese were attempting to free themselves from a century of Western condescension. Moreover, Bethune was viewed as an internationalist first and a Canadian second, if at all. He owes his fame in China to Mao's eulogy, written a decade before the Communists came to power. As for Ronning joking with Chou En-lai, Gilley's comment lacks knowledge of the depth of the personal relationship between the two men and the circumstances surrounding that particular meeting.

It is not clear how Gilley can characterize Canadian approaches to the United States on the question of China as "quiet remon- strance" when one recalls the outbursts of presidents Eisenhower and Johnson, and secretaries of state Dulles and Rusk, when Pearson and Diefenbaker raised with them the possibility of recognizing Beijing. Perhaps it was because the Canadian leaders remained quiet when they were berated. The term "crude" befits the comments of Lyndon Johnson better than they do representatives of Canada. It is also odd for Gilley to link Trudeau and Ronning together, since Ronning had left government service before Trudeau was elected and his speeches in Canada and the United States, in which he criticized America's China policy and its war in Vietnam, were made as a private citizen. Others were doing the same. It might be argued that Trudeau and Ronning, each in his own way, were trying to challenge American con- descension of Canada.

Ronning was also very fortunate in his son-in-law, Seymour Topping, a journalist and China Hand in his own right, who later worked for the *New York Times*. Ronning and Topping shared China experiences. The two of them were in Nanking in 1949 and witnessed the collapse of the Nationalist government and the arrival of the Communists. At the time, Topping was reporting for Associated Press. Ronning liked Topping; they held similar views on China. He was very pleased when Seymour married his daughter Audrey, who, among his children, most reflected his love of China. Formerly a student in Nanking, she became a widely recognized expert on modern China. Thanks to the doors opened to her by her father, her photos and arti- cles on China were to scoop the Western media.

During the period 1951–66, Topping was assigned to bureaus in regions where Ronning served as a diplomat. He was in Vietnam when Ronning exited China in 1951, in London when Ronning was in Norway and Geneva, in Moscow when Ronning was in India, and in Hong Kong when Ronning made his special missions to Hanoi in 1966. Ronning was important to the *New York Times* because as a Canadian diplomat he had access to areas where Americans did not. This applied particularly to the People's Republic of China where Ronning, because of his friendship with Chou En-lai, facilitated visits by *New York Times* correspondents prior to the Nixon visit of February 1972. Before this, the only paper north of the Rio Grande to be represented in Beijing was the *Globe and Mail*, whose correspondents had been reporting from China for over a decade. The American government had had a policy forbidding American reporters to visit the People's Republic. Huang Hua, an ambassador and later Foreign Minister, regarded both Ronning and Topping with friendship and respect. Needless to say, Ronning's observations and opinions on China and on Vietnam found their way into the columns of the *New York Times*, both directly and indirectly.

Ronning was a family man, and the most painful times of his life were when he was separated from his wife and children, whether it was in Ottawa, Chungking, or Nanking. He was proud of all of his children, although he talked most about Audrey for reasons already mentioned. Her adult life intersected with his more than any of the others, apart from Sylvia who lived not far from him in Camrose. Ronning was also a bit uxorious. He doted on Inga Marie, at times with a touch of competitiveness and teasing. He also adored his mother, and likely saw many of her qualities in Inga. He often spoke proudly of his mother's riding skills, skills that Inga shared.

When Inga and Chester danced on the night of their wedding at Valhalla early in September 1918, they could not have possibly imagined the life they would lead. Unlike Inga, Chester, at the time of marriage, was a world traveller. Perhaps this was why he was not fully sensitive to the bewildering impact a first visit to China would have on Inga. Quite understandably, she was uneasy and often frightened by China. With all his optimistic explanations, Chester could not completely allay her fears. When, after his posting to China as a diplomat, he worked hard for Inga and the children to join him in Nanking, her previous experience made her reluctant to come. She did, however, and less than two years later she and their children were evacuated by plane to Japan. When she arrived back in Camrose, for the first and only time, she ventured a public comment on the situation in China. Her comments did not deviate from the views of her husband, but the uniqueness of them adds weight to Ronning's comment: "Inga did all the talking inside the home and I did all the talking outside."[9]

This remark need not be taken too literally, but it implies that Inga's words carried the most weight in the home. If true, it is understandable, because Ronning was absent for long periods, leaving Inga the day-to-day care of the children. A woman of quiet, almost regal, dignity, she appeared content to let the spotlight shine on her husband. A proud mother, she derived great strength from her children. She once said that the greatest handicap of their diplomatic life was that her children were scattered around the globe, which meant she did not see them and her grandchildren as often as she would have liked. Forced by circumstances to share Chester with China during long stretches of their married life, she counted on him receiving a posting to Norway as a form of compensation. There is little doubt that the three years in Norway were, for her, the highlight of their diplomatic career. The two of them, dressed for a gala evening in Oslo, were a sight to make Canadians proud of their representatives abroad. Inga passed away in Camrose in 1967 at age seventy-two, surrounded by her beloved family, leaving Chester another eighteen years on his own—years when he came to rely increasingly on his children.

Ronning's energy and stamina were remarkable, even more so as he grew older. He attributed his ability to maintain such a hectic pace to proper food and a set of exercises of his own devising, which he did each morning in the bathtub. He would prepare Chinese food for himself, singing the chants he had heard the family cook recite in his childhood as he chopped vegetables. He did not suffer from high blood pressure, although he had some asthma and did not take heat well, something that plagued him both in China and India. All his life, it seems, he was able to drive himself to the limit and beyond, following such extreme efforts with periods of physical and nervous exhaustion when he took to his bed to recover.[10]

Following his retirement from the DEA, Ronning became a veritable whirling dervish of activity, addressing groups scattered about North America. From Canadian Club lunches to small Lutheran colleges, he carried his messages of how to win peace in Vietnam, how vital it was to understand China and to recognize its government and to seat it in the UN, and how important India was to our collective futures. He pressed these topics on a willing public with zeal akin to the way his father approached the conversion of heathens. As already mentioned, his efforts to put forth a Chinese point of view undercut his previous status as an objective diplomat. He was so engaged with the land of his birth that he was willing to overlook, or at least to put into a broader context, personal affronts he and his friends received at the hands of agents of the People's Republic. And sometimes, he mistook the treatment he received as a guest of Chou En-lai as normal. One thing is clear: after he retired from diplomatic service, Ronning became Beijing's best unofficial ambassador in Canada.

By any measure, Ronning was an extraordinary person who led an extraordinary life during extraordinary times. It is unlikely that a Canadian diplomat today could become as close to the premier of China and to the prime minister of India as did Ronning. At best, such opportunities are open to prime ministers through state visits, or G8, G20, Commonwealth, and Francophonie meetings. Moreover, Canada's diplomatic stature is not what it used to be. Canada's post-1945 strength provided a unique opportunity for Canada to play an important role on the world stage. Today, Canada is a middle-sized power doing middling things, straying somewhat from Pearson's description: "We have always been ready to be a 'mediator,' even at risk of becoming a busybody."[11] Diplomacy has changed. Canadian diplomats today do not enjoy the international stature of the Ronning generation.

Today, nearly thirty years after his death, as Canada–China relations enjoy a renaissance, Ronning is little remembered in Canada, even though the Asia Pacific Foundation of Canada named him as one of the ten top people to influence Canada–Asia relations in the twentieth century. *China Mission* (1980), Tom Radford's film examining Ronning's life, is available on the Internet and sometimes appears on television, but, outside Camrose, Alberta, the town Ronning called home and where he is buried, his name is not well known. Most long-term residents of Alberta over fifty are familiar with the name Chester Ronning, and many hold fond personal memories of him. It can be argued, however, that for today's younger generations, Ronning remains little known, and that his importance is more widely recognized in China.[12]

Ronning gave his all for the development of the CCF in Alberta, yet summaries of his life in books and government handouts often omit this phase of his life. Except among the inner circles of the Alberta New Democratic Party, his contribution remains virtually unknown. His name appears on local schools, and the Augustana Campus of the University of Alberta (formerly Camrose Lutheran College) uses his little white house as its alumni office. Augustana is also the home of the Chester Ronning Centre for the Study of Religion and Public Life. But there is nothing to mark his extraordinary diplomatic career and his international achievements. There is no university chair, no annual lecture, and no scholarship, not even an essay contest. The extraordinary and remarkable Chester Alvin Ronning deserves better.

# Notes

## Preface
### Chester Alvin Ronning

1. Chester A. Ronning, *A Memoir of China in Revolution* (New York: Random House, Pantheon Books, 1974).
2. Audrey Topping, *Dawn Wakes in the East* (New York: Harper and Row, 1973).
3. I made this trip courtesy of a Canada-China academic exchange program grant.
4. Brian L. Evans, "Ronning and Recognition," in *Reluctant Adversaries*, ed. Paul M. Evans and B. Michael Frolic (Toronto: University of Toronto Press, 1991), 148–67.
5. Liao Dong, "Chester A. Ronning and Canada–China Relations, 1945-1954" (master's thesis, University of Regina, 1983).
6. Liu Guangtai, *Chester Ronning* (Hebei: Xinhua Publishers, 1999).
7. Andrew Preston, "Operation Smallbridge," *Pacific Historical Review* 72, no. 3 (2003): 353–90.

## I
## Chinese Childhood

1. On days when the sun shone, the remains of crashed aircraft glinted on the valleys and mountains below.
2. The route followed was Montreal to Cairo, stopping in the Azores, Rabat, and Malta; Cairo to Karachi, stopping at the Dead Sea, Lake Habbaniyah, Basra, Bahrein, and Fort Sharjah; Karachi to Calcutta, stopping at Rajamund and Allahabad.
3. In 1949, the two cities were brought under one jurisdiction called Xiangfan.
4. Kenneth Scott Latourette, *A History of Christian Missions in China* (1929; repr., Taipei: Ch'eng-wen Publishing Company, 1966), 418–19 gives a generic description of a typical Protestant mission station: "The mission station was usually made up of a preaching hall, a church building, a school or schools, a

dispensary and perhaps a hospital, and residences for missionaries and their Chinese colleagues and assistants. Not all these buildings and institutions were necessarily within one enclosure or even in the same part of the city. The residences, usually in Occidental style and surrounded by a wall, were, with their gardens and lawns, attractive even if unpretentious bits of the West set down in China....From the central stations journeys were made to neighboring cities and villages and in time a network of congregations, each with its chapel and often with its school, came into existence....In deference to Chinese conceptions of propriety, men and women sat on opposite sides of the room, sometimes separated by a high screen."

5. I am grateful to Audrey Topping for providing additional information on her grandfather's family.

6. Nils Nilius Ronning, *The Gospel At Work* (Minneapolis: N.N. Ronning, 1943), 28.

7. Ibid., 31.

8. Actually, her brothers supported her. It was said that missions did not like self-supporting missionaries, as they could be difficult to direct.

9. Without funds to pay to get to America, the Rorem family repaired a derelict sailing vessel in return for free passage to New York. They took their own food in the form of dried fish and lefse in chests on the deck of the ship.

10. Ronning, *The Gospel At Work*, 36.

11. The main impetus was from Britain and its white dominions, with the ensuing rush to convert being described by a modern American historian as "this Anglo-Saxon Islam," the torch being passed to the United States in 1910. See James Reed, *The Missionary Mind and American East Asia Policy 1911–1915* (Harvard: East Asian Monographs 104, 1983), 12.

12. In addition to the Ronnings and Miss Rorem, the members of the mission were Mr. and Mrs. S. Netland, Mr. and Mrs. D. Nelson and four children, and Misses Olive Hodnefield and Oline Hermanson.

13. There was one more city at this point on the Yangtze: Hanyang, situated across the mouth of the Han River opposite Hankou. In 1927, the three cities were grouped together to form present-day Wuhan.

14. Olive T. Christensen, "Language Study," in *White unto Harvest: The China Mission of the Norwegian Lutheran Church of America*, ed. T. Ekeland, Albert Anderson, and Olive T. Christensen (Minneapolis: Board of Foreign Missions, 1919), 187.

15. Ronning, *The Gospel At Work*, 40–44.

16. The British concession was the oldest, but the French, Germans, Russians, and Japanese each had one. In time, following the suppression of the Taipings, Hankou became a major base for both Catholic and Protestant missions that were establishing stations up and along the Yangtze to Szechuan and into neighbouring provinces. Protestant colleges and an excellent Catholic hospital were established in Hankow.

17. John was a thirty-five-year veteran of missionary work in China. CIM was a nondenominational Protestant society. Taylor began his missionary work in China in 1855. A visit by him to Norway in 1889 led to the Norwegian mission in China.

18. John and Taylor more or less directed the assignment of mission fields to Protestant missionaries by country. Swedish missionaries were assigned, like the Norwegians, to Hupei and Honan provinces.

19. The Taiping Rebellion (1850–64) is considered the major revolt among many in China during the nineteenth century that threatened the rule of the Ch'ing imperial government. It broke out in the south near Canton, which had been greatly affected by the turmoil surrounding the First Opium War. Gathering strength, it moved north to the Yangtze valley, where it established a capital at Nanking. Because its leader claimed to be Christian, foreign missionaries and foreign diplomats toyed with the idea of giving him support, but such ideas were short-lived and foreign soldiers of fortune supported the Ch'ing troops sent to suppress the revolt. Among these "foreign advisors," as they would be called today, was Charles Gordon of England, who became known as General Chinese Gordon. Still later, he became Gordon of Khartoum, where he died in January 1885. Twenty million people are said to have died or been misplaced by the Taiping Rebellion and the accompanying plague and famine.

20. For a detailed picture of the history of Hankow during the nineteenth century, see William T. Rowe, *Hankow: Conflict and Community in a Chinese City, 1796–1895* (Stanford: Stanford University Press, 1989).

21. All male Chinese were obliged to wear their hair braided in a queue as a sign of their submission to the Ch'ing (Manchu) rulers who became rulers of China in 1644. In order to further their work, missionaries chose to attempt to blend in, rather than to stand out.

22. Chester witnessed one of those times:

    One day a large crowd of people had followed Father when he was returning from a visit to the shopping centre of Fancheng. The crowd suddenly became a mob. Shouting "*yang jen*," foreigner, or "*yang kuei*," foreign devil, they chased him up the street leading to our mission compound. Our gatekeeper heard the unpleasant noise and quickly barred the gate, unaware that my father was involved. Seeing the gate closed, Father made a desperate leap at the compound wall. As he scrambled up the wall, a ruffian grabbed his queue and yanked it off, together with his skullcap. The angry mob suddenly began to laugh at my father, who sat disheveled, without a queue, straddling the wall. The crowd roared with laughter. The man who had snatched the queue, now stared at the object in his hand, apparently suspecting some evil foreign magic, and quickly carried the dangling queue to the gate. The gatekeeper was too frightened to do anything. Father descended from the wall, opened the gate, and thanked the frightened man for returning his precious queue. He then expressed gratitude to the smiling crowd for their kindness, placed the cap and queue back on his head, and invited them to visit him some time when they were not in such a hurry.

    Ronning, *A Memoir of China*, 7.

23. In all, Hannah bore seven children, four boys and three girls, before she died, following bouts of illness, in February 1907. She was thirty-six.

24. Ronning interview with author (RIA), 13 May 1980.

25. Ronning papers (RP), from the undated essay, "The Convent of Scattering Clouds."

26. Ibid.

27. The Ch'ing government sought to remain in control of China despite growing foreign intervention in China's internal affairs, domestic rebellions, and general unrest. First, it tried to revitalize Confucianism and combine it with Western technology and science. This approach proved unsatisfactory and there was growing agitation for reform of China's educational system, and to reject Confucius in favour of Western science, economics, and education, particularly after Japan defeated China in a war over Korea in 1895. The young Kuang hsu (Guangxu) emperor, who came of age in 1889, proved to be reform-minded and on the advice of intellectuals, launched, in 1898, A Hundred Days of Reform. Horrified, the empress dowager, his aunt, had him removed from power and imprisoned, ending the reforms. Instead, she later embraced the antiforeignism of the Boxer movement, thinking that the Westerners could be driven from the country.

28. Ronning, *A Memoir of China*, 30.

29. Ibid., 7.

30. Nils Nilius Ronning, *Fifty Years in America* (Minneapolis: Friend Publishing Company, 1938), 68–69.

31. Ronning, *A Memoir of China*, 7–8.

32. RP.

33. Ronning, *A Memoir of China*, 4, 27.

34. The disaster of World War I, however, brought disillusionment among the Chinese, with the vaunted superiority of the "all-powerful West."

35. Ronning, *The Gospel At Work*, 81.

36. Ibid., 82.

37. For a background on the growth of revolutionary movements in Hubei during this period, see Joseph W. Esherick, *Reform and Revolution in China: The 1911 Revolution in Hunan and Hubei* (Berkeley: University of California Press, 1976).

38. When Halvor left the mission in 1908, "there were four main stations and 39 outstations, 567 native church members, 1,150 children in the mission schools, including boys and girls in orphanages and high schools. There were 24 students in the school for evangelists and 14 students in Bible school for women. In all 82 native workers: evangelists, 29; men teachers, 33; women teachers, 6; Bible women, 14. Of physical plants and equipment: homes for missionaries and native workers, churches, schools, a hospital and a doctor's residence. Estimated value $23,000. Total expenses the last year, $20,167.00, of which $6,350.00 represented missionaries' salaries." Ronning, *The Gospel At Work*, 86.

39. RIA, 29 May 1980.

40. Ibid.

41. Ronning, *A Memoir of China*, 10.

42. To Chester, she appeared to retain traces of a Norwegian accent, but this was not apparent to others.

43. RIA, 29 May and 3 June 1980.

## 2
## Bucolic Youth

1. N.N. Ronning, *The Gospel At Work* (Minneapolis: N.N. Ronning, 1943), 88.
2. Ronning papers (RP), "Free Homesteads in Peace River," n.d. For an excellent account of the opening and early development of the Peace River area, see David W. Leonard, *The Last Great West: The Agricultural Settlement of the Peace River Country to 1914* (Calgary: Detselig Enterprises, 2005), note particularly Valhalla, 580–84. In China, Halvor yearned to bring Christianity to the heathen, but in northern Alberta, the home of Cree and Beaver Aboriginals, he only wanted to tend to the spiritual needs of Norwegian settlers.
3. The land became available as free homestead, or through South African land scrip, which was offered to all veterans and nurses who had served in the Boer War (1899–1902). The scrip was to be used to acquire 320 acres of land, free of fees but under homesteading regulations. Those who did not use the scrip sold them to others. Halvor bought enough scrip to provide land for himself, Gunhild, Nelius, and Chester; at least ten homesteads. See Provincial Archives of Alberta (PAA), *Alberta Homestead Records 1879–1930*.
4. Ronning, *The Gospel At Work*, 90.
5. I am grateful to David Leonard for providing me with details on the Ronnings' homestead claims from Alberta homestead files.
6. This trail went from Athabasca Landing up the Athabasca River and Slave River over Lesser Slave Lake and across the Little Smoky River, Sturgeon Lake, and Big Smoky River to Grande Prairie.
7. *Kavring* are wheat rusks that they served with loaf sugar and coffee during the day. Ragna Steen and Magda Hendrickson, *Pioneer Days in Bardo Alberta* (Tofield: Historical Society of Beaver Hills Lake, 1944), 197–98.
8. Ronning interview with author (RIA), 28 August 1980. The journey was a coming of age experience for the two older Ronning boys. Later in life, Chester described the trek in great detail. The trail remained the link to the south until the railway to Grande Prairie, fifty miles from Valhalla, was completed in 1916. The link to Hythe, fifteen miles from Valhalla, was not completed until 1928, by which time Valhalla was a thriving community.
9. A Minnesota settler in Grande Prairie around 1911 once told a journalist that to start breaking a homestead and live for a year, a farmer needed about $375, i.e., $225 for oxen, and $150 for equipment and food. See Leonard, *The Last Great West*, 189.
10. RIA, 28 August 1980.
11. University of Alberta Archives (UAA), university calendars and registration records. Ronning did well in his courses at the university, finishing regularly near the top of Class II (an upper second in British parlance) and finished ahead of Nelius in those courses they both attended. The early calendars list all examination results. In later years, examination results were published each spring in the Edmonton papers.

12. Chester A. Ronning, *A Memoir of China in Revolution* (New York: Random House Pantheon Books, 1974), 13.

13. See Bradford James Rennie, *The Rise of Agrarian Democracy: The United Farmers and Farm Women of Alberta 1909-1921* (Toronto: University of Toronto Press, 2000).

14. Alberta held an election on 7 June 1917. There were three candidates in the riding of Peace River. The winner was William Rae, a Liberal. Dan Minchin, a Conservative, finished second, and Harry Adair, Independent, finished last.

15. *Apostles donks* refers to being on foot.

16. Rev. A.H. Solheim, teacher at the college.

17. RP, copy of letter loaned by James Stolee, son of Peter Stolee.

18. RIA, 13 May 1980.

19. Ibid.

20. 272562 Chester Alvin Ronning and 173481 Nelius Theodore Ronning were demobilized with honourary commissions as second lieutenants.

21. RIA, 13 May 1980.

22. *Believe me Zantippe*, (or Xantippe) was a 1913 farce staged in Boston and New York starring John Barrymore. It was regarded as more or less a collection of jokes with little in the way of a plot. It was made into a silent film in 1918. I do not believe Ronning is doing anything more than using a catchy phrase popular at the time.

23. Underlined in the original.

24. RP.

## 3
## Return to Fancheng

1. N.N. Ronning, *The Gospel At Work* (Minneapolis: N.N. Ronning, 1943), 118.

2. Ibid., 117.

3. In 1917, in order to relieve a labour shortage behind the lines in France and to free up Allied soldiers to serve at the front, Britain, France, and the United States recruited Chinese men from north China to serve as workers in France. Some 120,000 were recruited, with nearly ninety thousand of them being shipped via Canada to Europe. Chinese missionaries were recruited to act as interpreters and to work with the labour corps, some of whom stayed on in France after the war. A number of cemeteries in France contain the bodies of Chinese workers who died during the final two years of the war.

4. Ronning, *The Gospel At Work*, 118.

5. Ibid., 121. On receipt of the telegram announcing Nelius's death, Halvor "looked up to heaven and said; 'My boy is in glory.'"

6. Nelius's body was found the following summer, but that of J.C. MacDougall was not. The Ronning Formation at Pine Point is named in honour of Nelius and a mound after MacDougall.

7. *The Gateway*, 2 October 1920.

8. Ronning, *The Gospel At Work*, 121, letter from Shi Cun-ching.

9. Ronning was to write much later that if it had not been for the death of Nelius, he likely would not have gone back to China: "If he had returned, the chances are that I would not have been here today." Ronning papers (RP), letter from Ronning to parents, 22 January 1947, from Chungking.

10. During this time, he became involved in union activities as an organizer in the less militant of the two unions vying to improve the working conditions for teachers.

11. The Hakka are a group of people within China who are said to have moved from north-central China to the southern part of China. *Hakka* translates to "guest people." They are justly famous for having produced a number of prominent Chinese revolutionary leaders.

12. This is a very complex period in modern Chinese history with so many bit players competing for major roles. There is no need to delve deeper for the purposes of discussing Ronning's life, but more detailed accounts of the warlord period can be found in John King Fairbank, ed., *The Cambridge History of China*, Vol. 12, Pts. I & II, Republican China 1912–1949 (Cambridge: Cambridge University Press, 1983). A full flavour of the times can be found in the pages of the *North China Herald*, a weekly published in Shanghai.

13. The *North China Herald* listed all passengers arriving and departing Shanghai and the ships they travelled on. The 11 November 1922 issue notes that Rev. and Mrs. O. Ronning [*sic*] and Miss S.A. Ronning arrived from Vancouver on the *Empress of Canada* on 3 November.

14. An interesting look at the lives and activities of foreigners in China in the 1920s and '30s is available in Carl Crow, *Foreign Devils in the Flowery Kingdom* (New York: Harper & Brothers, 1940).

15. Ronning interview with author (RIA), 11 May 1980, and RP. One of the famous bandits, familiar to Ronning, was known as the Old Foreigner (Lao Yangren), because he was tall and thin, with a white face, big eyes, and long lashes. Bandits were such a familiar problem at this time that a two-volume work designed to train people in the Chinese language contained exercises dealing with them. (See J.P. Ratay, *Current Chinese* [Shanghai: Kelly and Walsh, 1927]). Insight into the true nature of the bandit problem can be gained from Phil Billingsley, *Bandits in Republican China* (Stanford: University Press, 1988).

16. See *North China Herald*, 4, 11 November and 16 December 1922.

17. RIA, 13 May 1980.

18. There were a number of Protestant churches and compounds in Peking at this time, but the precise location of the hostel is not given.

19. Chester A. Ronning, *A Memoir of China in Revolution* (New York: Random House, Pantheon Books, 1974), 97. In 1924, in a coup, Feng expelled P'u-i, the last emperor of China, from the Forbidden City, where he had been confined since the Ch'ing abdicated in 1912.

20. As a youngster, Ronning learned a rhyme that told you where to sit on the back of various animals. Translated from the local Hupei Chinese dialect, it goes: You ride a horse at the front, a cow on the hump, and a donkey on the smelly rump. Ronning, *A Memoir of China*, 287–88. Ronning advised Anvil that the spoken Chinese language needed to be sung. He, in turn, surprised Ronning

with his skill in writing and understanding Chinese characters. "He was a Kalgren genius." RIA, 13 May 1980.

21. Ronning, *A Memoir of China*, 16.

22. This is not to disguise the fact that real wars, destructive, devastating, and deadly, were fought among the warlords, who sought more and more ways—some ingenious—of taxing the people to pay for the expense.

23. As reported in the *North China Herald*, 10 March 1923.

24. Chiang, as a young man, went to Japan for military training. Later he gained experience in the financial world of Shanghai, and perhaps in its underworld. Still later, he became a follower of Sun's.

25. "There is a Chinese saying that 'bandits and soldiers are breath from the same nostrils,' and it is certainly true that they are frequently indistinguishable. In fact, many warlords started their careers as bandits....The bandit had no official position, he killed and stole and fled. The warlord had military rank; he killed and stole and stayed." James E. Sheridan, *China in Disintegration: The Republican Era in Chinese History 1912–1949* (New York: The Free Press, 1975), 92.

26. Known for over 1,400 years to the Chinese for its beauty, it was first visited by Westerners in 1903. Two hundred and twelve of the over three hundred Western-style buildings constructed there subsequently have survived and are preserved like exhibits in a museum of foreign architecture.

27. Ronning was familiar, since his childhood, with every type of boat plying the Han River. For centuries the Chinese have been building ships, including ocean-going ones, with a hull full of a series of watertight compartments. Should the hull be breached, only one compartment flooded and the ship stayed afloat.

28. RIA, 13 May 1980.

29. Ibid.

30. Ibid.

31. T. Ekeland, Albert Anderson, and Olive T. Christensen, eds., *White unto Harvest: The China Mission of the Norwegian Lutheran Church of America* (Minneapolis: Board of Foreign Missions, 1919), 117.

32. Ibid., 170–71.

33. Since Halvor Ronning's day, the three Lutheran missions—the Hauge Synod Mission centred at Fancheng; the American Lutheran Mission, a continuation of the American-Norwegian China Mission, which began in Hankow; and the later arriving Norwegian Synod Mission had joined forces in 1917 to become the Lutheran United Mission, covering an area of Hupei and Honan provinces 450 miles long and 110 miles wide. Later, at a general assembly held in 1920 at Chi-kung shan, the Lutheran missions in China united to form the Lutheran Church of China (LCC).

34. Today, a column commemorating Hannah Rorem is located in the schoolyard, replaced there by Ronning on a visit to Fancheng in 1971 after he could not find the original marker. He was unable to locate her grave.

35. Ronning, *A Memoir of China*, 17–18.

36. This was done with solemn ceremony on 1 June 1929, two years after the Republic of China was established with its capital at Nanking. Sun's death was mourned among Chinese overseas communities worldwide.

37. Ronning, *A Memoir of China*, 33–34.

38. Canada had no diplomatic ties with China at this time (not until 1941) and the British handled its affairs.

39. Audrey Topping, *Dawn Wakes in the East* (New York: Harper and Row, 1973), 3.

40. RP. The story of Ronning's encounter with the Red Spears is told in detail in an undated, draft essay on the Red Spears.

41. Quoted in Topping, *Dawn Wakes in the East*, 3–4.

42. RP, letter to family, 2 February 1949; RIA, 22 May 1980.

43. The book *Sand Pebbles*, written by Richard McKenna, was published in 1962 and the movie of the same name followed in 1966. They depict the fictionalized adventures of an American gunboat, the USS *San Pablo*, during the events at this time.

44. The *North China Herald* of March and April 1927 carries many first-hand accounts by refugees from Nanking.

45. Outward and inward passenger lists, *North China Herald*, 9 April 1927. Liao Dong takes Ronning to task for his seeming acceptance of the shelling of Nanking and of the deaths of Chinese as a result. He observes that Ronning at the time was not yet completely anti-imperialist. "It seems that for him, it was intolerable that the foreigners should have extra-territoriality, but it was more intolerable that the Chinese should be xenophobic." Liao Dong, "Chester A. Ronning and Canada–China Relations, 1945-1954" (master's thesis, University of Regina, 1983), 40. It is perhaps a bit much to expect a young husband and father seeking safety at a time of nascent civil war and revolution to question the motives of the protectors of his family and himself.

46. Chinese politics at this time were even more complex than usual. Chiang's actions and motivations are best outlined in Jay Taylor, *The Generalissimo* (Cambridge, MA: Belknap Press of Harvard University Press, 2009), 49-96.

47. André Malraux, *La condition humaine* (1933) translated into English as *The Human Condition*, and as *Man's Fate*, is a fictionalized account of the events in Shanghai in 1927.

48. There is reputed to be an ancient Chinese curse that went "May you live in interesting times."

49. Topping, *Dawn Wakes in the East*, 3.

# 4
# Principal and Politician

1. Roger Epp, *We Are All Treaty People: Prairie Essays* (Edmonton: University of Alberta Press, 2008), 60.

2. See Lewis Gwynne Thomas, *The Liberal Party in Alberta* (Toronto: University of Toronto Press, 1959).

3. George Oake, "With Neither Policy nor Leader the Farmers Take Over Alberta," in *Alberta in the 20th Century*, Vol. 5, ed. Ted Byfield (Edmonton: United Western Communications, 1996), 54-73.

4. Epp, *Treaty People*, 60.

5. The next year they moved into the small house they had built. It was to be home in Camrose for the Ronnings and their six children. It was the house he retired to after his diplomatic career ended and would be his home until his death in 1984. It is now Alumni House for the Augustana Campus of the University of Alberta.

6. The foregoing descriptions of the Ronnings' first home and of Chester's first day at the college are taken from Ronning interview with author (RIA), 5 June 1980.

7. Haugeans were followers of Hans Nielsen Hauge (1771-1824). See Chapter One.

8. This terse summary of the college, its founding, and its early history is based on John Johansen, "A History of Augustana/CLC," written to celebrate its one hundredth anniversary in 2010-11. Available at http://www.augustana.ualberta.ca/100/history/. In January 1936, the college opened a new department based on the folk school idea from Scandinavia. *Camrose Canadian* (CC), 15 January 1936.

9. Ronning papers (RP), radio station CFCW 790 Wetaskiwin, transcript of taped interviews with friends of Ronning, 1984.

10. Audrey (Ronning) Topping, "Chester Ronning's Daughter Reflects on Her Father and Life in Camrose," [Augustana] *Express* 14, no. 1 (2003): 16-17.

11. Bertie (Anderson) Fowler, "Chester Ronning's Compassion Compelled Attention," [Augustana] *Express* 14, no. 1 (2003): 17-18.

12. RIA, 5 June 1980.

13. Ibid.

14. Ibid.

15. CC, 12 June 1930.

16. For greater detail, see Epp, *Treaty People*, 61-65, and Bradford James Rennie, *The Rise of Agrarian Democracy: The United Farmers and Farm Women of Alberta 1909-1921* (Toronto: University of Toronto Press, 2000), 179-206.

17. Ronning was to stand for election many more times for both the UFA and the CCF. Each time his candidacy was unopposed.

18. CC, 28 September 1932.

19. RIA, 5 June 1980.

20. Chester A. Ronning, *A Memoir of China in Revolution* (New York: Random House, Pantheon Books, 1974), 18-19.

21. CC, 12 October 1932. Underlined in original.

22. Reprinted in CC, 15 February 1933.

23. The original text of Ronning's speech is preserved in Archives of the Glenbow Institute (AGI), Walter Norman and Amelia Turner Smith Fonds, M-1157-106, UFA and CCF proposals, 1933.

24. Ibid.

25. CC, 8 March 1933.

26. Ibid.
27. cc, 15 March 1933.
28. cc, 29 March 1933.
29. cc, 7 March 1934. The article was based upon a glowing report of Ronning's speech published in the *Edmonton Bulletin* that called the speech outstanding.
30. cc, 4 April 1934.
31. Ibid.
32. Provincial Archives of Alberta (paa), audiotape of Howard Leeson interview with Ronning, 1976.
33. Ibid.
34. Ibid.
35. cc, 9 May 1934.
36. cc, 27 July 1934.
37. cc, 25 July 1934.
38. "Civil War in Social Credit," cc, 12 September 1934.
39. cc, 9 May 1934.
40. cc, 10 October 1934.
41. McPherson was involved in a divorce scandal, and, as noted earlier, Brownlee was accused of having an affair with his secretary.
42. Reid was the main architect of the Sexual Sterilization Act of 1928.
43. 17 April 1935.
44. cc, 7 August 1935.
45. cc, 14 August 1935.
46. Quoted in cc, 13 January 1937.
47. cc, 12 January 1938.
48. cc, 12 April 1939.
49. cc, 28 June 1939.
50. It was made up of Conservatives and Liberals who felt tainted by those labels, instead calling themselves independents.
51. cc, 9 August 1939.
52. cjca and cfrn are both Edmonton radio stations.
53. Ronning was in my hometown of Taber on 16 March 1940, but being only seven years old at the time, I did not attend the meeting.
54. The Alberta election was held on 21 March, while the federal election was held on 26 March 1940.
55. cc, 6 and 13 March 1940. The 13 March ccf ad attempted to counter these comments.
56. cc, 16 October 1940.
57. Quoted in cc, 31 December 1940.
58. cc, 29 January 1941 carried the poster and a report of a Ronning speech comparing the ccf to the British Labour Party. Underlined and emphasis in original.
59. cc, 12 February 1941.
60. ria, 5 June 1980.

## 5
## Diplomat in China

1. For example, among the first ambassadors from Canada to the People's Republic of China were three sons of Protestant missionaries: Ralph Collins (1971–72); John Small (1972–76); and Arthur Menzies (1976–80).

2. George Frederick McNally, "Odlum: Canada's First Ambassador to China" (master's thesis, University of Alberta, 1977).

3. I wrote elsewhere that the department considered Ronning to be a "one trick pony," a phrase that raised eyebrows in light of his diplomatic career, but at the time, the appointment was short-term and solely for China work. Brian L. Evans, "Ronning and Recognition," in *Reluctant Adversaries*, ed. Paul M. Evans and B. Michael Frolic (Toronto: University of Toronto Press, 1991), 148–67.

4. Ronning interview with author (RIA), 9 August 1980.

5. Odlum was an odd choice for ambassador since his business and military qualifications appeared to be outside the range of skills the DEA was advised to emphasize: academic, civilian. The process followed in selecting Odlum is discussed fully in McNally, "Odlum."

6. Ronning papers (RP), letter to family, 17 March 1946.

7. Tao Xisheng had an interesting history. A former close associate of Chiang's, he defected to serve Wang Jingwei, who headed the puppet regime set up by the Japanese in occupied east China. Disillusioned, he fled to Hong Kong and after making public amends, he returned to be Chiang's secretary. *China's Destiny* was Chiang's response to Mao's *On the New Democracy*. Although published in China in 1944, *China's Destiny* was not translated into English because Madame Chiang feared that it would be upsetting to China's American supporters. An authorized English translation with an introduction by the popular writer Lin Yutang was published in January 1947. That same year and month, a second translation, edited and with notes by Philip Jaffe, was published in England and America.

8. Memo from Norman Robertson, USSEA, to prime minister, 18 January 1943, quoted in McNally, "Odlum," 11.

9. The quoted portions of the sentence represent a Chinese aphorism.

10. The German military advisors returned to Germany, following the signing of the Japan-German pact of September 1937.

11. *Camrose Canadian* (CC), 22 December 1943.

12. Canada, at Britain's urging, had sent troops to Hong Kong to defend the colony against Japanese attack, hence the earlier declaration of war.

13. Madame Chiang Kai-shek gave a speech entitled "Role of Law: Democracy vs. Ochlocracy" to a joint session of Parliament on 16 June 1943. The text of the speech is in *Hansard* for that day.

14. No one knows who coined the phrase, but Hannah Pakula, *The Last Empress* (New York: Simon and Shuster, 2009), 564, refers to Truman's use of it. In Britain, it gained popularity when used on the radio comedy series of the 1950s, *The Goon Show*.

15. The China Lobby effectively blocked relations between Washington and Peking from 1950 to 1979, maintaining that the Nationalist government of Taiwan spoke for all of China.

16. RP, "Canada via Cairo to China."

17. RP, letter to family, 4 December 1945. Ronning wrote a weekly letter to his wife and children, usually with a copy to his parents, reporting on his activities. Summaries of his first series of letters appeared in the local weekly *Camrose Canadian* early in 1946.

18. Theodore H. White and Annalee Jacoby, *Thunder Out of China* (New York: William Sloane Associates Inc., 1946) 5, 9-10.

19. Patterson was recruited to the DEA from the YMCA in Toronto. He was offered the position of ambassador to China but rejected it as being too temporary. Instead, he was brought into the career diplomatic service and sent out as counsellor. From China, he was posted to Japan after the war. See John Hilliker, *Canada's Department of External Affairs*, Vol. I, *The Early Years 1909-1946* (Kingston: McGill-Queen's University Press, 1990), 266.

20. Chester A. Ronning, *A Memoir of China in Revolution* (New York: Random House, Pantheon Books, 1974), 58.

21. RIA, 13 May 1980.

22. Tessie joined the embassy staff in December 1945 shortly after Ronning arrived. Her sister was already employed there. The Wong sisters were from an upper-class Cantonese family. Tessie was married but had left her husband, a professor in Hong Kong, and her young daughter in Canton with her mother, to strike out on her own. See Camrose Burdon, "Left Behind in Nanjing," *bout de papier* 21, no. 5 (2005): 9-15.

23. RP, letter to family, 4 December 1945.

24. Ibid.

25. RP, letters to family, 11 and 18 December 1945. Dr. James G. (Jim) Endicott was a charismatic United Church (Methodist) minister and missionary who had worked with Madame Chiang on the New Life Movement. Disillusioned, he quit and became increasingly involved with the Communists. His subsequent activities, speeches, and writings were to make him a very controversial figure during the Cold War.

26. RP, letter to family, 1 January 1946.

27. Yeh participated in the 1 August 1927 uprising with Chou En-lai, later becoming a general in the Red Army (later the People's Liberation Army [PLA]). He was in Chungking assisting Chou in negotiations with the KMT.

28. RP, letter to family, 1 January 1946.

29. There is confusion as to when Ronning first met Chou. In his *A Memoir of China*, 75, he says he had only been in Chungking a few days when he and the ambassador were invited to dine with Chou. As Liao Dong has pointed out, this was not possible because Chou was away from Chungking when Ronning first arrived. In his letter to his family dated 1 January 1946, Ronning indicates that the next night Chou and his wife were coming to dinner. There is no indication that they had met before. In a letter on 15 January, written after he had spent

a week in bed from 6 to 13 January, he refers to having previously spent half an hour with Chou, presumably at the aforementioned dinner. Yet, in his *A Memoir of China*, 76, he makes passing reference to the 2 January dinner, but dates it after 15 January, when the ceasefire between the KMT and CPC was signed and after his description of the dinner at Chou's "a few days after he arrived in Chungking." One is forced to conclude that Ronning first met Chou on 2 January and that the conversation he describes as having taken place at Chou's actually took place on 9 April 1946, when he and Odlum were guests of Chou. This was a few days after Ronning returned to Chungking from his two-month visit to Nanking.

30. RP, letters to family, 1 and 16 January 1946. These letters were summarized and printed in CC, 27 March 1946.

31. RP, letter family, 10 April 1946. Ronning incorrectly identifies Nanking as the place from which he is writing, but he was, in fact, back in Chungking as he states in the letter itself. With the passage of time, his memory of the evening underwent a change: "Chou Enlai invited the two of us to dinner and Chou sat at one end and Odlum the other and Chou's interpreter acting for both sides facing me. The interpreter softened down something Chou had said, but I told Odlum the precise terms that Chou had said. Then Chou said: You interpret for me too! The interpreter was softening things down because he wanted to have an agreement, but I felt they should face the worst aspects of the situation before the agreement." RIA, 27 May 1980.

32. Ronning, *A Memoir of China*, 75–76.

33. Ibid., 86.

34. Ibid., 63.

35. Kung was a direct descendant of Confucius, a former Finance Minister, and reputedly the richest man in China. He was married to Soong Ailing, Madame Chiang's sister.

36. RP, letters to family, 1 January and 26 February 1946. A *ma kua* is a loose, short, silk jacket.

37. RP, letter to family, 30 April 1946.

38. RP, letter to family, 15 January 1946.

39. RP, letter to family, 9 February 1946.

40. Graham Peck, *Two Kinds of Time* (Boston: Houghton Mifflin, 1950), 683. When the Communists took over China in 1949, the KMT gave Okumura a quick trial, exonerated him, and repatriated him to Japan.

41. RP, letter to family, 9 February 1946.

42. RP, letter to family, 30 March 1946.

43. RP, letter to Odlum, 5 May 1946.

44. Canada, Department of Foreign Affairs and International Trade (DFAIT), Documents on Canadian External Relations (DCER), Vol. 12-1107 DEA/4558-Q-49 Despatch 530, Odlum to Secretary of State for External Affairs, 14 May 1946.

45. The loan was from three Canadian banks, guaranteed by the Canadian and Chinese governments. The Communist victory in 1949 complicated repayment. See Maurice Copithorne, "The Settlement of International Claims

between Canada and China: A Status Report," *Pacific Affairs* 48, no. 2 (1975): 230–37.

46. Ronning, *A Memoir of China*, 98.
47. RP, letter to family, 1 June 1946.
48. RP, letter to Lily, 26 June 1946. All through his time in China, Ronning was also bothered by sciatica.
49. RP, letter to Odlum, Ottawa, 6 April 1952, and Odlum to Ronning, 29 April 1952.
50. The ship travelled through the gorges during the day, tying up each night at a river port.
51. RP, letter to family, 1 June 1946.

# 6
# Nanking Forever

1. Ronning papers (RP), letter to family, 10 April 1946.
2. RP, letter to family, 27 June 1946.
3. RP, Memo: "Protocol and the Diplomatic Corps Dinner," June 1946.
4. Ronning described the week in a letter to his family, also published in the *Camrose Canadian*, in a section in his *A Memoir of China in Revolution* (New York: Random House, Pantheon Books, 1974), 112–14, and in Ronning interview with author (RIA), 6 May 1980. What follows draws on all of these accounts.
5. Chiang was not a linguist. Although he studied in Japan, he did not speak Japanese with any facility. There are many stories of his struggles with English, such as when he greeted the British ambassador one morning with "Kiss me," when he meant "Good morning." Chiang was fifty-eight at the time of Ronning's visit in 1946, seven years Ronning's senior.
6. Rumours were circulating about the state of their marriage and the possible infidelity of Chiang. It was common practice in China to carry your own sheets when travelling.
7. RP, letter to family, 27 June 1946.
8. RP, note, 9 July 1946.
9. RP, letter to family, 28 August 1946.
10. RP, letter to family, 4 September 1946.
11. In Japan, he was the Canadian representative on the United Nations Temporary Commission on Korea (UNTCOK).
12. RIA, 27 May 1980.
13. Pai was a warlord who later co-operated with Chiang Kai-shek. His ancestors were reputed to be Persian merchants. His Muslim name was Omar. Although he was regarded as second-in-command after Chiang, he did not hesitate to criticize Chiang's handling of the civil war.
14. RP, letter to family, 26 September 1946.
15. RP, letter to family, 19 September 1946.
16. This, and the previous quotation, are from RP, letter to family, 17 December 1946. The family left Camrose on 6 November, making their way by train to San Francisco to board the *Marine Lynx*. America controlled shipping across

the Pacific at this time and space for civilians was difficult to obtain. The *Lynx* had a terrible reputation, such that one passenger, having survived the passage from San Francisco, declared that he would stay in China rather than return on the *Lynx*. Also on the *Lynx* with the Ronnings was Mary Endicott, wife of Rev. James Endicott, who, at the request of Chou En-lai, was in Shanghai publishing a pro-Communist newsletter. Because of the great competition for space on the *Lynx*, Mary Endicott appealed to her old classmate Lester B. Pearson for assistance. Pearson, who was number two in the Canadian Embassy in Washington, managed to get her on board by claiming that she was the nursemaid to the Ronning children. See Stephen Endicott, *Rebel out of China* (Toronto: University of Toronto Press, 1980), 240 and note. There is no indication that the Ronnings were aware of Pearson's stratagem.

17. On 28 February 1947, Nationalist troops began a bloody suppression of native Taiwanese in Taibei, giving the Nanking government a black eye internationally. In attempting to put things right, martial law was imposed and was not lifted until 1987.

18. Documents on Canadian External Relations (DCER), Vol. 12, Document 1134, Memorandum from Director, Trade Commissioner Service to Assistant Deputy Minister of Trade and Commerce, Ottawa, 10 December 1946.

19. RP, note, Nanking, 21 January 1947.

20. RP, letter to family, 15 September 1947.

21. Under the earlier Ch'ing dynasty (1644–1912), the full *kowtow* was described as three kneelings and nine knockings of the head on the ground.

22. RIA, 27 November 1979.

23. Ibid.

24. DCER, Vol. 13, Document 954, 2 June 1947.

25. The 1923 Chinese Immigration Act put an end to the infamous head tax, which had been in effect since 1885 and was imposed on Chinese workers, but not on merchants. The 1923 act, however, forbade the admission into Canada of females who were not born in Canada, or were not Canadian citizens. It became impossible for Chinese men in Canada to bring their families over to join them, or to return to China to marry and bring their brides into the country. For all intents and purposes, it was an act of exclusion.

26. Ronning, *A Memoir of China*, 124–26.

27. DCER, Vol. 14, Document 1115, Secret Memo from Acting Under-Secretary of State for External Affairs to Acting Secretary of State for External Affairs, 15 December 1948, and Document 1116, Top Secret Extract from Cabinet Conclusions, 16 December 1948.

28. RIA, 6 May 1980.

# 7
## The Coming of the People's Republic of China

1. Seymour Topping, *Journey between Two Chinas* (New York: Harper & Row, 1972), 49.

2. From Japan, they took a Norwegian freighter to Vancouver, arriving back in Camrose early in January 1949. "Mrs. Ronning and 3 Children Evacuated Home from China," *Camrose Canadian* (CC), 5 January 1949. Inga ventured the opinion "that the Chinese Communists are not necessarily Russian in their inspiration."

3. Ronning papers (RP), letter to family, 2 February 1949.

4. Ibid.

5. John (Jack) Ryerson Maybee came to the embassy in 1948 as a junior officer along with Nevitt Black, his Chinese-speaking wife. When she resisted the evacuation order of November 1948, Ronning is reported as saying, "Nevitt, if you women stay here and things get tough, they'd send a plane from Hong Kong to get you out. We men would stay and get shot! Go home!" *Globe and Mail*, 10 July 2009.

6. Documents on Canadian External Relations (DCER), Vol. 15, Document 1032, Secret Memorandum from Special Assistant to Acting Under Secretary of State for External Affairs to Secretary of State for External Affairs, Ottawa, 28 January 1949. Also US Department of State, *Foreign Relations of the United States* (Washington, DC: GPO, 1949), Vol. 8, 653–55.

7. RP, letter to family, 21 April 1949.

8. RP, excerpts from "Fall of Nanking," personal memorandum, 28 April 1949.

9. RP, "First Impressions of Communists in Nanking," 13 May 1949.

10. See beginning of Chapter One.

11. RP, letter to family, 22 June 1949.

12. DCER, Vol. 15, Document 1037, Secret: Memorandum from Under-Secretary of State for External Affairs to Secretary of State for External Affairs, Ottawa, 3 June 1950 [*sic*].

13. Ibid.

14. DCER, Vol. 15, Document 1043, Secret telegram: Ambassador in China to Secretary of State for External Affairs, Nanking, 27 August 1950 [*sic*].

15. DCER, Vol. 15, Document 1045, Telegram: Memorandum from Under-Secretary of State for External Affairs to Secretary of State for External Affairs, Ottawa, 2 September 1950 [*sic*].

16. Ronning, *A Memoir of China in Revolution* (New York: Random House, Pantheon Books, 1974), 170, and Ronning interview with author (RIA), 28 May 1980.

17. Huang Hua, *Memoirs* (Beijing: Foreign Languages Press, 2008), 118.

18. DCER, Vol. 15, Document 1047, Secret: Memorandum from Under-Secretary of State for External Affairs to Secretary of State for External Affairs, Ottawa, 13 October 1950 [*sic*]. In the published text, Ronning is referred to as "Mr. Running" and as "Mr. Roaring."

19. Cabinet meetings, 16 November and 20 December 1949, as noted in DCER, Vol. 16, Document 1015, Secret: Memorandum from Secretary of State for External Affairs to Cabinet, Ottawa, 17 February 1950.

20. RIA, 6 May 1980. There appears to be no confirmation in Department of External Affairs (DEA) records of the suggestion that he move to Peking at this time.

21. Ronning's view was belatedly proven true when documents of the Mao-Stalin meetings surfaced in 1995. His mention of warming relations between Peking and Moscow was seen as an effort to scare Ottawa into action. See John Holmes, *The Shaping of Peace*, Vol. 2 (Toronto: University of Toronto Press, 1982), 136.

22. DCER, Vol. 16, Document 1015, Secret Cabinet Document No. 55, Ottawa, 17 February 1950.

23. Ibid.

24. One of them, Arthur Menzies, another China "mish kid" (a term for children of missionaries), pointed to the hazards internationally if Peking was recognized and assumed seats on international bodies sensitive to Cold War issues. Ronning was twenty-two years Menzies's senior, but not his equal in time served in the department. They were both China-born and spoke Chinese. Ronning called the plump Menzies "little dumpling" and Menzies called Ronning "elder brother." They did not see eye to eye on Mao's China and as a result Ronning did not trust Menzies fully. RIA, 27 November 1979.

25. Ronning, *A Memoir of China*, 173.

26. RP, letter to family, 17 March 1950.

27. RIA, 29 May 1980.

28. Holmes, *The Shaping of Peace*, 138–39.

29. During the war in the Pacific (1941–45), the American public had been led to believe that the Nationalist government in China would emerge from the fighting as a democratic state and ally of America. The corrupt conditions of the Chinese government were not reported on until after the war. These reports shocked the American public and when the Communists emerged in 1949 as the winners of a civil war, a number of members of the US Congress looked for reasons why the American policy had failed. Those American politicians, missionaries, and business people whose futures had been closely tied to the Nationalist government roundly condemned the US government for its failure and worked hard to block recognition of the Maoist government and any relations with it. As mentioned previously, they made up what was generally called the China Lobby. They looked for those American advisors whose opinions had contributed to the failed policy and to the "loss of China." This charge, along with the onset of the Cold War with the USSR, gave opportunities for individuals such as Senator Joseph McCarthy to launch a hunt for "traitors and communists" in the US State Department, and more broadly among people within academia and the entertainment industry who had espoused leftist views. The federal civil service was purged of its best China experts as America turned its back on the new People's Republic of China.

30. Holmes, *The Shaping of Peace*, 141.

31. Peter Stursberg, *Lester Pearson and the American Dilemma* (Toronto: Doubleday, 1980), 91.

32. Senior Canadian diplomats thought the UN resolution to be ill-advised, and even stupid.

33. Ronning, *A Memoir of China*, 143.

34. DCER, Vol. 16, Document 1025, Secret: Heeney to Secretary of State for External Affairs, Ottawa, 4 July 1950.
35. Ronning, *A Memoir of China*, 150.
36. Ibid., 151–52.
37. CC, 29 November 1950.
38. The consulate in Shanghai remained open for another year.

# 8

# A Long Way to Norway

1. The house was rented for US$100 a month from a Mrs. Liang who had since taken up residence in Brazil. When the Communists arrived, they took possession of the house and charged the embassy US$30 a month. When she heard the embassy had left, Mrs. Liang attempted to collect rent for the weeks after Ronning and Staines vacated the house. She was directed to the Communist government. Ronning papers (RP), letter from George S. Paterson to Ronning, Hong Kong, 20 January 1952.
2. Chester Ronning, *A Memoir of China in Revolution* (New York: Random House, Pantheon Books, 1974), 153–57.
3. "Menzies Bones," as they came to be known, represented one of the largest collections of oracle bones. The bones are significant because they proved the existence of the Shang Dynasty, previously thought to be mythical. Menzies's house in Anyang was opened in 2004 as the James Mellon Menzies Memorial Museum for Oracle Bone Studies.
4. A "name chop" is usually called a seal. It is made up of a piece of ivory, semiprecious stone, or metal with one's name in Chinese carved on its face. When pressed into ink and pressed on paper, a name chop is as good as a signature.
5. Ronning, *A Memoir of China*, 166. A full account of Ronning's and Staines's exit from China is covered on pages 157–66.
6. Department of External Affairs (DEA) to Ronning, telegram, 7 March 1951, quoted in Alwyn J. Austin, *Saving China: Canadian Missionaries in the Middle Kingdom 1888–1959* (Toronto: University of Toronto Press, 1986), 312.
7. Arthur Menzies, "Chester Ronning, a Recollection," *bout de papier* 3, no. 1 (1985): 17.
8. Ronning, *A Memoir of China*, 152, letter dated 24 January 1951.
9. Ronning interview with author (RIA), 29 May 1980. Ronning said it first in Norwegian, and then translated it for the author's benefit.
10. John Hilliker and John Barry, *Canada's Department of External Affairs: Coming of Age 1946–1968*, Vol. II (Montreal: McGill-Queen's University Press, 1995), 58.
11. Arthur E. Blanchette, "Indochina: From Desk Officer to the Acting Commissioner," in *Special Trust and Confidence*, ed. David Reece (Ottawa: Carleton University Press, 1996), 33, 35.

12. Chester Ronning, "Canada and the United Nations," in *Canada's Role as a Middle Power*, ed. J. King Gordon (Toronto: Canadian Institute of International Affairs, 1966), 42; Reid was senior to Ronning, see 171.

13. RP, letter from George S. Patterson to Ronning, Hong Kong, 20 January 1952.

14. RP, letter from Panikkar to Ronning, Peking, 25 June 1951.

15. RP, letter from Odlum to Ronning, Ankara, 28 September 1951.

16. RP, letter from Ronning to Odlum, Ottawa, 6 July 1952.

17. Chester Ronning, "Canada and the United Nations," 37.

18. Denis Stairs, *The Diplomacy of Constraint* (Toronto: University of Toronto Press, 1974), 277–78.

19. Reg Whitaker and Gary Marcuse, *Cold War Canada: The Making of a National Insecurity State, 1945–1957* (Toronto: University of Toronto Press, 1994), 399.

20. Sidney Freifeld later recounted a story about Ronning at this time. Freifeld was working for the DEA as a young man and went fishing in Algonquin Provincial Park in Ontario with Charles Eustace McCaughey (called McGuff) who was in the Far Eastern section under Ronning. McGuff cleaned a dozen speckled trout for Freifeld to deliver to Ronning. Ronning was delighted with the gift and a decade later when Freifeld, now a young DEA officer, visited Delhi, India, Ronning arranged a fishing trip in the Himalayas for him as a surprise. Sidney Freifeld, "Chester Ronning: A Canadian Diplomat," *bout de papier* 10, no. 3 (1993): 22.

21. Pearson, in a statement to the House of Commons, remembered Patterson as "a quiet, sincere and dedicated man, whose whole life was devoted to the service of his fellow men...[whose] life was shortened by his refusal to recognize any limitations on the energy and hours he gave to his work." Department of Foreign Affairs and International Trade (DFAIT): *Statements and Speeches*, No. 54/5, Survey of World Affairs, Statement by Secretary of State for External Affairs, Mr. L.B. Pearson, 29 January 1954.

22. When Norway separated from Sweden in 1905 and ceased to be under the Swedish monarchy, it turned to a Danish prince who agreed to be selected as the first of a new line of Norwegian monarchs.

23. RIA, 29 May 1980. In fact, the Norwegian Foreign Minister had been alerted to Ronning's circumstances, but it was the local custom not to approach the king for an appointment until the ambassador had arrived. RP, Memorandum for File, Ottawa, 26 March 1954.

24. Holmes had boarded a ship in Genoa and was well on his way to Canada when the surprising news reached him. John W. Holmes, "Geneva 1954," *International Journal* 22, no. 3 (1967): 457–83. John Wendell Holmes joined the DEA in 1943 two years before Ronning. He quickly became known for his diplomatic skill and wisdom. He has been called the epitome of what is good in the Canadian diplomatic tradition. He left the DEA for academia in 1960, following an RCMP-conducted purge of homosexuals from among the civil service under the direction of Cabinet. See Hector MacKenzie, "Purged...from Memory: The Department of External Affairs and John Holmes," *International Journal* 59, no. 2 (2004): 375–86.

25. Han Suyin, *Eldest Son: Zhou Enlai and the Making of Modern China 1898–1976* (New York: Hill and Wang, 1994), 234. One of Chou's first guests was Charlie Chaplin, of whom Chou was a great fan.

26. Holmes, "Geneva 1954," 457–83.

27. Douglas A. Ross reports it this way based on a communication with Ronning in June 1976. See *In the Interests of Peace: Canada and Vietnam 1954–1973* (Toronto: University of Toronto Press, 1984), 71, note 10.

28. Lester B. Pearson, *Mike: The Memoirs of the Rt. Hon. Lester B. Pearson*, Vol. 2 (Toronto: University of Toronto Press, 1975), 120–21.

29. Seymour Topping, *On the Front Lines of the Cold War* (Baton Rouge: Louisiana State University Press, 2010), 333.

30. Ronning, *A Memoir of China*, 181.

31. "The special treatment accorded him [MacKenzie] was undoubtedly attributable to the Chinese regard for Ronning and probably also the strikingly different personal disposition of the Canadians in Geneva compared with the Americans, all of whom were forbidden to converse with the Chinese." See John Holmes, *The Shaping of Peace*, Vol. 2 (Toronto: University of Toronto Press, 1982), 195.

32. James Eayrs, *In Defence of Canada*, Vol. 5, *Indochina: Roots of Complicity* (Toronto: University of Toronto Press, 1983), 50.

33. Stairs, *The Diplomacy of Constraint*, 294.

34. DFAIT: *Statements and Speeches*, No. 54/32, Statement at Geneva, C.A. Ronning, 11 June 1954.

35. Canada's reputation for balance and fairness, along with a pool of military and diplomats who were bilingual, were more substantial reasons. See Holmes, *The Shaping of Peace*, 205.

36. Ronning, *A Memoir of China*, 181. Pearson was assisted notably by John Holmes and Chester Ronning.

37. Documents on Canadian External Relations (DCER), Vol. 21, Document 301, Top Secret: Cabinet Conclusions, Visit of the United States Secretary of State to Ottawa, 17–19 March 1955, (18 March 1955).

38. RP, Audrey Topping, "An Account of the Events of the Queen's Visit."

39. Ronning, *A Memoir of China*, 5.

40. RIA, 29 May 1980.

41. Ronning, *A Memoir of China*, 181–82. Pearson, in his memoirs, makes no direct reference to this incident.

42. DCER, Vol. 22, Document 632 contains Ronning's notes on meetings regarding the visit.

43. *High commissioner* is the term used for ambassadorial-level appointments within the Commonwealth.

44. "Ronning, speech to Camrose Rotarians, 8 April 1957," CC, 10 April 1957.

# 9
## Delhi, Nehru, and Dief

1. Ronning papers (RP). His departure was noted in the *Hindustani Times* of 11 May 1964, and he received a short note of appreciation from Indira Gandhi.

2. Ronning interview with author (RIA), 22 July 1980.

3. Ibid.

4. John G. Diefenbaker, *One Canada, Memoirs of the Right Honourable John G. Diefenbaker: The Years of Achievement 1956 to 1962* (Toronto: Macmillan, 1976), 106.

5. Ibid.

6. H. Basil Robinson, *Diefenbaker's World: A Populist in Foreign Affairs* (Toronto: University of Toronto Press, 1989), 75.

7. Department of Foreign Affairs and International Trade (DFAIT), Documents on Canadian External Relations (DCER), Vol. 25, Document 469, Personal and Secret, Ronning to Norman Robertson, 28 November 1958.

8. Ibid.

9. Ibid.

10. Ibid.

11. Diefenbaker recruited Smith from the University of Toronto where he was president, but he died suddenly on 17 March 1959 before he realized his potential as Minister for External Affairs.

12. Diefenbaker, *One Canada*, 152.

13. Robinson, *Diefenbaker's World*, 51. For a balanced discussion of Canada and China during this period, see John W. Holmes, *The Better Part of Valour* (Toronto: McClelland and Stewart, 1970), Carleton Library No. 49, 201-17.

14. A tiger hunt in honour of distinguished visitors and high officials was a fixture of India under British rule, and continued after Independence in 1947. Diefenbaker was worried about what his participation would do to his image in Canada, "but when the time came he surrendered happily enough to the excitement." See Robinson, *Diefenbaker's World*, 76. Ronning, a lifelong game hunter, as high commissioner, happily accompanied the Canadian prime minister, each seated atop an elephant. Later, toward the end of his term as high commissioner, Ronning was given his own tiger hunt. The head of the tiger he shot was mounted on the wall of his home in Camrose. The five tigers and two leopards was the total for the entire hunting party. RIA, 27 November 1979.

15. The naming of a school and, later, an area called Ronning Town is evidence of Ronning's popularity. Indian scholars and diplomats the author has met have confirmed Ronning's popularity in India.

16. DCER, Vol. 27, Document 412, Despatch 461, Ronning to Under-Secretary of State for External Affairs, New Delhi, 19 May 1960.

17. Campbell was critical of India's action in Goa and as a result, Canada was attacked in the Indian press for aligning itself with imperialists like the British, who had also objected.

18. Peter Stursberg, *Lester Pearson and the American Dilemma* (Toronto: Doubleday, 1980), 270.

19. John Kenneth Galbraith, *An Ambassador's Journal* (Boston: Houghton Mifflin, 1969), 177–78.

20. Robert Burns, "To A Mouse," 1785. The line can be translated as "Often go awry, wrong, or are derailed."

21. RIA, 22 July 1980; Seymour Topping, *On the Front Lines of the Cold War* (Baton Rouge: Louisiana State University Press, 2010), 234.

22. Galbraith, *An Ambassador's Journal*, 435. Entry for 25 October 1962.

23. The phrase "the helpful fixer" can perhaps be attributed to Canadian diplomat and academic John Wendell Holmes, but, regardless, it was used to describe the pre-Trudeau era of Canadian diplomacy when Canada appeared to put its national interests after those of achieving solutions to world problems. A prime example of this was the creation of the concept of "peacekeeping" following the Suez Crisis, which is credited to Lester Pearson. In those years, Canada acted as an honest broker in disputes. Pierre Trudeau rejected this approach in favour of putting Canada's interests first.

24. Canada sent India $6 million worth of military aid made up of eight Dakota airplanes, five Otters, five hundred tons of electrolytic nickel, and $2 million of winter clothing. Separately, Canada sold India sixteen Caribou planes on easy credit, loaning India $12 million to pay for them and a $2 million outright grant to reduce the interest to less than 3 per cent. Peyton V. Lyon, *Canada in World Affairs*, Vol. 12, *1961–63* (Toronto: Oxford University Press, 1968), 488–89.

25. RIA, 22 July 1980. Ronning had had close contacts with the Chinese delegation at the Geneva meeting on Laos.

26. Lyon, *Canada in World Affairs*, 488–89.

27. During his final year in India, Ronning was being thought of in Ottawa as a possible envoy to Peking to negotiate recognition. France recognized China in the spring of 1964 and sparked some rethinking of the China question within the DEA. Paul Martin, the Liberal Minister for External Affairs, pursued the question of China's admission to the UN, which his department officials recommended as a necessary step before Canada sought recognition. Martin became a promoter of a One China/One Taiwan solution, but he did not receive a positive international response and recognition went no further. President Lyndon Johnson and Dean Rusk definitely did not think it a good idea. Paul Martin, *A Very Public Life*, Vol. 2 (Toronto: Deneau, 1985), 510–12.

## 10

## A Smallbridge Too Far

1. Pearson's exact words were: "There are many factors which I am not in a position to weigh. But there does appear to be at least a possibility that a suspension of such air strikes against North Vietnam, at the right time, might provide the Hanoi authorities with an opportunity, if they wish to take it, to inject some flexibility into their policy without appearing to do so as the direct

result of military pressure." Peter Stursberg, *Lester Pearson and the American Dilemma* (Toronto, Doubleday, 1980), 217.

2. It was also said that Johnson grabbed Pearson by the lapels. Pearson, with his usual style, wrote Johnson a letter to thank him for his hospitality, but their relations were never quite the same again. Ibid., 223.

3. Complete text of Ho's letter and Pearson's reply can be found in Department of Foreign Affairs and International Trade (DFAIT): *Statements and Speeches,* No. 66/14, "A Review of the Situation in Vietnam," statement by Paul Martin, 4 April 1966.

4. Ronning interview with author (RIA), 5 June 1980. According to Douglas Ross, there was a shouting match (comment based upon Ronning's communication to Ross, June 1976), *In the Interests of Peace: Canada and Vietnam 1954-1973* (Toronto: University of Toronto Press, 1984), 285.

5. Stursberg, *Lester Pearson,* 271.

6. Paul Martin, *A Very Public Life,* Vol. 2 (Toronto: Deneau, 1985), 438. The Cultural Revolution officially began in mid-May 1966. Ronning's mission was in March. See also Stursberg, *Lester Pearson,* 272-74.

7. Andrew Preston, "Operation Smallbridge," *Pacific Historical Review* 72, no. 3 (2003): 367, note 35.

8. Ho begged off seeing Ronning on grounds that he was preparing for a major meeting and had no time.

9. RIA, 5 June 1980.

10. Martin, *A Very Public Life,* 439.

11. RIA, 5 June 1980.

12. Rangoon was the capital city of Burma (now Myanmar) from 1948 to 2006. At the time, it was seen to be suitably neutral.

13. Martin, *A Very Public Life,* 442; Stursberg, *Lester Pearson,* 274.

14. RIA, 5 June 1980.

15. Chester A. Ronning, *A Memoir of China in Revolution* (New York: Random House, Pantheon Books, 1974), 267-68, and RIA, 5 June 1980.

16. US Department of State, *Foreign Relations of the United States 1964-68,* Vol. 4, Vietnam, 1966, 50.

17. Ibid., Document 97, 288-89. Delivering "a feather" refers to a Tang dynasty story of an official charged with delivering a white goose to the emperor as a gift from his master. En route, the official stopped to wash the goose in a lake to clean it up for presentation. The goose got away, leaving only a feather. Determined to complete his mission, the official took it to the emperor with a note emphasizing the sincerity of the giver, no matter the size of the gift. No doubt Ronning was alluding to the fact that although what he delivered was little, it was sincerely meant.

18. Ibid.

19. See George C. Herring, ed., *The Secret Diplomacy of the Vietnam War: The Negotiating Volumes of the Pentagon Papers* (Austin: University of Texas Press, 1983), 160, the Ronning missions section, 159-207. The *Pentagon Papers,* a study on the American involvement in Vietnam from 1945 to 1967, were leaked to

the *New York Times* by Daniel Ellsberg of the State Department, unleashing a firestorm of criticism because they showed how successive American administrations had lied to the American people. The complete *Pentagon Papers* were declassified in June 2011.

20. DFAIT: *Statements and Speeches*, No. 47/1, "Canadian Diplomacy," address by L.B. Pearson to University of Toronto Alumni, Ottawa, 11 January 1947, 3.

21. The author can attest to doing this himself, having been at the Banff conference watching Ronning perform.

22. Ronning papers (RP), "Is the West Drifting to Inevitable War with China?" University of Calgary, 15 November 1967.

23. Seymour Topping, *On the Front Lines of the Cold War* (Baton Rouge: Louisiana State University Press, 2010), 240.

24. Robert McNamara, *In Retrospect: The Tragedy and Lessons of Vietnam* (New York: Random House, Times Books, 1995), 247.

## II

# Unfinished Business

1. Pacem in Terris II was one of a series of meetings inspired by the encyclical written by Pope John XXIII of 11 April 1963 that began "Peace on Earth."

2. Seymour Topping, *Journey between Two Chinas* (New York: Harper & Row, 1972), 391. At a dinner late in May 1971, Chou En-lai quizzed Topping about Henry Kissinger who, unknown to everyone at the time, was shortly to visit Peking. Topping was visiting China in May 1971 as part of the family group with Ronning, enabling him to compare the new China with the old through his own eyes and Ronning's.

3. Ronning interview with author (RIA), 5 June 1980; George C. Herring, *Secret Diplomacy of the Vietnam War: The Negotiating Volumes of the Pentagon Papers* (Austin: University of Texas Press, 1983); Charles Taylor, *Snow Job: Canada, the United States and Vietnam* (Toronto: Anansi Press, 1974); David Kraslow and Stuart H. Loory, *The Secret Search for Peace in Vietnam* (New York: Random House, 1968); House of Commons, *Debates*, 28 Oct. 1966, 27 Feb. 1967, 12 Nov. 1968, 1 May 1970. Diefenbaker's calls to send Ronning on further missions continued into the Pierre Trudeau period.

4. J. King Gordon, ed., *Canada's Role as a Middle Power* (Toronto: Canadian Institute of International Affairs, 1966), 38.

5. He gave the Tory Lecture, named after the first president of the university, Henry Marshall Tory.

6. *Manitou Messenger*, 19 January 1968.

7. *Calgary Herald*, 8 July 1964.

8. *Edmonton Journal*, 9 March 1966 and *Globe and Mail*, 12 March 1966, respectively.

9. *Washington Post*, 26 June 1966.

10. *Edmonton Journal*, 12 March 1966.

11. *Canada Month* 6, no. 12 (December 1966): 13–17.

12. Editorial, *Montreal Star*, 18 December 1967.

13. *Globe and Mail*, 30 July 1968; *Vancouver Province*, 28 May 1969.

14. Unfortunately, in his *A Memoir of China in Revolution* (New York: Random House, Pantheon Books, 1974), 185, Ronning gives the date of recognition as 13 October 1971, a date that has become embedded in many books since. He gives the correct date later on page 270.

15. He had been the interpreter for Chou En-lai in Chungking.

16. Endicott was a missionary, but never a diplomat.

17. Huang Hua, *Memoirs* (Beijing: Foreign Languages Press, 2008), 238–39.

18. A. Doak Barnett and E.O. Reischauer, eds., *The United States and China: The Next Decade* (New York: Praeger, 1970), 167–72. Alvin Hamilton, who had negotiated the original Canada-China wheat deals, and David Oancia, a *Globe and Mail* correspondent in Beijing, were the other Canadian contributors.

19. The negotiations that brought the Vietnam conflict to a close are covered in the previous chapter.

20. *Ottawa Journal*, 25 February 1971.

21. The film was shown on CTV/*W5* in October 1971.

22. The *Times* began publishing the *Pentagon Papers* on 13 June 1971. Seymour Topping was very much involved in the process. Topping, *Journey between Two Chinas*, 376–80.

23. Peter Stursberg, "China: A Traveller's Diary," *Newsweek*, 17 May 1971; Audrey Topping, "A New Interview with Chou," *Detroit Times*, 21 May 1971, with photo of Chou and Ronning.

24. *New York Times*, 7 June, 11 July 1971.

25. *New York Times*, 10 October 1971.

26. *Boston Sunday Globe*, 9 January 1972.

27. Typical of these accounts was the one in *The Blade* (Toledo, Ohio) of 15 March 1973 taken from Associated Press reporting "U.S. Leaked Peace Data, Ellsberg Trial Is Told: Retired Canadian Diplomat Says 1966 Mission Not Secret When Papers Copied."

28. *Montreal Gazette*, 6 May 1970.

29. "The Apologist," *St. John's Edmonton Report* (later *The Alberta Report*), 2 December 1974, 5.

30. *Globe and Mail*, 13 July 1974; *Toronto Sun*, 27 September 1974.

31. *Vancouver Sun*, 6 September 1974; *Kitchener-Waterloo Record*, 9 November 1974.

32. *Ottawa Citizen*, 16 November 1974.

33. *Meunster Prairie Messenger*, 15 September 1974.

34. *Edmonton Journal*, 31 August 1974.

35. *Calgary Herald Magazine*, 6 September 1974.

36. The sources referred to in this paragraph are, respectively, *China Quarterly*, March 1976, 137–38; *New York Times*, 22 September 1974; *Coffeyville Journal* [Kansas], 25 April 1974; *Washington Post*, 23 July 1974; *Los Angeles Times*, 17 September 1974; *Fresno Bee*, 1 December 1974.

37. Ronning papers (RP), CFCW 790, Wetaskiwin, transcript of taped interviews with friends of Ronning, 1984.

38. Ronning had no recollection of such a conversation in the summer of 1980 during interviews with the author.
39. RP, Liao Dong, "Chester A. Ronning," unpublished essay. House of Commons, *Debates*, 6 February 1967.

## 12
## Returning Home

1. Ronning papers (RP), "Is the West Drifting to Inevitable War with China?" University of Calgary, 15 November 1967.
2. Ronning, *A Memoir of China in Revolution* (New York: Random House, Pantheon Books, 1974), 270.
3. Audrey Topping, "Return to Changing China," *National Geographic* 140, no. 6 (December 1971): 811. Topping was freelancing for the *New York Times* and *National Geographic*. Her reports of the visit appeared in the *New York Times* shortly after and in *National Geographic* in December 1971. Her most famous photo of Chou En-lai laughing appeared on the cover of *Life Magazine*.
4. Ibid.
5. Audrey Topping, *Dawn Wakes in the East* (New York: Harper and Row, 1973), 42-44. *Moutai* is also known as *Maotai*.
6. Some accounts say Lin was innocent and it was his overly ambitious son who did the plotting.
7. Ronning told this story often. The author heard it first during a conversation with him in Camrose, Alberta, 27 November 1979.
8. Ronning, *A Memoir of China*, 282.
9. Topping, *On the Front Lines of the Cold War* (Baton Rouge: Louisiana State University Press, 2010), 367-68. Topping reports the date incorrectly as 14 October and says that this was Teng Hsiao-p'ing's first public appearance after his rehabilitation. Teng actually appeared in April 1973 at a Cambodian reception. Trudeau and Ivan Head in *The Canadian Way: Shaping Canada's Foreign Policy, 1968-1984* (Toronto: McClelland & Stewart, 1995), 235, put Ronning at a lunch in the Summer Palace on the afternoon of 13 October 1973, which was clearly impossible. Neither this book, nor Trudeau's *Memoirs* (Toronto: McClelland & Stewart, 1993) make note of the meeting with Ronning at the railway station. A photo of the meeting was published in the *People's Daily* the following day.
10. Deng Rong, *Deng Xiaoping and the Cultural Revolution: A Daughter Recalls the Critical Years* (Beijing: Foreign Languages Press, 2002), 347-48.
11. Seymour Topping gives Audrey's first-hand description of these events. See *On the Front Lines*, 369-70.
12. Huang Hua, in an interview with the author in the Great Hall of the People in November 1984, talked of the relationship between Chou and Ronning. "I believe that Premier Chou was genuinely fond of Ronning," he said.
13. RP, "Talk to Scarsdale Congregational Church New York, on Chou Enlai, 18 January 1976," by Chester Ronning, handwritten text.

14. I was in the audience and heard the exchange. The Sproule Lecture is sponsored by the University of Calgary alumni. Ronning also gave seminars during his visit.

15. Bethune is honoured in China as a hero for sacrificing his life in November 1939 when tending to Chinese Communist soldiers who were wounded in battles with Japanese invaders.

16. The author was there to see this occur first-hand.

17. Strictly speaking, both sides were Maoists, but each emphasized a different part of his legacy.

18. Chester Ronning, "In Memoriam: Chairman Mao Tse-tung: He Knew the Peasant," *International Perspectives* (September/October 1976): 57-59.

19. Han Suyin and Paul T.K. Lin, observers with good connections with the Chinese leadership, were among them. Pierre Ryckmans (aka Simon Leys) was one of the few who predicted otherwise.

20. *Camrose Canadian* (CC), 27 October 1976.

21. Arthur Menzies, "Chester Ronning, a Recollection," *bout de papier* 3, no. 1 (1985): 18.

22. Chiao was too closely associated with the Gang of Four. He was China's foreign minister and travelled to the UN in the fall of 1976 only to lose his job on his return.

23. Camrose Burdon, "Left Behind in Nanjing," *bout de papier* 21, no. 5 (2005): 15.

24. Liu Gengyin, "Founder of Sino-Canadian Friendship: Chester Ronning," Beijing, February 2006 (posted November 2009), http://voice.7xi8.com/archives/128.html. See also Audrey Topping, "Pilgrimage to China: A Canadian Goes 'Home,'" *The Gazette*, Montreal, 3 March 1984.

25. Ronning was fond of quoting, in his Hubei accent, a saying from his home province that translates as "In the sky is a nine-headed bird, and on earth are its equals, the guys from Hubei."

26. CC, "Ronning's Passing Is Mourned by Nations," 8 January 1985.

27. "Canadian Friend Remembered," Letter to the Editor, *China Daily*, Beijing, 16 January 1985.

## 13
## Taking His Measure

1. Letter to the *New York Times*, 11 March 1984. Tran left the diplomatic service in 1963 and became a professor of international politics and communications at Temple University, Philadelphia. He came from a family of Confucian and Buddhist scholars and Daoist poets.

2. Provincial Archives of Alberta (PAA). Ronning expressed these thoughts in his interviews with Howard Leeson in 1976 as part of a project to interview people involved in the early years of the CCF/New Democratic Party (NDP) movement in Alberta.

3. At least two other prominent Canadian diplomats at this time held degrees from the University of Alberta: Ralph Collins and Roland Michener. Collins went on to study at Harvard and Oxford; Michener was a Rhodes Scholar.

4. Douglas A. Ross, *In the Interests of Peace: Canada and Vietnam, 1954-1973* (Toronto: University of Toronto Press, 1984), 18–22, 157. The other two members were E.H. Norman and Escott Reid.

5. Sir Walter Crocker, draft essay on Chester Ronning, *Crocker Papers*, Special Collections, University of Adelaide Library, Adelaide, Australia, 1. I am grateful to Ms. Susan Woodburn, Special Collections librarian, for making this available to me.

6. Arthur E. Blanchette, "Indochina: From Desk Officer to the Acting Commissioner," in *Special Trust and Confidence*, ed. David Reece (Ottawa: Carleton University Press, 1996), 35.

7. The "golden age" is generally considered to be from 1946 or 1948 to 1957, ending with the Suez Crisis and the Nobel Peace Prize for Lester B. Pearson. Recent discussions of the period cast doubt on the use of the term.

8. Bruce Gilley, "Middle Powers during Great Power Transitions: China's Rise and the Future of Canada–US Relations," *International Journal* 65, no. 2 (2011): 255, 264.

9. Ronning interview with author (RIA), 27 November 1979.

10. Ronning's day-to-day routines were as the author observed him, in addition to comments made off-tape during the interview sessions.

11. DFAIT, *Statements and Speeches*, No. 47/1, "Canadian Diplomacy," address by L.B. Pearson to University of Toronto Alumni, Ottawa, 11 January 1947.

12. The only biography of Ronning that has been published previously is in Chinese—Liu Guangtai, *Chester Ronning* (Hubei, 1999). Several Chinese students have written theses on aspects of Ronning's life, both in English and Chinese.

# Bibliography

Austin, Alwyn J. *Saving China: Canadian Missionaries in the Middle Kingdom 1888–1959*. Toronto: University of Toronto Press, 1986.

Billingsley, Phil. *Bandits in Republican China*. Stanford, CA: Stanford University Press, 1988.

Blanchette, Arthur E. "Indochina: From Desk Officer to Acting Commissioner." In *Special Trust and Confidence: Envoy Essays in Canadian Diplomacy*, edited by David Reece, 33–48. Ottawa: Carleton University Press, 1996.

Burdon, Camrose. "Left Behind in Nanjing." *bout de papier* 21, no. 5 (2005): 9–15.

Byfield, Ted, ed. *Alberta in the 20th Century*. Vol. 5. Edmonton: United Western Communications, 1996.

Canada. Department of Foreign Affairs and International Trade. Documents on Canadian External Relations (DCER). http://www.international.gc.ca/department/history-histoire/dcer/details-en.asp?intRefid=11084.

Chiang Kai-shek. *China's Destiny*. Translated by Wang Chung-hui. New York: Macmillan, 1947.

———. *China's Destiny*. London: Dennis Dobson, 1947.

Copithorne, Maurice D. "The Settlement of International Claims between Canada and China: A Status Report." *Pacific Affairs* 48, no. 2 (1975): 230–37.

Crow, Carl. *Foreign Devils in the Flowery Kingdom*. New York: Harper & Brothers, 1940.

Deng Rong. *Deng Xiaoping and the Cultural Revolution*. Beijing: Foreign Languages Press, 2002.

Diefenbaker, John George. *One Canada: Memoirs of the Right Honourable John G. Diefenbaker: The Years of Achievement 1956 to 1962*. Toronto: MacMillan, 1976.

Donaghy, Greg. *Tolerant Allies: Canada and the United States 1963–1968*. Montreal and Kingston: McGill-Queen's University Press, 2002.

Durdin, Tillman, James Reston, and Seymour Topping. *The New York Times Report from Red China*. New York: Quadrangle Books, 1971.

Eayrs, James. *In Defence of Canada*. Vol. 5, *Indochina: Roots of Complicity*. Toronto: University of Toronto Press, 1983.

Ekeland, T., Albert Anderson, and Olive T. Christensen, eds. *White unto Harvest: The China Mission of the Norwegian Lutheran Church of America*. Minneapolis: Board of Foreign Missions, 1919.

Endicott, Stephen. *James G. Endicott: Rebel out of China*. Toronto: University of Toronto Press, 1980.

Epp, Roger. *We Are All Treaty People: Prairie Essays*. Edmonton: University of Alberta Press, 2008.

Esherick, Joseph W. *Reform and Revolution in China: The 1911 Revolution in Hunan and Hubei*. Berkeley: University of California Press, 1976.

Evans, Brian L. "Ronning and Recognition." In *Reluctant Adversaries: Canada and the People's Republic of China 1949-1970*, edited by Paul M. Evans and B. Michael Frolic, 148-67. Toronto: University of Toronto Press, 1991.

Fairbank, John King, ed. *The Cambridge History of China*. Vol. 12, Parts I & II, "Republican China 1912-1949." Cambridge: Cambridge University Press, 1983.

Fowler, Bertie. "Chester Ronning's Compassion Compelled Attention." [Augustana] *Express* 14, no. 1 (2003): 17-18.

Freifeld, Sidney. "Chester Ronning: A Canadian Diplomat." *bout de papier* 10, no. 3 (1993): 22.

Galbraith, John Kenneth. *An Ambassador's Journal: A Personal Account of the Kennedy Years*. Boston: Houghton Mifflin, 1969.

Gilley, Bruce. "Middle Powers during Great Power Transitions: China's Rise and the Future of Canada-US Relations." *International Journal* 65, no. 2 (2011): 245-64.

Gordon, J. King, ed. *Canada's Role as a Middle Power*. Toronto: Canadian Institute of International Affairs, 1966.

Han Suyin. *Eldest Son: Zhou Enlai and the Making of Modern China 1898-1976*. New York: Hill and Wang, 1994.

Head, Ivan, and Pierre Trudeau. *The Canadian Way: Shaping Canada's Foreign Policy, 1968-1984*. Toronto: McClelland & Stewart, 1995.

Herring, George C., ed. *The Secret Diplomacy of the Vietnam War: The Negotiating Volumes of the Pentagon Papers*. Austin: University of Texas Press, 1983.

Hilliker, John. *Canada's Department of External Affairs*. Vol. I, *The Early Years, 1909-1946*. Montreal and Kingston: McGill-Queen's University Press, 1990.

Hilliker, John, and Donald Barry. *Canada's Department of External Affairs*. Vol. II, *Coming of Age, 1946-1968*. Montreal and Kingston: McGill-Queen's University Press, 1995.

Holmes, John W. "Geneva 1954." *International Affairs* 22, no. 3 (Summer 1967): 457-83.

———. *The Shaping of Peace: Canada and the Search for World Order 1943-1957*. Vol. 2. Toronto: University of Toronto Press, 1982.

Huang Hua. *Memoirs*. Beijing: Foreign Languages Press, 2008.

Irving, John A. *The Social Credit Movement in Alberta*. Toronto: University of Toronto Press, 1959.

Johansen, John. "A History of Augustana/CLC." http://www.Augustana.UAlberta.ca/100/history/.

Kraslow, David, and Stuart H. Loory. *The Secret Search for Peace in Vietnam*. New York: Random House, 1968.

Latourette, Kenneth Scott. *A History of Christian Missions in China*. Taipei: Cheng-wen Publishing, 1966. First published 1929 by Society for Promoting Christian Knowledge, London.

Lenker, J.N. *Lutherans in All Lands: The Wonderful Works of God*. Milwaukee: Lutherans in All Lands Company, 1896.

Leonard, David W. *The Last Great West: The Agricultural Settlement of the Peace River Country to 1914*. Calgary: Detselig Enterprises, 2005.

Liu Gengyin. "Founder of Sino-Canadian Friendship: Chester Ronning." Beijing, February 2006 (posted November 2009). http://voice.7x18.com/archives/128.html.

Liu Guangtai. *Chester Ronning*. Shijiazhuang: Hebei Xin Hua Press, 1999.

Lyon, Peyton V. *Canada in World Affairs*. Vol. 12, *1961–63*. Toronto: Oxford University Press, 1968.

MacKenzie, Hector. "Purged...from Memory: The Department of External Affairs and John W. Holmes." *International Journal* 59, no. 2 (2004): 375–86.

Martin, Paul. *A Very Public Life: II, So Many Worlds*. Toronto: Deneau, 1985.

McNally, George Frederick. "Odlum: Canada's First Ambassador to China." MA thesis, University of Alberta, 1977.

McNamara, Robert S. *In Retrospect: The Tragedy and Lessons of Vietnam*. New York: Random House, Times Books, 1995.

Menzies, Arthur. "Chester Ronning, a Recollection." *bout de papier* 3, no. 1 (1985): 17.

Pakula, Hannah. *The Last Empress: Madame Chiang Kai-shek and the Birth of Modern China*. New York: Simon & Shuster, 2009.

Pearson, Lester B. *Mike: The Memoirs of the Right Honourable Lester B. Pearson*, Vol. 2. Toronto: University of Toronto Press, 1971.

Peck, Graham. *Two Kinds of Time*. Boston: Houghton Mifflin, 1950.

Pioneer History Society and Area. *Pioneer Roundup—A History of Albright, Demmitt, Goodfare, Hythe, Lymburn, Valhalla*. Calgary: D.W. Friesen & Sons, 1972.

Preston, Andrew. "Operation Smallbridge." *Pacific Historical Review* 72, no. 3 (2003): 353–90.

Radford, Tom. *China Mission: The Chester Ronning Story*. National Film Board of Canada, 1980.

Ratay, S.J. *Current Chinese*. Shanghai: Kelly and Walsh, 1927.

Reed, James. *The Missionary Mind and American East Asia Policy, 1911–1915*. Cambridge, MA: Harvard University Press, 1983.

———. "China on Our Minds." *International Journal* 61, no. 2 (2006): 453–67.

Rennie, Bradford James. *The Rise of Agrarian Democracy*. Toronto: University of Toronto Press, 2000.

Robinson, H. Basil. *Diefenbaker's World: A Populist in Foreign Affairs*. Toronto: University of Toronto Press, 1989.

Ronning, Chester A. "Canada and the United Nations." In *Canada's Role as a Middle Power*, edited by J. King Gordon, 37–50. Toronto: Canadian Institute of International Affairs, 1966.

———. "Nanking 1950." *International Affairs* 22, no. 3 (1967): 441–56.

———. *A Memoir of China in Revolution: From the Boxer Rebellion to the People's Republic*. New York: Random House, Pantheon Books, 1974.

Ronning, Nils Nilius. *Fifty Years in America*. Minneapolis: Friend Publishing Company, 1938.

———. *The Gospel at Work*. Minneapolis: N.N. Ronning, 1943.

Ross, Douglas A. *In the Interests of Peace: Canada and Vietnam 1954-1973*. Toronto: University of Toronto Press, 1984.

Rowe, William T. *Hankow: Conflict and Community in a Chinese City, 1796-1895*. Stanford, CA: Stanford University Press, 1989.

Sheridan, James E. *China in Disintegration: The Republican Era in Chinese Politics 1912-1949*. New York: The Free Press, 1975.

Spencer, Robert A. *Canada in World Affairs: From UN to NATO 1946-1949*. Toronto: Oxford University Press, 1959.

Stairs, Denis. *The Diplomacy of Constraint: Canada, the Korean War and the United States*. Toronto: University of Toronto Press, 1974.

Steen, Ragna, and Magda Hendrickson. *Pioneer Days in Bardo Alberta*. Tofield, AB: Historical Society of Beaver Hills Lake, 1944.

Stursberg, Peter. *Lester Pearson and the American Dilemma*. Toronto: Doubleday Canada, 1980.

————. *The Golden Hope: Christians in China*. Toronto: United Church Publishing House, 1987.

Taylor, Charles. *Snow Job: Canada, the United States and Vietnam [1954 to 1973]*. Toronto: Anansi, 1974.

Taylor, Jay. *The Generalissimo: Chiang Kai-shek and the Struggle for Modern China*. Cambridge, MA: Belknap Press of Harvard University Press, 2009.

Thomas, Lewis Gwynne. *The Liberal Party in Alberta*. Toronto: University of Toronto Press, 1959.

Topping, Audrey. *Dawn Wakes in the East*. New York: Harper and Row, 1972.

————. "A Canadian Goes 'Home.'" *The Gazette*, Montreal, 3 March 1984.

————. "Chester Ronning's Daughter Reflects on Her Father and Life in Camrose." [Augustana] *Express* 14, no. 1 (2003): 16-17.

Topping, Seymour. *Journey between Two Chinas*. New York: Harper and Row, 1972.

————. *On the Front Lines of the Cold War: An American Correspondent's Journal from the Chinese Civil War to the Cuban Missile Crisis and Vietnam*. Baton Rouge: University of Louisiana Press, 2010.

Trudeau, Pierre Elliott. *Memoirs*. Toronto: McClelland & Stewart, 1993.

Whitaker, Reg, and Gary Marcuse. *Cold War Canada: the Making of a National Insecurity State, 1945-1957*. Toronto: University of Toronto Press, 1994.

White, Theodore H., and Annalee Jacoby. *Thunder Out of China*. New York: William Sloane Associates, 1946.

# Index

role in Vietnam War peace proposal,
197–203
ties to Chinese Nationalist
government, 103, 125, 135, 136–37,
138
view of Ronning's advice on
recognizing China, 150, 153
*See also* Department of External
Affairs (DEA)
Canadian Embassy in China
closing of in 1951, 156–59, 164
and Communist takeover, 141
CR interviews candidates for, 98
life in, 108–11
move to Nanking, 111, 113, 116, 117–22
relations among staff, 106, 107–08, 133
*See also* Department of External
Affairs (DEA); Ronning, Chester;
Diplomatic Career
Cassady, Sylvia (Ronning)
birth, 35
life in Camrose, 194, 257
life in China, 39, 40, 47, 53, 54
pictures, 54, 62
visits China, 227, 229, 245
CCF. *See* Co-operative Commonwealth
Federation (CCF)
Chang Han-fu, 1, 145, 169
Chang Hsueh-liang (Zhang Xueliang),
101–02
Chang Tso-lin (Zhang Zuolin), 51
Chang Wen-chin (Zhang Wenjin), 214,
227, 241, 242
Chant, W.N., 88, 89, 90, 91
Chen, Mr. (embassy caretaker), 159, 164
Chennault, Claire L., 103
Chen Yi, 190, 200
Chen Zuyu, 247–48
Chiang, Madame (Soong Mei-ling),
100–01, 103, 126, 128, 130, 272n7
Chiang Ch'ing (Jiang Qing), 232
Chiang Ching-kuo, 130
Chiang Kai-shek (Jiang Jieshi)
and *China's Destiny*, 100, 129, 272n7
and CR's comment on visit to
Nanking, 117–18

CR stays in his house, 245
as disciple of Sun Yat-sen, 51
early life, 268n24
and German military advisors, 101,
272n10
as leader of China, 100–02, 107, 115,
116, 121, 133
meetings with Odlum and Ronning,
98, 100, 126, 128, 130, 275n5
negotiations with Mao, 108
relations with Communists, 58, 59,
61, 62–63, 103
relations with US, 103–04, 105
retires from government, 139–40
Chiao Kuan-hua (Qiao Guanhua), 227,
229, 244, 288n22
Chi-kung shan (Jigongshan), 44, 52,
268n26
China
agitation against Great Britain, 57, 58,
59
attacks on foreigners in, 8, 9, 11–12, 18,
43, 44, 56
awareness in Canada of crisis in,
102–03
banditry in, 43–44, 52, 53, 58–59
civil war in, 136, 138
foreign exodus in 1927, 61–63
immigration agreement with
Canada, 137, 276n25
Norwegian missions to, 3–4
political situation in 1890s, 6–7, 9, 11
political situation in 1930s, 100–02
political tensions in 1946, 123–24
politics from 1911 to 1917, 40–43, 52
politics of 1922–23, 50–52
treatment of prisoners in, 15–16, 17
and Versailles Treaty, 43, 50
during World War II, 103–05
*See also* Chinese Nationalist
Government; Ch'ing (Qing)
Government; People's Republic
of China
China Inland Mission (CIM), 7–8
China Lobby, 106, 154, 273n15, 278n29
*China Mission* (film), 243–44, 260

# Other Titles from
# The University of Alberta Press

Pursuing China
*Memoir of a Beaver Liaison Officer*
BRIAN L. EVANS

312 pages • Over 50 B&W photographs, notes, index
978-0-88864-600-2 | $34.95 (T) paper
978-0-88864-615-6 | $27.99 (T) EPUB
978-0-88864-680-4 | $27.99 (T) Amazon Kindle
978-0-88864-789-4 | $27.99 (T) PDF
Political Memoir/Foreign Relations/China Studies

The Lady Named Thunder
*A Biography of Dr. Ethel Margaret Phillips (1876–1951)*
CLIFFORD H. PHILLIPS

Brian L. Evans, Foreword
436 pages | B&W photos, index
978-0-88864-417-6 | $34.95 (T) paper
Biography

Emblems of Empire
*Selections from the Mactaggart Art Collection*
JOHN E. VOLLMER & JACQUELINE SIMCOX

368 pages | Full-colour throughout, colour
    photographs, map, index, glossary
Copublished with the University of Alberta
    Museums
978-0-88864-486-2 | $60.00 (T) cloth
Asian Art/Art History